THE ROYAL INDIAN NAVY

This book presents a comprehensive history of the Royal Indian Navy (RIN). It traces the origins of the RIN to the East India Company, as early as 1612, and untangles the institution's complex history. Capturing various transitional phases of the RIN, especially during the crucial period of 1920–1950, it concludes with the final transfer of the RIN from under the British Raj to independent India.

Drawn from a host of primary sources – personal diaries and logs, official reports and documents – the author presents a previously unexplored history of colonial and imperial defence policy, and the contribution of the RIN during the World Wars. This book explores several aspects in RIN's history such as its involvement in the First World War; its status in policies of the British Raj; the martial race theory in the RIN; and the development of the RIN from a non-combat force to a full-fledged combat defence force during the Second World War. It also studies the hitherto unexplored causes, nature and impact of the 1946 RIN Revolt on the eve of India's independence from a fresh perspective.

An important intervention in the study of military and defence history, this will be an essential read for students, researchers, defence personnel, military academy cadets, as well as general readers.

Kalesh Mohanan is a Commander in the Indian Navy as well as a naval historian. He is an alumnus of the Indian Naval Academy, Kerala, India. He was previously Head of the Department (Military and Maritime History) at the Indian Naval Academy (2015–16). He is a recipient of a Junior Research Fellowship from the Indian Council of Historical Research, Ministry of HRD. He has a PhD and has done his postdoctoral research in naval history from Jawaharlal Nehru University, New Delhi, India. He has several publications including *Maritime Heritage of India*.

THE ROYAL INDIAN NAVY

Trajectories, Transformations and the Transfer of Power

Kalesh Mohanan

LONDON AND NEW YORK

First published 2020 by Routledge

2 Park Square, Milton Park, Abingdon, Oxon OX14 4RN

605 Third Avenue, New York, NY 10017

Routledge is an imprint of the Taylor & Francis Group, an informa business

First issued in paperback 2021

Copyright © 2020 Kalesh Mohanan

The right of Kalesh Mohanan to be identified as author of this work has been asserted by him in accordance with sections 77 and 78 of the Copyright, Designs and Patents Act 1988.

All rights reserved. No part of this book may be reprinted or reproduced or utilised in any form or by any electronic, mechanical, or other means, now known or hereafter invented, including photocopying and recording, or in any information storage or retrieval system, without permission in writing from the publishers.

Notice:
Product or corporate names may be trademarks or registered trademarks, and are used only for identification and explanation without intent to infringe.

Publisher's Note

The publisher has gone to great lengths to ensure the quality of this reprint but points out that some imperfections in the original copies may be apparent.

British Library Cataloguing-in-Publication Data
A catalogue record for this book is available from the British Library

Library of Congress Cataloging-in-Publication Data
Names: Mohanan, Kalesh, author.
Title: The Royal Indian Navy : trajectories, transformations and the transfer of power / Kalesh Mohanan.
Identifiers: LCCN 2019030586 (print) | LCCN 2019030587 (ebook)
Subjects: LCSH: India. Royal Indian Navy—History—20th century. | India—History, Naval—20th century.
Classification: LCC VA643 .M64 2019 (print) | LCC VA643 (ebook) | DDC 359.00954/09041—dc23
LC record available at https://lccn.loc.gov/2019030586
LC ebook record available at https://lccn.loc.gov/2019030587

ISBN: 978-1-138-55495-5 (hbk)
ISBN: 978-1-03-217708-3 (pbk)
DOI: 10.4324/9780429355226

Typeset in Sabon
by Apex CoVantage, LLC

DISCLAIMER

The views expressed in the book are author's own, and it does not reflect the views of Government of India or the Indian Navy.

MY BELOVED MOM,
MRS SANTHAMMA MOHANAN

CONTENTS

	List of figures	x
	List of tables	xi
	Foreword	xiii
	Acknowledgements	xvi
	List of abbreviations	xviii
1	Introduction	1
2	Origin and development of RIN: post–First World War era (1920–1939)	14
3	Manpower and recruitment in the RIN during the war	55
4	Expansion of the Royal Indian Navy: growth of training and new establishments during the Second World War	110
5	Post-war plans, demobilisation, discontent and revolt	136
6	Indigenisation, partition, reconstitution and birth of a new Navy	178
	Bibliography	228
	Index	238

FIGURES

3.1	New recruits at the RIN Entry Camp	70
3.2	Issue of uniform kit to new recruits	76
3.3	Visit of FOCRIN to the Recruitment Centre	83
3.4	WRINS Officers	92
4.1	RIN establishments and bases during the war	118
5.1	Ratings standing in the queue for food	149
5.2	The RIN Uprising Memorial erected by the Indian Navy at Colaba, Mumbai	169
6.1	Indian Navy receives the President's Color on 26 January 1950	216

TABLES

2.1	Net capital cost in lakhs of rupees	40
2.2	Net total capital cost	41
2.3	Net total capital cost year by year	41
2.4	Annual recurring cost of maintaining the Forces in crores of rupees	41
3.1	Recruitment status in 1942	62
3.2	Warrant Officers sanctioned and borne as on 30 September 1943	63
3.3	Increase in the reserves	65
3.4	Borne strengths of active service ratings at the outbreak of war and on 31 December 1939	69
3.5	Manpower status during the war	73
3.6	Number of HO ratings recruited between the outbreak of war and 31 December 1939	74
3.7	Minimum physical standards of the RIN recruits prior to the war	77
3.8	Modified physical standards of the RIN recruits during the war	78
3.9	Physical standards of the direct entry recruits	78
3.10	Modified physical standards of the direct entry recruits	78
3.11	Pay of seaman branch ratings	80
3.12	Pay of communication branch ratings	80
3.13	Wartime advertisements: posters	84
3.14	Wartime advertisements: booklets	84
3.15	Wartime advertisements: folders, leaflets, etc.	85
3.16	Wartime advertisements: press schemes	85
3.17	Wartime advertisements: cinema slides	86
3.18	Shortage of officers	88
3.19	Shortage of ratings	89
3.20	Strength of officers and Women's Royal Indian Naval Service (WRINS)	91
3.21	Zone-wise manpower representation	93

TABLES

3.22	Communal development – Communication (C.S) & Supply and Secretariat (S.S) ratings	94
3.23	Communal representation in the RIN – ratings	94
3.24	Locality-wise representation – ratings	95
3.25	Development area-wise – C.S & S.S ratings	95
3.26	Recruitment and wastage during the war – active service ratings	97
3.27	Manpower status of Hostilities Only ratings during the war	98
3.28	Manning Progress of RIN during the war	99
3.29	Increase in the strength of officers during the war	100
3.30	Increase in the strength of warrant officers during the war	100
3.31	Increase in the strength of ratings during the war	100
3.32	Number of RIN officers of different nationalities	101
3.33	Manpower development (sailors) during the war	102
4.1	Warships of RIN prior to the war	111
4.2	Wastage of manpower during the war	133
5.1	Demobilisation – officers	145
5.2	Demobilisation – Phase 'A'	145
5.3	Planned strength of RIN warships	146
6.1	RN officers on secondment to RIN in February 1947	183
6.2	Time scale for promotion	184
6.3	Partition of RIN ships	198
6.4	Transfer of RIN ratings to Pakistan	201
6.5	Provincial aspect of active service ratings	201
6.6	Communal composition of active services ratings	202
6.7	Borne strength of officers in the post-Independence era	202
6.8	Borne strength of warrant officers in the post-Independence era	203
6.9	Provincial composition of Indian commissioned and warrant officers as on 1 July 1948	204
6.10	Post-Independence major naval plans – Cochin	214
6.11	Post-Independence major naval plans – Bombay	214
6.12	Post-Independence major naval plans – Vizagapatam	214
6.13	Warships of the Indian Navy in 1950	217

FOREWORD

It was during my first appointment as a non-specialist Navigating Officer of minesweeper *Bhavnagar*, just after award of full naval "watchkeeping certificate", that I came across a document called 'Letter of Proceedings' that was required to be prepared once a month and once every quarter. The format of the monthly and quarterly LOPs were promulgated by Naval Headquarters and the Commanding Officer of this ship, and every other ship that I navigated subsequently as a specialist, went through these reports with such a fine-toothed comb, splitting hairs over every comma, full stop and construction of every sentence, that it was clear to me from *Bhavnagar* itself that LOPs were taken far more seriously than any other document sent from the ship. It was only much later, as Principal Director Naval Operations at NHQ, that I realised that LOPs were essentially meant for the Naval History Division. And Captains did not want history to 'log' them, or their ships, in any manner other than that desired.

It was as PDNO at NHQ that I first ran into a very earnest, committed and diligent young naval officer for whom naval history was the *only* cause worth living, breathing and, maybe, even dying for. The young officer was Lieutenant Commander Kalesh Mohanan, a Deputy Director at the Naval History Division which was then placed under the PDNO. The officer was pursuing his PhD at the prestigious Jawaharlal Nehru University, New Delhi. He later reported to the Indian Naval Academy, Ezhimala, in the Humanities faculty when I was the Deputy Commandant and Chief Instructor. He remained as focussed, involved and assiduous in getting the young, testosterone-driven naval cadets deeply involved in pursuing a BTech curriculum with all the other outdoor, extra-curricular and necessary work to graduate from the academy, to also delve into aspects of naval history with more than cursory interest. I must place on record that his efforts bore fruits, and the papers on maritime history presented by different cadets at each of the academy's annual Dilli seminars, since his arrival, have been of excellent quality.

As the officer had been deeply involved with the writing of the official Indian Navy history with late Vice Adm Hiranandani (Retd) while borne

FOREWORD

on the books of the Naval History Division, it was inevitable that the Navy would like to rope him in to write the next edition too. While the Indian Naval Academy was poorer by the assignment of Lt Cdr Kalesh Mohanan as Assistant Editor to the Indian Naval History Project covering the period 2001–2010, the Indian Navy's history was chronicled with considerable dexterity, precision and élan by Vice Admiral Anup Singh (Retd), ably assisted by Kalesh. The Indian Navy correctly leveraged the author's deep passion and consistent involvement with the Indian Navy's history and the same is very clearly reflected in this labour of his love.

I consider it a privilege, and singular honour, to pen the foreword for his brilliant work: *The Royal Indian Navy: Trajectories, Transformations and the Transfer of Power*

The evolution of the Royal Indian Navy was primarily driven by the colonial self-interests of Britain. The British East India Company set up its own 'navy', called the Honourable East India Company's Marine, in 1612 to protect its shipments from India from local pirates and the elements of its ravaging colonial competitor, the Portuguese sea power. The fledgling force subsequently grew to become the Bombay Marine in 1686, which fought the Maratha and the Sidhis in the contested waters of the Konkan coast of India. The Bombay Marine then evolved to become His Majesty's Indian Navy in 1830 to take care of Britain's interests east of Aden, reverted to Bombay Marine in 1863 and then to Her Majesty's Indian Marine in 1877, to take care of Britain's interests off the Indian subcontinent and was based in Kolkata and Mumbai. By 1892, the force had over 50 vessels and was christened the Royal Indian Marine.

During World War I, from 1914 to 1918, the Royal Indian Marine played a sterling role in transporting over 1.5 million Indian Army troops and animals, and over 3.5 million tonnes of war stores, on troop carriers to Africa, Mesopotamia and France. The force was also involved in minesweeping operations off Mumbai and Aden and carried out riverine, inshore and offshore patrols with their smaller vessels. The force suffered over 300 casualties and 90 personnel were also decorated.

In 1934, the Royal Indian Marine became the Royal Indian Navy (RIN) and the ships of the force carried the prefix 'HMS'. The force, which was a small force with just eight ships at the commencement of the war, underwent rapid expansion during the war as Britain foresaw a major threat to its Sea Lines of Communication (SLOCs) from India to Britain, carrying raw material supporting the war effort.

While the force did a magnificent job during the war, Britain had begun to have second thoughts on the feasibility of continued rule over India once the sailors of the RIN mutinied against what was, initially, service conditions onboard HMIS *Talwar*, but soon took the shape of aligning with the Indian national freedom movement. There were similar mutinies in the Indian Army units too, the information on which was buried. While the narrative in India

FOREWORD

has tended to give short shrift to the contribution of the naval mutiny to speeding up the exit of Britain from India, official records in the United Kingdom have clearly recorded that it was the mutiny in the RIN in 1946 which led the British to conclude that they would not be able to "hold on to India for too long", once the "Indian soldier had begun to revolt against the British rule." The end of the British rule over India, thus, came not from the 'Quit India' or such other many freedom movements by various Indian political parties and groups that mushroomed all over India during that time but from the Indian sailor and soldier joining the freedom movement, which has been largely ignored in the existing narratives of India's freedom movement. The division of the RIN between the Indian Navy and the Pakistan Navy was yet another painful process the proud force had to undergo but was carried out with typical professional finesse, notwithstanding the machinations in Whitehall, London.

I commend this book by the lone professional historian currently in Indian Navy uniform, to both, casual and involved, readers of matters maritime and followers of the development of the Indian Navy from a humble, coastal defensive force to the proud, confident and growing, fifth largest navy in the world.

Rear Admiral M.D. Suresh, AVSM, NM
Assistant Chief of Integrated Defence Staff
Defence Intelligence Agency
New Delhi

ACKNOWLEDGEMENTS

This study has been a result of my analysis of numerous primary documents and interaction with several scholars, retired Defence personnel at various ranks. I had the opportunity to explore various reports and diaries pertaining to the period of 1920–1950 in relation to the various developments in Indian Defence Forces especially in context of Royal Indian Navy (RIN) in the United Kingdom. I visited various libraries, archives, war museums and also various war memorials in London. All this has helped me to a great extent to explore various private papers, personal memoirs, primary reports of various committees and commissions on Indian Defence Forces in general and RIN in particular. The whole journey of my research has been very exciting and incited with new thoughts and ideas. All these documents have a vital role in completion of my research.

I consider myself fortunate having the opportunity to work under the supervision of Professor Sucheta Mahajan, Centre for Historical Studies, JNU. She has always been kind, and her caring behaviour has been a source of inspiration for me, so the credit of this humble endeavour goes to her. In spite of all my shortcomings, the guidance and co-operation that she extended towards me has given shape to my ideas and insights.

Indeed, all credit goes to my Mom and the Almighty. My family, especially my Mother, Smt. Santhamma Mohanan – her support always made me stronger to face challenges in difficult situations. Dr. Krishnan and Prof. Vijayaramaswamy have always encouraged me to work dedicatedly. They were always beside me in their support. I owe my work to them though this is not enough in comparison to their love and affection. Also I want to express my sincere gratitude to Rear Admiral M. D. Suresh for his help, support and valuable suggestions during my research and taking out time from his busy schedule to pen down the foreword of this book. I would like to thank Dr. Narender Yadav (Deputy Director, MoD History Division) for his brotherly attitude and constant support from the very beginning of research. I want to thank my old friends, Dr. Nazia Khan (Dept of Political Science, Jamia Millia Islamia, New Delhi) and Gibu Sabu (Amity University) for their help and support.

ACKNOWLEDGEMENTS

I would like to give special thanks to all the faculty and staff members of Centre for Historical Studies (CHS/JNU), Indian Council of Historical Research (ICHR), History Division of the Ministry of Defence, Naval History Division, The National Archives of India, Maritime History Society (MHS) (Mumbai), Central Secretariat library, The National Archives (Kew, London), British Library (London), The Caird library of National Maritime Museum (Greenwich), Historical Branch of the Royal Navy (Portsmouth), Imperial War Museum (London). Also, my sincere gratitude to Admiral D. K. Joshi (former Chief of the Naval Staff), (Late) Vice Admiral G. M. Hiranandani (former Vice Chief of the Naval Staff), Prof. Gopinath (former Member Secretary ICHR), Rear Admiral Kishan. K. Pandey, Rear Admiral Sanjay J. Singh, Rear Admiral Atul Anand, Commander Mohan Narayan (former Curator, Maritime History Society), Commodore K. S. Noor, Captain Edwin. J. Rajan, Commander Pradumn Joshi, Capt Prashant Mohanan, Capt Navtej Singh, Dr. Reva Dhanadhar (former Director, History Div. Ministry of Defence), Commander Ashish Kale, Lt Commander Divyajot, Dr. Jyotsna Arora (Dy. Director ICHR), Dr. Nupur Singh (ICHR), Mrs. Jaya Prabhakar (National Archives of India), Dr. Gavin Rand (University of Greenwich), Shailendra Nirwal (Petty Officer) and Bhasker Tayal (Petty Officer) of Naval History Division and the list is endless . . .

Without mentioning Alan Jeffreys (Curator, Imperial War Museum, London) and Mrs. Lorren Jeffreys for their kind help and support in the UK, this acknowledgement would not be complete.

Needless to say, my friends and colleagues have always been my constant support and source of relief for me. Merely saying thanks to them is not enough; they have always encouraged me and provided their helping hand to me as and when I wanted them. I recognize the support they have extended to me.

ABBREVIATIONS

AA	Anti Aircraft
Adm	Admiral
AFNC	Armed Forces Nationalisation Committee
AFRC	Armed Forces Reconstitution Committee
AG	Adjutant General
ASW	Anti Submarine Warfare
BTE	Boys' Training Establishment
Capt	Captain
Cdr	Commander
Cmde	Commodore
CPO	Chief Petty Officer
EA	Electrical Artificers
Ed	Education
ERA	Engine Room Artificer
FOB	Flag Officer Bombay
FOCRIN	Flag Officer Commanding Royal Indian Navy
HA	High Angle
HDML	Harbour Defence Motor Launch
HMIS	Her /His Majesty's Indian Ship
HMS	Her /His Majesty's Ship
HO	Hostilities Only
IAOC	Indian Army Ordnance Corps
IC	Indian Commissioned
IECO	Indian Emergency Commission Officer
IEME	Indian Electrical and Mechanical Engineers
IMD	Indian Medical Department
IMMTS	Indian Mercantile Marine Training Ship
IMS	Indian Medical Service
INA	Indian National Army
Inst	Instructor
KC	King's Commission
LA	Low Angle

ABBREVIATIONS

LCA	Landing Craft Assault
LCA (HR)	Landing Car Assault (Hedgerow)
LCC	Landing Craft Control
LCE	Landing Craft Emergency
LCH	Landing Craft Headquarters
LCI (L)	Landing Craft Infantry (Large)
LCM	Landing Craft Mechanised
LCN	Landing Craft Navigation
LCP	Landing Craft Personnel
LCQ	Landing Craft Administration
LCS	Landing Craft Support
LCT	Landing Craft Tank
LCVP	Landing Craft Vehicle Personnel
LCW	Landing Craft Wing
Ld Sig	Leading Signalman
Ldg	Leading
LSD	Landing Ship Dock
LSI (L)	Landing Ship Infantry (Large)
LST	Landing Ship Tank
Lt Cdr	Lieutenant Commander
Lt	Lieutenant
MCPO	Master Chief Petty Officer
ML	Motor Launch
MoD	Ministry of Defence
M/S	Minesweeping
MTB	Motor Torpedo Boat
MTE	Mechanical Training Establishment
NCSC	Naval Central Strike Committee
NHQ	Naval Headquarters
NWFP	North Western Frontier Province
PO	Petty Officer
RAdm	Rear Admiral
RAOC	Royal Army Ordnance Corps
RIAF	Royal Indian Air Force
RIM	Royal Indian Marine
RIN	Royal Indian Navy
RINFR	Royal Indian Navy Fleet Reserve
RINR	Royal Indian Navy Reserve
RINVR	Royal Indian Navy Volunteer Reserve
RMO	Regimental Medical Officer
RN	Royal Navy
RRC	Regional Recruitment Centre
SBA	Sick Berth Attendant
SS	Special Service

ABBREVIATIONS

SS	Supply & Secretariat
SSC	Short Service Commission
Spl	Special
Tel	Telegraphist
TS	Torpedo School
VAdm	Vice Admiral
VC	Viceroy's Commission
WAC (I)	Women's Auxiliary Corps (India)
WRINS	Women's Royal Indian Navy Service
W/T	Wireless Transmitting
Wtr	Writer

1
INTRODUCTION

1. Historical background

The genesis of a naval force by the British in India can be traced back to the formation of the Indian Marine raised by East India Company (EIC) at Surat in 1612. The East India Company in India was established in the seventeenth century to serve its economic interests. They very soon realised the need for a naval force in India to protect their mercantile interests against the Portuguese, the Dutch and also the pirates who infested the coasts of India. Subsequently, in 1612, two of the East India Company's merchant ships, the *Dragon* and *Hoseander*, and two smaller vessels were converted into fighting ships.[1] This small squadron was the birth of the Royal Indian Navy; it was called the Honorable East India Company's Marine and was placed under the command of Captain Thomas Best.[2] These ships arrived off Surat, which was the headquarters of the Company at that time, in October 1612. After acquiring Bombay, the Company moved its headquarters on the Western Coast from Surat to Bombay. The Indian Marine also moved to Bombay.

The evolution of the Royal Indian Navy from the Indian Marine, Bombay Marine, Bombay Marine Corps, Indian Navy, Bombay Marine, Bengal Marine (non-combatant), His Majesty's Indian Marine (a combatant force with two divisions at Bombay and Calcutta), Royal Indian Marine (combatant, reversion to a non-combatant role and again combatant) and Royal Indian Navy. Her Majesty's Indian Marine was constituted as the Royal Indian Marine in 1892 with a strength of 240 British officers and 2,000 Indian sailors, and it functioned as a non-combatant force. The RIM did not make much of a contribution to India till the outbreak of First World War.[3] Till 1914, the RIM was mainly concentrated on marine surveys, transportation of troops and the maintenance of lighthouses.

When the First World War broke out, the British Government realised the need for a combatant navy in the Indian Ocean. Subsequently the status of RIM was upgraded, and her ships were fitted with guns. During the war, RIM was utilised in various theatres of wars for transportation of Indian

INTRODUCTION

troops, arms, ammunitions and rations to Egypt, Iraq and East Africa.[4] RIM ships landed troops in Mesopotamia, and its smaller ships, designed for operations in inland waters, rendered service in the Euphrates and Tigris rivers. During 1914–1918, the six ships of the Royal Indian Marine served as auxiliary cruisers, and the officers of the service served at sea with the Royal Navy in many theatres of war. The total manning strength of the RIM at that time was 240 officers, 60 warrant officers and 2,000 ratings.[5] Without RIM the utilisation of Indian manpower and material in various theatres of war would not have been possible.

The post-war economic situation forced the RIM to revert to a non-combatant force. The post-war period witnessed a large demobilisation (including the reserve list). The RIM was once again reverted to its non-combatant role when the war ended in 1918. The RIM remained as a minor component of the Indian Army and its director was subordinated to the Army's Commander-in-Chief.[6] Till the beginning of the Second World War, the Royal Indian Marine was an amphibious force; the main tasks assigned to the RIM were marine survey, maintenance of lighthouses and transportation of troops, arms, ammunition and stores.

On 2 October 1934 the RIM was re-designated as the Royal Indian Navy. Prior to the Second World War, Britain's Royal Navy was responsible for the overall maritime defence of India. The naval defence of India and its maritime commerce were taken over by the Royal Navy for this service The government of India had to pay an amount of £100,000 annually to the British Government.[7] Many committees were formed between 1925 and 1939 to find the feasibility of a re-organisation of the navy in India but the British Government could not implement any of those recommendations. The outbreak of the unforeseen Second World War forced the British Government to expand the RIN, in haste, to protect the colonial interests in the Indian Ocean. During the war period the British followed a massive expansionist policy towards the RIN. By the end of the war, manpower, establishments and ships increased to almost fifteen to twenty times that of the pre-war situation. In the post-war economic situation the British went on to demobilise the massive naval force in India. The naval revolt of 1946 led the British realise that Indian Armed Forces could not be trusted anymore. Historians have different opinions about the nature and causes of this incident. However, there is a commonality in the views of most of the scholars that the post-war demobilisation and discrimination against the Indians in the RIN were the main causes of the 'mutiny'.

The focus of my book is the crucial years when the Royal Indian Navy went through major phases of developments and change. In some way this book hopes to look at the course taken by the Navy in terms of attitude of the British towards the development of the Royal Indian Navy, the history of its subalterns, the Indian sailors. The Navy, being one of the largest

INTRODUCTION

Government employers, had to decide whom to recruit and on what basis. The Government had vast demographic resources at its disposal, so the naval authorities carried out debates and discussions on how get the best materials out of the countless communities of South Asia. Moreover, their perception about the importance of different indigenous groups within the Navy changed with the function of the Navy.

The aim of the book is also to show the various transitional phases of the Royal Indian Navy, what the Navy officers thought about various potential recruits in the subcontinents and how their beliefs and convictions shaped the establishment policy of the Raj, the growth of the RIN from a non-combat force to a full-fledged combat defence force during the war, discontent within the Navy which led to the revolt of 1946 and the reaction of political leaders towards it. At a broader level the book will examine five major phases in the history of the Royal Indian Navy. Finally the book talks about the partition of RIN, the question of Commonwealth and the final transfer of the Navy from the Royal Indian Navy under the Raj to the Indian Navy in Independent India.

2. Historiography

The period 1935–1950 has a vital role in the history of the world, especially in the case of the Indian subcontinent. It was the period of many major changes. This period witnessed many new developments and striking incidents like the rise of powers called Axis and Allied Powers, rise of armies, navies and air forces, the Second World War, the Pearl Harbour attack followed by the atomic massacre of millions of people, liberation of many nations from the century-old colonial rule at the end of the war. In the case of India, it was a period of transition. The struggle for freedom from the colonial regime was at its climax; without the concern for India, Britain declared the involvement of India in the Second World War and began the reorganisation of the armed forces in the colonial state. This period witnessed great recruitment of Indian manpower and the utilisation of the Indian economy for the imperialist war in the name of 'the protection of India'. India's contribution in the Second World War was appreciated by many British officials. When the war ended in 1945, the world scenario had changed. The socio-economic-political and military situation worsened in the post-war period; the armed forces did not remain untouched, and it led to many revolts in the armed forces. The RIN revolt of 1946 made a new chapter in the history of India. The British plans for the nationalisation of the armed forces were never realised due to the immediate plan for the partition of India and reconstitution of the armed forces. In the post-independence era, the Indian armed forces kept some of the senior British defence personnel for almost for a decade to fully nationalise the Indian armed forces.

INTRODUCTION

Between 1930 and 1941, 15 native navies were raised in the British colonies to protect the imperial interest during the war. Britain could not have fought the Second World War without exploiting the men and material available in India. Historians have looked at this period from different angles. The studies of British policy in India between 1935 and 1950 are characterised by different schools of thought and ideologies. In 1945, when the Second World War was nearing the end, the Government of India set up an office to collect and collate material for writing the history of the operations conducted by the Indian Armed Forces in various theatres of War. This office was subsequently designated as the War Department Historical Section, and Major General T. N. Corbett was appointed as the Director. In August 1946 Brigadier Cordon took over as the Director. Meanwhile, in March 1946, the Section was shifted to Shimla as the climate of Delhi was not considered conducive for quality academic work. However, in 1951, the Section was shifted back to Delhi. Meanwhile, the partition of the country took place and the Section was re-designated as the Combined Inter-Services Historical Section (India and Pakistan). The writing of the history of the Second World War now turned out to be a joint effort of India and Pakistan. Efforts to write the history of the Second World War started in 1948 after Dr. Bisheshwar Prasad, a reputed academic, was appointed as the Director of the CIS Historical Section. Later this office was re-designated as the History Division under the Ministry of Defence. The Division eventually came out with a series of books on the contribution of the Indian Armed Forces in the Second World War. Most of these works mainly focus on the Indian Army in various theatres of war. The History Division has published 25 volumes covering not only the campaigns of the Indian Army but also the history of the Indian Air Force and the Corps of Engineers and a series of volumes on the medical services. *The Royal Indian Navy,* by Instructor Lieutenant D. J. E. Collins, is a unique work on the Royal Indian Navy.[8] However it mainly focusses on the operational history of the RIN. Another work by the MoD History Division, *Expansion of the Armed Forces and Defence Organisation, 1939–1945,* by Sri Nandan Prasad, gives information on the development of the RIN during the Second World War.[9] These two official history books by the History Division of the Ministry of Defence give the primary information but do not provide an academic perspective. Another work of MoD History Division by S. C. Gupta discusses the formation of Indian Air Force Volunteer Reserve (IAFVR), recruitment and training during wartime.[10] He says that the Pownall Sub-Committee recommendation to form auxiliary Air Force units for the coast defence could not be given effect to for lack of funds. According to him "On the outbreak of war the immediate expansion of the Service resulted in an urgent need of officers, and their recruitment."[11]

In 1968, the Naval History Cell was created at Naval Headquarters, New Delhi, to document the history of the Indian Navy. Subsequently,

INTRODUCTION

the history of the Navy has been published in five volumes covering the period from 1945 to 2000. The official history of the Indian Navy, *Under Two Ensigns: Indian Navy, 1945–1950*, by Rear Admiral Satyindra Singh, throws some light on the origin and development of the Indian Navy during the war years.[12] This work focuses on the post-war period and dedicates a chapter on the RIN Mutiny. Satyindra Singh considers the RIN incident of 1946 a mutiny on the similar lines to the colonial masters. The *History of the Pakistan Navy* by the Historical Cell of the Pakistan Navy too does not discuss much about the pre-war period and expansion of the Royal Indian Navy during the course of the war and in the post-war era events.

Rear Admiral Sreedharan gives an idea about the genesis and birth of the Royal Indian Navy and its role in the First and Second World Wars in his work. It helps the reader to understand the morphology of the Indian Navy; however, it lacks the in-depth study on some areas such as Indianisation, recruitment, post-war issues and the Commonwealth. Brigadier Dr. Noor-ul-Haq's work, *Making of Pakistan: The Military Perspective*,[13] focusses on the British attitude towards the demand for Pakistan, the Muslim element in the British Indian Armed Forces, the strategic location of the Muslim majority provinces and the division of the British Indian Army on communal lines. Another work on the Indian Navy by James Goldrick[14] throws light on the development of navies in South Asia in the post–Second World War era. It is on the navies and about navies working with very limited resources in less than ideal circumstances. Goldrick says, "The RIN lacked not only a clear way ahead but any substantial degree of political support or appreciation of its problems."[15]

Commander E. C. Streatfield James of the RIN held many important appointments, including Assistant Adjutant General (Recruiting) and Deputy Chief of Staff (Administration, Naval Headquarters) during the Second World War. He wrote the book[16] from his personal experience, and it gives many insights into the Royal Indian Navy. He relates the evolution of a comprehensive, effective naval force in a colonial state (India) and what happened to the RIN when the axe of partition fell on it.

Memoirs of naval officers throw some light on the subject matter. Autobiographies like of Admiral Ram Dass Katari, the first Indian Chief of the Naval Staff,[17] and Vice Admiral N. Krishnan[18] give the information on the operational aspects of RIN and post-war issues and on partition and its impact on the armed forces.

Sucheta Mahajan's scholarly work discusses the most historically important event of the century, the partition of the Indian subcontinent.[19] Her book explores the post–Second World War imperial strategy for India and the national and popular anti-colonial movements during the freedom struggle. The book discusses the colonial 'Divide and Quit' policy and Hindu and Muslim communal identities, which made the partition

INTRODUCTION

of India unavoidable. In one of the chapters on popular movements, she discusses the Indian National Army (INA) trials, the RIN Revolt of 1946 and the workers, peasants and tribal movements as a prelude to partition. Regarding the RIN revolt, Mahajan says that "though it was easily crushed and remained confined to a section of the navy, was a portent for the future. Anger at racial discrimination and poor service conditions and ill-defined but strong patriotic feelings, produced an explosive situation."[20] She differs from the general leftist view that the British had lost their trust in the Indian Armed Forces in the post 'mutiny' period. She says that "The soldier-Viceroy, Wavell, gave a clean chit to the army a few days after the naval strikes." "Those who believed that the British would succumb to popular pressure, if only it was exerted forcefully, were proved wrong."[21] According to her, Jinnah's demand for partition triumphed over Gandhi's vision for a united India. British wanted strategic and defence alliances with both dominions in the post-partition period. Further, she discusses the British withdrawal from India, transfer of power and the post-partition relationship between India and Britain. Lastly the book examines the aftermath of the hasty transfer of power and the partition of the subcontinent. "The decision to partition India was not only the consequence of past actions and present needs, it was influenced by future prospects."[22] The British were not sure about the membership of an undivided India under the Congress in the Commonwealth defence; therefore they kept open the option of Pakistan as a future strategic partner in the Indian Ocean.

Anirudh Deshpande, in his book *British Military Policy in India, 1900–1945: Colonial Constraints and Declining Power*,[23] discusses the colonial defence policy in the 20th century up to the end of the Second World War. He analyses the military reforms, Indian armed forces in the inter-war period, modernisation during the Second World War and recruitment and demobilisation at the end of the war. He discusses the Indian Army and Royal Indian Marine in the pre–First World War scenario and the Esher Committee recommendations for the military reforms in India. He says that the report of the Esher Committee was based on the financial and political conditions prevalent in India in the post-war period. Regarding the RIM, Deshpande says that "the scope of the Esher recommendation was broad and included the RIM."[24] In 1919 Lord Jellicoe recommended the expansion of RIM and, due to Army dominance over the budget, it was never realised. He says that Esher Committee and its report constituted the British perspective on Indian military reform with all its limitations. He points out that even at the peak of manpower shortage in officer cadres, the Esher Committee did not envisage the indigenisation and modernisation of Indian armed forces, and it failed to consider the social changes in the armed forces. The British could not implement the recommendations, due to the post-war economic condition of the Raj and on the basis of the recommendations of the Indian

INTRODUCTION

Retrenchment Committee. Further, he discusses the Indianisation and the 'martial race' theory in the Indian Army. Indianisation emerged 'in opposition to the pseudo-scientific colonial discourse' of martial race theory, as a 'subaltern' attempt to fashion, and even historically reclaim, identities denied to most Indians by colonial ideology.[25] He says, "After the Mutiny of 1857 the British had gradually evolved the theory of the 'martial races' hand in hand with the Punjabization of the Indian Army to pursue their military and political interest in India."[26] However, Deshpande does not discuss the 'martial race' theory and Indianisation of the Royal Indian Marine. He concludes the 1946 naval 'mutiny' started as a 'Strike' and ended as an 'Uprising'. He discusses the post war demobilisation, discontent among the naval ratings, anti-colonial feeling and their protests against the colonial hegemony for their rights.

The unpublished Ph.D. thesis of V. M. Bhagwatkar focuses on the RIN Mutiny based on primary sources and largely on the RIN Enquiry Commission Report.[27] According to Bhagwatkar, the RIN Uprising was the struggle for the freedom of the country.[28] He says that the Congress and the Muslim League opposed the RIN uprising because "they did not want freedom through struggle of the people but through negotiations with British imperialists."[29] The Congress leadership was influenced by the Indian bourgeoisie and petty bourgeoisie classes, who wanted the future Government of India to safeguard their vested interests. He criticises Gandhi and Jinnah. He says that, for Gandhi "the struggle of the ratings for their demands or for the freedom of the country was not important. Only the problem of violence or non-violence was the main issue before him."[30] According to Bhagwatkar, Jinnah adopted a communal approach by addressing his appeal only to the Muslim ratings to call off the strike. He says that Communist Party of India was the only party which gave its wholehearted support to the RIN uprising, and Aruna Asaf Ali had played a major role in it. He considers racial discrimination to be one of the main reasons behind the ratings' discontent and one of the cardinal causes of the RIN uprising. Even though Bhagwatkar discusses the RIN episode at length, the thesis does not give an analytical view, especially about the causes, character and nature of the event.

Personal accounts of ex-RIN ratings, who were part of the revolt, on the RIN episode are valuable sources of information. Balai Chandra Dutt, ex-communication rating of the RIN, actively took part in the RIN revolt and was thrown out of the naval service. He has extensively written about the episode of RIN Revolt from his personal experience. In his book,[31] Dutt says that in the last hundred years of British rule the Indian armed forces had clashed with the Raj twice before the sepoys in 1857 and with the INA during the Second World War. The RIN uprising was a sequel to the struggle of the INA against British rule. It was not the struggle of the British patronised officers and the privileged ranks, but it was a struggle of the subaltern. He claims that the ratings were politically conscious and their nationalist feelings motivated them to go for a strike with an aim to throw the British from India, and it helped for an early transfer of power. He emphasises that the ratings were not fighting for better food and other amenities. Their ultimate goal was to convert themselves into the navy of a free India, taking orders only from the national leaders. But he feels that the ratings were expecting political support, but they were betrayed by the national leaders. According to him, it was probably the greatest single factor in hastening our freedom. As a result of the revolt, the British were largely convinced that they had lost the control over the military to hold a colonial state anymore. Dutt criticises the Indian officers of the RIN, saying that they were "loyal to the British crown and not nationalist" during the mutiny, and had not done anything for the 'innocent' ratings in the post-war period.

Other RIN 'mutiny' participants, like, Biswanath Bose[32] and Subrata Banerjee[33] too discuss the causes behind the revolt and how it shaped the British decision to leave India.[34] Dipak Kumar Das discusses the RIN episode of 1946 at length in his book.[35] According to Das, "The fact among others gave the RIN strike so vehemently an anti British character as British domination seldom did an anti authority outbreak in colonial society at large. The British top brass sought to explain away the 'mutiny' as a 'war mortality'."[36] Percy. S. Gourgey, who was a Sub-Lieutenant in the Royal Indian Navy Volunteer Reserve and was posted at HMIS *Talwar* during the 'mutiny', discusses the RIN revolt from his personal experience of the incident and interactions with RIN 'mutineers'.[37] According to him, the RIN ratings believed that they were taking part in a 'strike' and they were very decent in their behaviour to British officers. He quotes M. S. Khan, President of the Central Strike Committee:

> Some of our friends got in touch with members of the Congress and other nationalists amongst the civilians. . . . They suggested plans for a mass strike. The authorities may call it 'mutiny' but we understand mutiny to be the violent and bloody overthrow of the officers commanding us. On the other hand, our original intention was, and still is, to have a mass sit-down strike in all ships and establishments, until the authorities take sincere, concrete steps to settle our grievances. But we want this strike to be peaceful. If we can achieve on our aims peacefully, why should we want any harm to come to our superior officers?[38]

Gourgey tries to show that the RIN 'mutiny' aimed for better service conditions and did not aim to throw the British from India.

Lt General S. L. Menezes discusses the history of the Indian Army during the two world wars.[39] It shows the recruitment of the native soldier, racial and martial theory in recruitment, induction of Indians into the officer cadre, nationalisation of the army, partition and aftereffects. Another work on the Indian Army by Byron Farwell talks about the distinction between the Indian Army, British Army in India, independent native armies, Indian Army in the two World Wars, Indianisation, and the INA.[10] Byron says that "In the final decade of the British raj, the Army in India faced four major crises: (1) the need to expand, reorganise and modernize for the exigencies of another world war; (2) the struggle to hold at bay the nationalist in India and to defeat the foes of Empire abroad, particularly the Japanese; (3) the problems presented by the Japanese inspired Indian national Army: and (4) finally the need ultimately to come to terms with the splitting asunder of the Indian Army by the political partition of the subcontinent and the independence of Pakistan and India."[41]

Indigenisation of the Indian Armed Forces was always a question for the British Government. Regarding Indianisation, Pandit Motilal Nehru said that "Indianisation is a word I hate from the bottom of my heart. I cannot understand that word. What do you mean by Indianising India? . . . The Army is ours; we have to officer our own army, there is no question of Indianising there. What we want is to get rid of the Europeanisation of the army."[42] The first Indian officer, Sub Lt D. N. Mukherji, commissioned into the Royal Indian Marine in 1928. In accordance with the policy of nationalisation, the British officials recruited one Indian officer against two British officers. This policy later affected the RIN badly in the post-partition period. Lt. Colonel Gautam Sharma discusses the nationalisation of the Indian Army in his well-researched book *Nationalisation of the Indian Army (1885–1947)*.[43] Even though the book focuses on 'nationalisation', it does not touch upon the Navy and Air Force.

When the unexpected partition and independence of India and Pakistan became realistic, the question of keeping the newly born dominion states in the Commonwealth became a matter of concern for the British Government. The British wanted India to continue in the Commonwealth in order to have armed forces in the Indian Ocean for any future war. Anita Inder Singh's articles throw light on the partition and Commonwealth. According to her, the Britain wanted a unified army and wanted India to be part of the Commonwealth. Anita shows with the colonial primary sources the colonial interests in the Indian armed forces and their hidden agendas to utilise India as a base in the Far East. She says, "The chief advantage of India to Britain was strategic; India was the only base from which the British could sustain large-scale operations in the Far East."[44] According to Singh, Mountbatten played a major role in persuading the Indian leaders to "remain in the Commonwealth and to shake Jinnah's obduracy."[45] "Mountbatten's tactic was to warn the Congress that India would be militarily vulnerable outside the Commonwealth; and to threaten them that the British would probably accept Pakistan's plea for Dominion status, which would give Pakistan full access to British military facilities and aid."[46] Singh says that "The loss of

INTRODUCTION

India would weaken the British position in the Middle East and the Indian Ocean."[47]

3. Chapterisation

Chapter 1 is the Introduction.

Chapter 2, 'Origin and Development of RIN: Post–World War I Era (1920–1939)', deals with the post-war Policies of the British Raj with respect to the defence strategy, geo-political scenario, transition of the Royal Indian Navy from a non-combat force to a combat navy, various committees and recommendations for the development of RIN prior to the war. This chapter tries to analyse the British naval perceptions/policies with respect to the Indian Ocean, what the reasons were behind the delay in the reorganisation of the Royal Indian Marine even after many committees and recommendations, and what was the prevailing situation of RIN at the outbreak of the war.

Chapter 3, 'Manpower and recruitment in the RIN during the war', explicates the changes in the policies and attitude of the colonial regime, the policy of induction of the officer cadre and the entry of Indians, RIN's new induction of Indian sailors (ratings) and how different it was from the previous ideologies behind recruitments. Why did the Indian youth join a colonial defence force during the peak of the national movement? What were sailors' attitude towards the British Raj and the Royal Crown's policies towards India during wartime?. Thus the policies towards recruitment as well as its social implications for the newly recruited Indian sailors are the major thrust of my arguments.

Chapter 4, 'Expansion of the Royal Indian Navy: growth of training and new establishments during the Second World War', enumerates the training of new Indian recruits and growth of establishments during World War II. This chapter is purely based on the primary sources (which are not available in the public domain). Because of this and my official obligation to the Indian Navy, I could not give the source of reference. This chapter enumerates the expansion of the Royal Indian Navy in the fields of vessels, equipment, training and establishments during wartime and how these developments were utilised by the colonial government to the fullest for the protection of the imperial interest.

Chapter 5, 'Post-war plans, demobilisation, discontent and revolt', deals with the Royal Indian Navy during the post-war period. It discusses the British policy of demobilisation at the end of the war, the policies of the resettlement of demobilised ratings, the nature, causes and aftermath of the Royal Indian Naval 'Mutiny' of 1946, the service conditions and the main reasons behind the discontent among the ratings. Was it a mutiny or a revolt? Did the RIN ratings have nationalism on their minds? Was it a strike for better service life? Were they influenced by any political

INTRODUCTION

ideologies? What was the response of the national leaders towards the Mutiny and the impact of the Mutiny on the Armed Forces?

Chapter 6, 'Indigenisation, partition, reconstitution and birth of a new Navy', explores the post war situation of the RIN. This chapter tries to analyse the indigenisation of RIN, the question of the partition of Armed Forces in 1947, and the views of Congress and the Muslim League on the division of Armed Forces. What was the British stand on the division of Armed Forces? What was the impact of partition on RIN? It addresses the question of Commonwealth in contest of Indian Armed Forces, and lastly gives an analysis of the post-independence situation of RIN.

4. Sources and research methodology

The research is based on both qualitative and quantitative research methodology. This research is largely dependent on colonial sources. and on less-used primary documents like the Royal Indian Navy Reports, RIN Mutiny Inquiry Reports, Chief of Staff's Committee Reports, Admiral Godfrey Papers, RIN job advertisements, Naval Plans Papers, letters of high ranking naval and civil service officers, unpublished historical records of the Royal Indian Navy and the service journals (like *RIN Log, United Services Institute of India Journal*). For the administrative policies, administrative structure and recruitment policy, I have used direct sources like the annual reports, RIN advertisement booklets and the books written by high ranking Naval Officers. But for the loyalty mechanism or command mechanism, to get a glimpse of the sailor's views, I have used secondary sources like memoirs of the officers, articles published in the naval journals etc. Apart from using the resources available at the National Archives (Kew, UK), Caird Library of the National Maritime Museum (Greenwich, UK), Naval Historical Branch of the Royal Navy (Portsmouth, UK), I have used unpublished documents available at the History Division of Ministry of Defence (New Delhi), and the Naval History Division of the Indian Navy (New Delhi).

Notes

1 Papers of Commander G. E. Walker, RINVR, 'File of Historical Notes', 1944, RIN/16/2, Caird Library, National Maritime Museum, Greenwich, UK.
2 Ibid.
3 Rear Admiral Satyindra Singh, *Under Two Ensigns, the Indian Navy 1945–50*, Oxford Publications, New Delhi, 1986, p. 19.
4 Ibid.
5 Sailors of the Royal Indian Marine/Royal Indian Navy were known as Ratings.
6 James Goldrick, *No Easy Answers: The Development of the Navies of India, Pakistan, Bangladesh and Sri Lanka: 1945–1996*, Lancer, New Delhi, p. 3.

INTRODUCTION

7 Rear Admiral Satyindra Singh, *Under Two Ensigns, the Indian Navy 1945–50*, Oxford Publications, New Delhi, 1986, p. 20 and R. D. Katari, *A Sailor Remembers*, Prabhat Prakashan, New Delhi, 2012.
8 Instructor Lieutenant D. J. E. Collins, *The Royal Indian Navy*, Orient Longmans, New Delhi, 1964.
9 Sri Nandan Prasad, *Expansion of the Armed Forces and Defence Organisation: 1939–45*, MoD History Division, New Delhi, 1956.
10 S. C. Gupta, *Official History of the Indian Armed Forces in the Second World War 1939–45*, 'History of the Indian Air Force: 1933–45', Orient Longmans, New Delhi, 1961.
11 Ibid., p. 31.
12 Rear Admiral Satyindra Singh, *Under Two Ensigns: Indian Navy 1945–1950*, Oxford & IBH Publishing Co., New Delhi, 1986.
13 Dr. Noor-ul Haq, *Making of Pakistan: The Military Perspective*, Reliance Publishing House, New Delhi, 1997.
14 James Goldrick, *No Easy Answers: The Development of the Navies of India, Pakistan, Bangladesh and Sri Lanka, 1945–1996*, Lancer, New Delhi, 1997.
15 Ibid., p. 7.
16 Commander E. C. Streatfield James, *In the Wake, the Birth of the Indian and Pakistani Navies*, Charles Skilton, Edinburgh, 1983.
17 Ram Dass Katari, *A Sailor Remembers*, Prabhat Prakashan, New Delhi, 2012.
18 Vice Admiral N. Krishnan, *A Sailor's Story*, Punya Publishing Private Limited, 2011. New Delhi, 2011.
19 Sucheta Mahajan, *Independence and Partition: The Erosion of Colonial Power in India*, Sage Publications, New Delhi, 2000.
20 Ibid., p. 383.
21 Ibid., p. 100.
22 Ibid., p. 386.
23 Anirudh Deshpande, *British Military Policy in India, 1900–1945: Colonial Constraints and Declining Power*, Manohar, New Delhi, 2005.
24 Ibid., p. 53.
25 Ibid., p. 88.
26 Ibid.
27 V. M. Bhagwatkar, Ph.D thesis submitted to Nagpur University, *The Role of the R.I.N. Mutiny of Feb. 1946 (Royal Indian Navy Uprising) in the Indian Freedom Struggle* (Year not known).
28 Ibid., p. 260.
29 Ibid., p. 262.
30 Ibid., p. 224.
31 Balai Chand Dutt, *Mutiny of the Innocents*, Sindhu Publications Pvt. Ltd, Bombay, 1971.
32 Biswanath Bose, *RIN Mutiny 1946*, Northern Book Centre, New Delhi, 1988.
33 Subrata Banerjee, *The RIN Strike (February, 1946)*, PPH, New Delhi, 1954.
34 Biswanath Bose and Subrata Banerjee actively participated in the RIN Revolt of 1946 and later they were dismissed from the service for their participation.
35 Dipak Kumar Das, *Revisiting Talwar: A Study in the Royal Indian Navy Uprising of February 1946*, Ajanta, New Delhi, 1993.
36 Ibid., p. 130.
37 Percy S. Gourgey, *The Indian Naval Revolt of 1946*, Orient Longman, Chennai, 1996.
38 Ibid., p. 23. Mistakenly the author calls him as Punnu Khan.
39 Lt General S. L. Menezes, *Fidelity and Honour: Indian Army from the Seventeenth to the Twenty-First Century*, Oxford University Press, New Delhi, 1999.

INTRODUCTION

40 Byron Farwell, *Armies of the Raj, from the Great Indian Mutiny to Independence: 1858–1947*, Viking, England, London, 1989.
41 Ibid., p. 303.
42 Legislative Assembly Debates, National Archives, New Delhi. Vol. 4, 1927, p. 3474.
43 Lt. Colonel Gautam Sharma, *Nationalisation of the Indian Army (1885–1947)*, Allied Publishers Limited, New Delhi, 1996.
44 Anita Inder Singh, 'Keeping India in the Commonwealth: British Political and Military Aims, 1947–49', *Journal of Contemporary History*, Vol. 20, No. 3, July 1985, p. 473.
45 Anita Inder Singh, 'Imperial Defence and the Transfer of Power in India, 1946–1947', *The International History Review*, Vol. 4, No. 4, November 1982, p. 584.
46 Ibid.
47 Ibid., p. 571.

2

ORIGIN AND DEVELOPMENT OF RIN

Post–First World War era (1920–1939)

1. Introduction

The need for a Navy for the naval defence of India in the 20th century was more of a necessity than it had ever been in the preceding centuries. The Indian Marine Service Act of 1884 defined the purpose for which the Royal Indian Marine Service exists, viz., the transport of troops; the guarding of the convict settlements; the suppression of piracy; the survey of coasts and harbours; the visiting of lighthouses; the relief of distressed and wrecked vessels and other naval establishments.[1] However, the suppression of piracy has never been handed over to the Royal Indian Marine as their exclusive duty.[2] It was the duty of the Royal Navy to suppress the piracy on the high seas.

The Royal Indian Marine was governed by the Indian Marine Act of 1887, which, although it was modelled substantially on the provisions of the Naval Discipline Act of 1884, remained nevertheless a purely local Act. Although it made special provisions for wartime, it did nothing to bring the ordinary peacetime discipline code of the Royal Indian Marine in line with the standard code embodied in the Naval Discipline Act.[3] In 1927 the British Parliament passed the Indian Navy Act, which empowered the Indian Legislature to adapt the Naval Discipline (Dominion Naval Forces) Act of 1911.[4] The policy was that, if and when the Indian Legislature availed itself of this power, the Royal Indian Marine would thereupon be entitled to rank as one of the 'Navies' of the British Empire because it would be conforming to the standard British Empire code of naval discipline.[5]

The RIM vessels were used to convey political officers and other high officials to and from the Persian Gulf and islands off the Indian coast, both when proceeding to take up appointments in such places and on inspection duty.[6] The RIM was given the task of the management of the dockyards at Bombay, Kidderpore and Mandalay. The Bombay dockyard was largely used by the ships of the East Indies Squadron of the Royal Navy. The RIM built launches for the customs and police and tugs for the Government of India and provincial governments.[7] The RIM had the charge of marine survey of India and used to carry out marine survey from the Persian Gulf to the Mergui Archipelago. A RIM vessel was deployed at Port Blair, the convict settlement on the Andamans, for police duty.[8] Apart from these duties, RIM was in charge of lighthouses on 1,200 miles of the Madras coast, on a portion of the Calcutta coast, on the whole of the Burmese coast and was also responsible for the floating lights in the Persian Gulf.[9]

In accordance with the recommendations of the Royal Commission of 1895, India had to pay £1,00,000 annually to the British Government for the naval defence of India.[10] The RIM functioned under the Commander-in-Chief in India, who was one of the four members of the Governor General's Council as the War Member. Sea power was strictly kept on a tight leash from England with the 'distant fleet' ensuring that the Britain's Navy ruled the waves.

Since the last decade of the 19th century, the Royal Indian Marine had given support to the Royal Navy in various British martial operations.[11] Most of these expeditions were in Africa, as a continuation of the colonial expansionist policy towards the continent. The RIM participated in the Suakin Expedition of 1896 (in Sudan), Mkwelo (East Africa) in 1897 and in the Second Anglo-Boer War (1899–1902). Till 1914, the RIM mainly concentrated on marine survey of India, transportation of troops and the maintenance of lighthouses. "On the outbreak of the South African War in 1899, the entire contingent from India was sent by the Director Royal Indian Marine from Bombay with unequalled celerity, and a considerable number of officers and seamen were employed in transport and allied duties."[12] The service received the thanks of both houses of Parliament for the celerity with which the troops from India were despatched to Natal.[13] The RIM again was deployed in the North China for the Boxer Rebellion in 1900 to 1901 and also in the various Somaliland Expeditions between 1902 and 1904 and in the gun running operations in the Persian Gulf between 1911 and 1912.[14] Prior to the war, the RIM was busy carrying out the responsibility of sea transportation. In February 1912, the RIM ships *Hardinge* and *Dufferin* had carried two Indian Infantry Battalions with transport carts and mules from Karachi to Hong Kong and *Northbrook* carried the 24th Mountain Battery from Rangoon to Hong Kong.[15] Between 1909 and 1914, RIM, as a non-combatant navy, was involved in the Joint Antigun Running Operations with the Royal Navy in the Gulf of Oman.

During the First World War, RIM was utilised in various theatres of war for transportation of troops, arms, ammunitions and rations to Egypt, Iraq and East Africa.[16] The Royal Indian Marine was a very useful adjunct to the Royal Navy in the First World War. RIM ships landed troops in Mesopotamia, and its smaller ships, designed for operations in inland waters, rendered excellent service in the Euphrates and Tigris rivers. During 1914–1918, the six ships of the RIM, fitted with arms, served as auxiliary cruisers, and the officers of the service served at sea with the Royal Navy in many theatres of war. On acknowledging the contribution of RIM in the First World War, the Mesopotamian Commission of 1917, recommended the RIM as a 'useful reserve'.[17]

Since the constitution of RIM in 1892, a senior officer of the Royal Navy used to be appointed as the Director RIM, as nominated by the Admiralty with concurrence of the Secretary of State for India. The Director had to submit his proposals to the Secretary of Army Department, who was from the Army, and who had taken his orders on marine questions from the Army Member. The Director, Army Department, was posted at Army Headquarters (Delhi and Shimla) and the Director RIM was in Bombay. The Admiralty had no responsibility for the training and efficiency of the RIM, though under the Indian Marine Act of 1884, Section 6, the Admiralty was authorised to take over the RIM, if considered necessary, in time of war.[18] Accordingly the RIM vessels were taken over by the Royal Navy during the First World War and deployed in the various theatres of war. The budget of the RIM was fully controlled by the army authorities, as a separate section of the military budget.[19]

In the post–World War I era, the strength of RIM was cut down to 131 officers, 57 warrant officers, and 1,360 ratings. In 1919, Admiral of the Fleet Viscount Jellicoe of Scapa was sent to India to study and propose the reorganisation of the RIM.[20] In the report, Jellicoe proposed the reorganisation and the increase of strength of RIM, which meant finding £3.5 million out of a massive Imperial Defence Budget for India of £30 million.[21] Admiral Chatterji, former Chief of the Naval Staff said that, "The Army hierarchy approved only a little over one tenth of this money on the pretext of rapid growth of Army expenditure."[22] Jellicoe's main objection was that the administration of a Marine service should not be under the Army member (the Commander-in-Chief, India) who viewed naval problems through army spectacles.[23] The Admiralty, who claimed jurisdiction over everything afloat and were anxious to bring the RIM under their control, failed to do so.[24] And the proposal of shifting the RIM Headquarters from Bombay to Delhi was also turned down.[25]

The Esher Committee of 1920 also recommended the continuation of RIM as an Indian service, so long as it was paid for and maintained by the Government of India.[26] The Committee recommended the following two alternative proposals, on the lines of the recommendations of the Report of the Mesopotamian Commission of 1917,[27] for the administration of the Royal Indian Marine and to give a higher status to the Director RIM in the Government of India:

1   The upgradation of the rank of Director RIM to Rear Admiral from the Royal Navy, with a status of Secretary to the Government of India, with his headquarters and residence at Bombay.[28] The Director RIM thus would be directly subordinate to the proposed civilian Member

ORIGIN AND DEVELOPMENT OF RIN

of Council for Munitions and Marine or to the Commander-in-Chief, and like other Secretaries would have the right of direct access to the Viceroy.[29]

2. The office of the Director RIM should be in Bombay, but there should be a RIM officer, holding the appointment of Deputy or Assistant Secretary to the Government of India.[30]

Further, the committee recommended that the Director RIM should have two Deputies, both officers of the RIM; one was to be his second-in-command, the other the Superintendent of the Bombay Dockyard, and it would be the duty of the Director, or his Deputies, to attend at the headquarters of Government (Delhi or Shimla), when any important case was under consideration.[31] In addition, the committee recommended the improvement of the conditions of the recruitment, training, service, pay and pension of the Indian personnel. The committee emphasized the existing recruitment from the seafaring communities, especially from the Ratnagiri on the Bombay coast.[32] The Committee discussed higher education in seamanship, marine engineering to the ratings (sailors) to make professionally sound Indian ratings in the RIM. However, the Committee did not discuss the promotion of the Indian ratings to officer rank or the Indianisation of the officer cadre.

The Esher Committee recommended the use of RIM in the policing of the Persian Gulf to relieve the British sailors. The recommendation said that "The climate is enervating, and the nature of the duties is such as can be performed by Indians, thus setting free British sailors. The Indian, trained and led by British officers, will be a match for any enemy that he is likely to encounter there. A few British naval ratings, such as first class petty officers for gunnery and drill instructors, supplied by the Admiralty, will be necessary for a few years."[33] The Esher Committee aimed to promote the efficiency and contentment of the Navy in India, and to secure that the Government of India would have at its disposal a well-trained and loyal Navy, fit to take its share in the defence of the British empire.

The role of Defence forces in India in the post–First World War period was defined by the Indian Legislative Assembly in 1921 as to be the defence of India from external aggression and maintenance of internal security.[34] For any other tasks involving co-operation with the British forces for imperial purposes, it was clearly stated that the obligation should not be more onerous than that of any self-governing dominion.[35] The defence forces of the Dominions were not available unconditionally for imperial interests. But in the case of India, her defence forces were utilised for the imperial interests, even after the iteration of the policy of 1921. Between 1921 and 1932 Indian troops were sent to Iraq, Persia and Singapore.[36]

The Commander-in-Chief had informed the Defence Secretary that "we have said more than one occasion that we aim, in an Imperial emergency, at placing the equivalent of one division at the disposal of His Majesty's

Government for overseas operations."[37] The Defence Policy of India of 1921 was summed up: "To the extent to which it is necessary for India to maintain an army for these purposes, its organisation, equipment and administration should be thoroughly up-to-date, and with due regard to Indian conditions, in accordance with present day standards of efficiency in the British Army so that when the Army on any occasion there may be no dissimilarities of organisation, etc., which would render such co-operation difficult."[38] The Garran Tribunal Report of November 1933 stated that "The Defence of India and the defence of the Empire cannot be dissociated. In a sense everything done in the defence of India is also done in the defence of the Empire, and everything done in the defence of the Empire, whether in India or elsewhere, is also done in the defence of India."[39]

By 1935, the developments of modern warfare, and the alteration in the world geographical distribution of naval power, had wrought a vital change in India's strategic situation. Britain and France were no longer the sole naval powers, with Germany as a strong potential contender; instead, the United States and Japan possessed strong and modern battle fleets, in the 1930s and Italian naval power was (by reputation at least) also a force to be reckoned with. The centre of gravity of any possible naval activity in a future war had shifted from the Northern European waters eastwards towards the Pacific, and consequently much nearer India. Three of the great naval powers – Britain, the United States and Japan – had vital interests, and ambitions, in the Far East, and any naval conflict involving these three was likely to approach much closer to India than ever before.

In addition to this factor, post-1914 developments in methods of waging war had made it at least as much a matter of material as of personnel, and in the former, India was notably lacking in self-sufficiency. This fact gave the Chatfield Expert Committee much anxiety in 1938–1939, and caused them to recommend considerable expenditure on the building and equipment of ordnance factories in India.[40] The obvious inference is that to a far greater degree than before, India was dependent on the Imperial Navy for keeping her lines of sea communication open and safe. There was little doubt in any future war, India's maritime supply routes would be one of her most vulnerable points, and one of the points at which her potential enemies would be most likely to direct their attention and most likely to injure her most.

This chapter examines how the problem of India's defence presented itself to those responsible for making the necessary plans, and what measures were taken to meet the potential dangers, in terms of seaward protection, in order to maintain the imperial hegemony over the Indian sub-continent.

2. Geo-political situation

The international situation had seriously deteriorated since 1930s, owing to the re-arming of Germany and Italy, the attitude of Japan and the failure of the League of Nations to restrain Italy in Abyssinia. The ambitions of Germany, Italy and Japan tended more and more to clash with the interests of the British Empire, and these three powers were temporarily grouped together. For Britain, the effect of this grouping in a war would be a serious threat to British communications with India and British interests in the Far East.[41] In this scenario Britain planned to utilise the Indian Defence Forces to reinforce British troops in Egypt, Palestine, Iraq, Malaya and the Far East, since India was the only source (temporarily at least) from which reinforcement could reach those areas.[42] The British believed that the Russian menace to the territorial integrity of India, though dormant, might arise again in the future in intensified form.[43] The changes in the international situation had materially increased India's vulnerability and her potential commitments.

The international political situation at the time of war also forced the British government to think about the need for expansion of a fighting force in India. The Soviet Russian–German Treaty of August 1939 created a threat of a Russian invasion of Afghanistan and India.[44] "The contingency of Russian aggression through Afghanistan, aimed at the overthrow of British rule in India, was considered as a 'Major Danger'."[45] At the same time the British Government considered there to be lesser likelihood of Afghan aggression against India. War with Afghanistan was classified as a '*Minor* Danger' and its prosecution was the responsibility of the Government of India without assistance from Imperial sources.[46] Till the end of 1936 the British had not foreseen any threat from Japan, because Japan was fully occupied with her nationalist policy of expansion in Eastern Asia and she was anxious for a political understanding with the British Government.[47] But the tripartite agreement between Germany, Italy and Japan had created a potential military combination against the Empire of a menacing character.[48] The British feared attack from Japan as well. They were afraid that Japan's operations in China might have decisive influence on her power to threaten India thereafter.[49] The British feared that Japan's attack on Singapore, in conjunction with one or more Western Powers, "which would vitally concern India as well as the rest of the Empire, and would directly menace sea communications, Sea borne raids on Indian coasts would inflict much material damage and cause serious alarm among the civil population, which would intensify the need for adequate Internal Security measures, and the Air attack on Burma and India from advanced land bases, possibly in Siam."[50] The Memorandum on the Defence Forces (1936) stated that "the scale of Japanese attack cannot be exactly determined but it would probably include sporadic raids by surface craft and by sea-borne aircraft from a raider, and submarine and mining activities."[51] The British expected such operations would not constitute a vital threat to the security of India, and it would be a serious danger to shipping, which would certainly affect the morale of the country. Moreover, the political situation inside the country was believed to aggravate the task of internal security[52] and these factors called for larger forces in India.

Apart from the aggression on India by Japan and Russia, the British were anxious about the threat from Italy. The Admiralty expected that the aggressive activities against India by Italian naval force operating from ports in Somaliland and Eritrea would be very largely, if not largely, neutralised by the British occupation of the Suez Canal zone and Aden, resulting in the British ability to maroon, in the Red Sea, Italian warships which happened to be in those waters on the outbreak of war.[53] Isolated and small scale attacks by submarines, surface craft and seaborne aircraft attack against shipping and coastal towns in India were expected to be possible during the very early stages of war, though the effect of such attacks would not be great. The Admiralty believed that a high standard of local naval defence was not required during the strained situation with Italy in 1935 and 1936.[54]

When the war broke out, the United Kingdom was in the midst of a rearmament programme.[55] The British Government had to procure the essential supplies of ammunition, aircrafts or vehicles at the outbreak of war from the United States or Canada. India was largely dependent on the supplies of technical equipment and trained officers from the United Kingdom. Without them, her immense potential of manpower could not be translated into natural fighting strength. The sea lanes carrying these vital supplies from the United Kingdom to India became more and more vulnerable as the war progressed. In order to avoid the attack from Italian ships and German U-boats (submarines) these ships had to follow a convoy system, which in itself reduced considerably the effective shipping space.

Till the beginning of the Second World War, the Imperial Government believed that the scale of seaborne attack to which India was liable was not such as would seriously threaten her security.[56] On the basis of the recommendations of the Imperial Conference of 1928, the British Government had regarded it as the duty of the Dominions and India to make provision for local naval defence of their ports and harbours in wartime.[57]

3. Economic factors

The post–World War I era was a period of economic recession, and it had a major impact on the defence forces of the colonial state. The British Government did not want to modernise or expand the defence forces of the colonies due to the economic crisis in the post War period. The Government of India was already paying to the Admiralty for naval defence of India an amount of £1,00,000 annually as recommended by a Royal Commission of 1895.[58] In 1857, this amount was reduced to £38,500 and in 1869 this was increased to £70,000 and later it was fixed at £100,000 confirmed by arbitration of Lord Rosebery in 1895 for 10 years. Since the amount was continued at a rate of £100,000 per annum.[59] In 1913 it was increased to £16,80,000 as capital outlay and £490,000 as annual payment.⁶⁰ At the end of the World War I the Royal Indian Marine was adversely affected by shortage of funds and extensive retrenchment. The combatant role of the RIM had been lost and the task of the naval defence of India was again entrusted with the Royal Navy. The RIM was reduced to a small non-combatant, auxiliary force and practically RIM had no role in the defence of Indian coasts.

In the post–World War I, Lord Jellicoe drew up a scheme for the re-organisation of the Royal Indian Marine, "but the Indian Government shelved the scheme and the Service fell on hard times, drastic retrenchment was necessary and the axe fell heavily."⁶¹ In the early 1920s Rear Admiral H. L. Mawbey, director of the RIM, had proposed a reorganisation scheme of the RIM, which recommended the raising of RIM to a full-fledged combatant naval force. In this period the Marine Administration was handled by the Army Administration. Mawbey emphasized the separation of Marine Administration from the Army Administration and the relieving of RIM from its duty of carrying troops and ammunition during peacetime.⁶² He recommended the upgradation of the post of Director RIM to that of Secretary to the Government of India to enable him to pursue the matter personally in the Viceroy's Council.⁶³ But the proposals of Mawbey were turned down by the Government of India on the ground of economic crisis, and as a protest Rear Admiral Mawbey resigned in April 1922.

On 25 May 1921, Sir Charles Walker, Deputy Admiralty Secretary, wrote to the Secretary of the Committee of Imperial Defence, in response to the letter received from the Treasury, No. S 7077, dated 14 May 1921, on the formation of an Indian Navy and an extension of annual subsidy the Government of India had paid for the services of the East Indies Squadron since 1869. He felt that this was a matter for Cabinet decision, and must await a definite proposal from the Government of India.⁶⁴ In 1922 the Government of India formed a committee under the chairmanship of Lord Inchcape,⁶⁵ as part of a general effort to reduce the governmental expenditure, to study the future of the Royal Indian Marine. Admiral Chatterji says, "The axe fell heavily on the Royal Indian marine."⁶⁶ The Inchcape Committee recommended the drastic curtailment and reorganisation of the RIM; particularly selling of its old ships and the commercialisation of its dockyards.⁶⁷ Further, the Committee recommended the abolition of the RIM troopships, stating the trooping could be far better run by ships taken under contract from the Merchant Service.⁶⁸ As a result of the Inchcape Committee recommendations, in 1923 the RIM was virtually reduced to a Marine Survey unit and a yacht squadron for the benefit of senior Government officials wishing to travel by sea.⁶⁹

The defence budget of India had passed through two periods of intensive retrenchment. The first was in 1923 when, as a result of arbitrary cuts recommended by the Inchcape Committee, the budget was reduced from Rs.65 crores to Rs.56 crores.⁷⁰ In 1927, the state of equipment and war reserves had fallen so much below the standard required under modern developments that it was necessary to embark on a special re-equipment programme in 1928, costing Rs.10 crores.

In 1928, the Committee of Imperial Defence recommended three phases for the Naval defence of India.[71] But the budget for all defence forces in India was under the heading of Defence and was controlled by the Defence Minister, by default, who was the Army Commander-in-Chief. Naturally the Defence Minister, the Army Chief, used to give priorities to the Army over the Navy and Air Force.[72] Owing to the financial stringency and the Indian General Staff's preoccupation with the North West Frontier problems, the first two phases of the naval defence have been badly neglected.

The retrenchment programme was supposed to be completed in four years, but in 1930 the second period of retrenchment started, owing to the general Economic Depression, and it culminated in 1934 with the reduction of budget from Rs.55 crores to Rs.45 crores.[73] During the period (1930–1934) the British Government was compelled to reduce mobilisation and Reserves.[74] The Secretary of State for India recommended to the Committee of Imperial Defence that the Imperial government agree to the request of the Indian government that control of the Royal Indian Marine not be transferred to the Commander-in-Chief East Indies Squadron without prior consultation with the Government of India.[75] So that the Royal Indian Marine could control merchant shipping, steps were taken to establish a Royal Indian Marine Voluntary Reserve.[76] Financial problems were so acute, however, that the formation of a Voluntary Reserve had to be deferred, and the fleet had to be reduced to eight vessels.[77]

4. Birth of the Royal Indian Navy

The public opinion against the 'wilful eradication of India's naval and maritime traditions'[78] and the protest of Mawbey led to the formulation of a Committee in 1925, under the chairmanship of General Lord Rawlinson, Commander-in-Chief India, to examine the future role of the RIM and its development.[79] The Rawlinson Committee looked into the reorganisation and reconstruction of the RIM as a combatant force so as to form the nucleus of an Indian Navy to undertake the local naval defence of India. Subsequently, the Committee recommended the reconstitution of RIM as a combatant force and its re-designation as Royal Indian Navy under a Rear Admiral of the Royal Navy.[80] The Committee recommended the strength of RIN as four sloops, two patrol craft vessels, four trawlers, two survey ships and one depot ship.[81] As per the recommendations, the peacetime functions of the newly constituted Navy were the training of personnel for service in wartime, the naval services required by the Indian Government in the Indian Ocean and Persian Gulf, Naval Defence of the Indian ports, survey work in the Indian Ocean and marine transport work for the Government of India.[82] Even though the combatant status was recommended to the RIM, the committee recommended the King's Commission to the British and Indian officers of the RIN, similar to the RIM officers' commission. The British Government always wanted to maintain disparity in the status of officers of the Royal Navy and naval officers of the colonies, even though they were largely British. The Rawlinson Committee recommended that "We strongly deprecate the use of any form of commission which might convey the impression that the officers of the Indian Navy held a purely subordinate status as is held by Viceroy's commissioned officers in the Indian Army."[83]

At the end of 1926 things began to move; all the station ship duties were taken over by the various local governments and the ships were concentrated in Bombay. Two officers were lent from the Royal Navy to commence the instruction and advice on the militarisation of the ships. Lt Holmstrom for Gunnery and Lt Knight for Minesweeping started their jobs in early 1927 in Bombay.[84]

On the basis of the recommendations of the Rawlinson Committee, the RIM was reorganised as a combatant force in 1928 and a White Ensign was hoisted on all RIM ships on 11 November 1928.[85] Subsequently the Indian Navy Discipline Bill was taken up by the Legislative Assembly in 1928, with an aim to re-designate the name of RIM as Royal Indian Navy (RIN). The bill was opposed by Shanmukham Chetty and it was defeated by one vote in the Assembly.[86] It did not lack supporters among the Indians, but the Swarajists, who were in a powerful majority, had decided to obstruct the passage of the Bill, not because they wanted to stop India having a navy of her own, but because they wished to force upon the Legislature the Indian Coastal Reservation Act which contained several drastic proposals for the coastwise shipping of India.[87] It can be assumed that the Swarajist would not consider the introduction of a new service unless the Indians were to have financial control. The Bill, however, was re-introduced again in 1934 and was passed by the Indian Legislative Assembly on 29 August 1934[88] and the Council of States on 5 September 1934. Later, on 2 October 1934, RIM was re-designated as the Royal Indian Navy and the King Emperor presented the King's Colours to the Royal Indian Navy, which was officially brought into existence with Naval Headquarters at Bombay under the command of Flag Officer Commanding Royal Indian Navy (FOCRIN).[89]

Rear Admiral Sir Humphery Walwyn became the first Flag Officer Commanding Royal Indian Navy and continued until November 1934, when he was succeeded by Rear Admiral A. E. F. Bedford. During his tenure, 1928–1934, Rear Admiral Walwyn made considerable changes and improvements to the RIM. Shortly after he came to India, he decided the uniform worn by the ratings was not in keeping with the Royal Navy. The uniform then consisted of blue jean baggy trousers and a long flowing smock with a stocking cap similar to that worn by lascars in the Merchant Service.[90] In due course

Royal permission was granted for the ratings to wear the same uniform as worn in the Royal Navy, except for the buttons.[91]

In the post–First World War era the purpose of the land and air forces in India was defined as 'the defence of India against external aggression and the maintenance of internal peace'.[92] This definition was supplemented by the limitation that the scale of forces was not calculated to meet external attack by a great power, though their duties might well include initial resistance to such an attack pending the arrival of Imperial reinforcement.[93] The purpose of the Royal Indian Navy was to co-operate with the Royal Navy and the other services in the defence of India's coastal harbours.[94] In practice, the role of the RIN was restricted to the Local Naval Defence of the Indian coast except during wartime. During peacetime, the Cabinet could always request the Governor General to release ships of the Royal Indian Navy in case of emergency. The British Government intended to legalise this state of affairs by means of Indian Legislation.[95] The Squadron of RIN before the outbreak of the war consisted of five sloops: *Clive*, *Lawrence*, *Hindustan*, *Indus* and *Cornwallis*. All vessels were armed with a broadside of two to four inches, except *Indus*, which had two 4.7-inch guns. As per the annual programme, the RIN squadron cruised around the coast of India and in the Mergup Archipelago from November to April. From May to October, more or less the monsoon season, the annual training was carried out. The squadron was generally based at Trincomali to Karachi in the height of the monsoon.

5. Plans for the development of RIN; committees and recommendations

Garran Award

The political leaders of India believed that India's military expenditure was a burden on the people, and that in particular the capitation charges were unfair and unjust.[96] The Indian unrest on this issue resulted in the formation of a Tribunal in 1932, under the chairmanship of Sir Robert Randolph Garran, former Solicitor General of Australia. Among four members, two were nominated by the British Government and two by the Government of India. Viscount Dunedin and Lord Tomlin were the British members and Sir Shadi Lal and Sir Shah Muhammad Sulaiman were the Indian members in the Tribunal.[97] This Tribunal was assigned to examine India's claim that a contribution should be made from Imperial revenues towards military expenditure from Indian revenues and to report the basis on which any contribution approved should be assessed.[98] The Tribunal assembled in London in November 1932 and submitted its final report in January 1933.

The Imperial War Office made a clear demarcation of responsibilities in terms of defence between India and Britain. The responsibility for 'minor danger', like internal security, defence against border tribes and war against Afghanistan, was vested with India and the 'responsibility of Major danger', any attack upon India by a superpower, was assumed by Britain.[99] For the British the defence of India by the Empire and the defence of the Empire by India was an impossible task and incapable of evaluation as a basis for monetary contribution.[100] A majority of the members of the Tribunal took the stand of the Imperial War Office on demarcation of responsibilities of India and Britain. But the Tribunal thought that this did not dispose of the question of contribution. The report stated that "it is doubtless impossible to weigh imponderables, but we all think there are certain aspects in which the advantages derived by Great Britain from army in India were distinctly ponderable, though there may be difficulty in assessing them precisely in terms of money." The majority of the Tribunal agreed on the following two grounds, on which they recommended a contribution to be made by the British Government:[101]

1   That the Army in India was a force, ready in an emergency to take the field at once, which does not exist elsewhere in the Empire, which is specially available for immediate use in the East, and which had on occasion been so used.
2   That India was a training ground for active service such as does not exist elsewhere in the Empire.

Even though the conclusions of the Garran Report were not unanimous, both the Governments accepted the unanimous recommendations of the Tribunal and agreed to act on majority recommendations. As a result of the implementation of the Garran Recommendations, India gained £1,417,000 a year towards the cost of defence of India from British revenues. The amount of British Government's contribution towards the defence expenditure was fixed at £1.5 million per year beginning from the year 1933–1934, and this amount was increased to £2 million from the year 1939–40.[102]

Government of India proposal of 1934

In June 1934 the Government of India proposed to the Secretary of State for India that the £100,000 subsidy paid to offset the cost of the Royal Navy's East Indies Squadron should be reduced temporarily so that money could be made available for the development of local naval defences, requiring guns and minesweeping equipment and the establishment of a Royal Indian Navy Voluntary Reserve, and for the acquisition of seagoing ships for the Royal Indian Navy.[103] The proposal aimed at India undertaking her own local naval defence and RIM's direct control over India's naval expenditure. The proposal requested the British Government to forgo India's annual subvention of £100,000 by stating "that, the amounts that we now pay towards the cost of His Majesty's Navy, however small they may appear, are yet sufficient to enable us to carry out the major portion of our responsibilities for local naval defence and would therefore be more usefully employed if placed at our disposal, instead of forming a comparatively negligible contribution towards the revenues of the United Kingdom."[104] The proposal further emphasized that "it is a transfer, and not a reduction, of expenditure that we have in view and that the funds that may be set free as a result of our recommendations will be utilised for naval purposes and not to lessen the burden of our defence expenditure."[105] The first and the foremost thing sought by the proposal was the equipment needed for the execution of local naval defence schemes and the personnel to use that equipment. The proposal sought one Mark II set and 23 Mark III sets of minesweeping gear, including winches, and 38 guns to equip the trawlers and other vessels which would be taken up from civil sources on mobilisation for minesweeping duties at the defended ports.[106] Further it brought out the importance of requisite personnel and the urgent constitution of the Royal Indian Navy Volunteer Reserve.[107] Although legislation was earlier undertaken in 1933 towards the formation of the Reserve Scheme (Act No. I of 1933), the financial situation had precluded the RIM from putting the scheme into force. Apart from the above recommendations, the proposal sought the expansion of the Royal Indian Marine, on similar lines as the recommendations of Vice Admiral Sir Humphery Walwyn, with a fleet of six sloops and four minesweepers, within a few years.[108]

Neville Chamberlain expressed the entirely unsympathetic attitude of the Treasury in his letter, and again reference was made to the unsympathetic attitude of the Public Accounts Committee.[109] He said in his letter that

> Dominions and Colonies generally are responsible for the cost of her own local defences; the proposal to provide such local defences at the expense of her (already inadequate) contribution to Navy Vote amounts in fact to an evasion of that responsibility. The attitude of India in this matter is in sharp contrast to that of other members of the British Commonwealth. While the Dominions generally have increased substantially their effective contribution to the naval defence of the Empire by maintaining naval units of their own and in some cases also by cash subventions to particular defence services, e.g. Singapore, and are at the same time spending large sums in bringing their coastal defences up to date, India's annual contribution has stayed at the same level for some 40 years, while the deficiencies in her coastal defences remain virtually untouched.
>
> . . . In recent years we have assumed a large additional liability by way of grant in aid of the defence of India; we have also agreed to take over sole financial responsibility for the defence of Aden. Notwithstanding these factors, and the growing burden of

our commitments at Singapore (to which India has not contributed) I can fairly claim that we have taken a not ungenerous line in recent adjustments between the two governments. . . . In the light of the above, I feel bound to make my protest against the apparent unwillingness of the Government of India to accept responsibilities which are unquestionably theirs. . . . [T]he Public Accounts Committee have recently shown an increasingly critical attitude towards financial adjustments of expenditure on defence between the Imperial Government and the Dominions, India and the colonies, on the ground that the mother country does not always insist on a good enough bargain from her point of view . . .[110]

Vice Admiral Arthur Bedford, the FOCRIN, wrote to the Admiralty pleading for an early decision, and pointing out that "Unless the RIN is to be abolished or die of stagnation it must go forward at least sufficiently far to carry out local Naval Defence properly. The proposed expansion is necessary to raise the reserves required and to make the service sufficiently attractive to exist."[111] "[T]he attitude of the Government of India is that they already pay enough for Imperial Defence by maintaining a large part of the British Army as much on Imperial account as on their own and they do not see why they should spend more on Imperial Defence by a subsidy towards the Royal Navy."[112] Bedford, in his letter, enclosed an appreciation drawn up for the Army Commander-in-Chief in which he referred to the C.I.D. Paper O.D.C.537M dated 19 March 1928, accepted policy for the development of Dominion Navies and pointed out that the four stages of development as follows:[113]

1   Phase I - Local Naval Defence in its narrowest sense
2   Phase II & III -Local Naval Defence in its widest sense
3   Phase IV - Units able to join the Royal Navy Main Fleet

Vice Admiral Bedford requested the early implementation of phase II & III stages through the acquisition of new sloops for RIN.[114] The Admiralty pleaded the importance to the United Kingdom by stating that, "It is of first importance to the United Kingdom that provision should be made for Indian local naval defence. If it is not made by the Government of India the liability will in the long run have to fall on the United Kingdom. In view of the importance of India to the Empire, there is everything to be said from the point view of the Admiralty, and we think also from the point view of the Government as a whole, for accepting this scheme for proving for this necessary service, in spite of its financial drawbacks."[115]

Despite Admiralty advice not to make the stipulation, the only terms on which the British Government would agree to letting part of the subsidy be used for construction and maintenance of sloops was that they should be made available unreservedly in wartime for use by the Royal Navy anywhere in the world.[116] In this regard Murray informed J. A. Barlow, that

> We estimate that the financial effect of including the cost of construction and subsequent maintenance of a sloop in the five year scheme would be to make the annual abatement from the Indian contribution of £66,000 out of £100,000 a year instead of £21,000 out of £100,000 a year.
>
> The only condition on which we could accept the reduction of our own shipbuilding programme by one sloop would be that the Government of India should agree to place the sloop, which they include in the 5 year scheme, unreservedly at the disposal of H.M. Government in the United Kingdom in the event of any war. It would not be enough that the Government of India should place the vessel at our disposal for use only in Indian waters.[117]

The India Office continued to press the proposal, and in January 1936, the Chancellor agreed that half of the cost could be taken from the subsidy by stating that "one half of the cost over the next two years of making good India's local naval defences should be met by a diversion from India's naval contribution, on the understanding that the other half is borne on Indian funds."[118]

In January 1938, the British Government agreed to forgo India's annual subvention of £1,00,000 and miscellaneous annual charges of £15,000 to £20,000 on the condition that the Government of India would maintain a seagoing squadron comprising not fewer than six modern escort vessels, which would take care of the naval defence of Indian ports and would be free to co-operate with the Royal Navy in the defence of India.[119]

During the 1930s the development of the Dominion navies was divided into four phases.[120] When the Royal Indian Marine became the Royal Indian Navy in 1934 as a combatant force, it was mainly concentrated on (Phases II and III of the development) acquisition of a few seagoing sloops, development of training, building of repair facilities and the formation of a seagoing squadron for service at the home station. In 1935 and 1936, the protection of shipping in the immediate approaches to the principal ports, including Bombay, Karachi, Madras and Calcutta, against attack by submarines and minelayers, leaving the security of Indian trade routes and protection against larger ships to the Royal Navy, became a serious concern to the Admiralty.[121] The existing resources of the Royal Indian Navy in 1936 so far as local naval defence was concerned were not sufficient to carry out this task, but negotiations were started with His Majesty's Government as a result of which the existing Indian contribution amounting in all to about £1,32,000 per annum towards the upkeep of the Royal Navy, and to spend it on local naval defence.

In 1936, the RIN was consisted of five sloops, one patrol vessel and one survey vessel.[122] The total establishment onshore and afloat consisted of about 170 officers and 1,100 men including boys under training. There were no reserves, and it was just possible to keep the crews of vessels up to establishment by frequently re-engaging time-expired men.[123] The Government of India was fully conscious of the deficiencies in this respect and had for so many years been considering, in consultation with the British Government, ways and means of bringing into existence a regular organisation for the protection of shipping against mines and submarines in the immediate approaches to the major ports of India. The main difficulties were mainly of a financial nature.[124] The Memorandum on the Defence Forces (1936) brought out that this expedient could not be repeated indefinitely and an increase of the training establishments to compete with wastage alone was an urgent necessity.[125]

The General Staff Memorandum entitled 'India's Defence Commitments and Her Ability to Implement Them' was submitted to the Secretary of State for issue to the Dominion delegates and it was discussed during the Imperial Conference held in March 1937. The paper informed the conference that RIN would continue depending on the Royal Navy for the protection of sea routes, and plans were in preparation to modernise and improve the Royal Indian Navy in order to enable it to provide adequately for the local naval defence of the main seaports.[126] To this end the plan for the RIN was concentrated on strengthening the active service and training establishments, This included organisation of a reserve of officers and trained ratings, building up of a stock of guns and other equipment for use on auxiliary vessels in war and replacement of obsolete combatant vessels of the RIN squadron.[127]

Nine Year Plan of 1937

In April 1937, the Government of India sent the draft Nine Year Plan for the development of the Royal Indian Navy to London and urged that it be paid for the complete abolition of the Indian subsidy, return for which the Royal Indian Navy would relieve the Royal Navy of the obligation to maintain three sloops in the Persian Gulf.[128] In July 1937, Simpson discussed the matter in his demi-official letter to the Admiralty and later Duff Cooper, Secretary of State for War, wrote to Sir John Simon, the Chancellor, urging that it was in Britain's interest to give up the subsidy if in return India committed to develop the Royal Indian Navy.[129] On 26 July 1937, Sir John Simon wrote to the Secretary of State for India, the Marquis of Zetland, agreeing to the policy, but he sought guarantees that political conditions in India would not prevent the transfer of tactical control of the Royal Indian Navy to the Admiralty in the event of war.[130]

In March 1938, Vice Admiral Fitzherbert, the Flag Officer Commanding the Royal Indian Navy, had submitted his comprehensive scheme for the reorganisation of the RIN to His Majesty's Government. The Nine Year Plan proposed an increase in the strength of the Royal Indian Navy as follows:[131]

Active service

1	Commissioned Officers	from 101 to 169
2	Warrant Officers	from 52 to 104
3	Ratings	from 1,140 to 2,562

Reserve service

1	RINR Officers	252
2	RINVR Officers	71
3	RINR Ratings	912
4	RIFR Ratings	593
5	Communication Reserve	286

This Nine Year Plan proposed a developed local naval defence, the establishment of training depots at Bombay, Cochin and Vizagapatam with sub-depots for subsidiary training of Reserve Officers at Calcutta, Madras and Karachi, the replacement of the old sloops *Cornwallis*, *Lawrence* and *Clive*, the rearmament with high angle (H.A.)/low angle (L.A.) guns on the two escort vessels, *Hindustan and Indus*, the construction of a sixth escort vessel and six minesweeping vessels, and the provision of eight Motor Torpedo Boats to provide offensive measures of local defence.[132] The estimated capital cost of these proposals was Rs.733.3 lakhs and recurring annual cost of Rs.64.1 lakhs.[133] This scheme was re-examined by the defence authorities in India in order that it might be brought into line with the conception governing the corresponding schemes for the Army and Air Force, namely, that of the minimum issuance which it was essential to provide. The Defence Authority in India concluded the proposal as follows:[134]

1. First in priority was placed the provision of adequate local naval defence. At the same time it was thought most undesirable that the Royal Indian Navy should lapse into a purely harbour defence form and that accordingly some type of seagoing vessels must be provided. The price of the Black Swan Class of escort vessel, which had risen to Rs.55 lakhs, was regarded as prohibitive. The alternatives were Bittern (Rs.47 lakhs) or Fleetwoods (Rs.35 lakhs), but the latter's speed of only 15 knots was held as a serious objection. A matter for consideration was whether the armament of six four-inch guns could be reduced to four guns, but as the savings would be very small, the reduction was depreciated.
2. The rearmament of *Indus* and *Hindustan* seemed most desirable but could, it was thought, be postponed if necessary.
3. It appeared that the six minesweepers would cost Rs.12 lakhs each. As regards the possibility of obtaining a cheaper type, the Flag Officer

Commanding had stated that the Mastiff type trawler, a possible alternative, was too small to accommodate the numbers of reservists to be trained in addition to the established complement.

4 While the Flag Officer's arguments for the provision of Motor Torpedo Boats were carefully considered, it was doubtful whether these vessels were essential, and, in any case, it was felt that they should have a low position in the priority list.

5 As regards local defence, it was considered that provision should be made for:

 a Auxiliary minesweepers for training and the necessary equipment for all auxiliary vessels.

 b Training of reservists to man auxiliary vessels, together with the provision of training establishments, instructional equipment etc.

As was to be expected, even this plan was not accepted by the Army dominated Executive Council on financial grounds.[135]

Chatfield Committee – 1938

During the discussions on defence in London, in the summer of 1938 the Commander-in-Chief had initiated a new and a comprehensive review of India's local defence requirements by the General Staff in India and his naval and air advisers.[136] The results of the review were embodied in proposals for the reorganisation of the local defence forces and subsequently the constitution of a committee was recommended to look in to this matter. The Viceroy wrote to the Secretary of State, on 24 August 1938, regarding the scope of a committee/commission to look into the matter of development/expansion of defence forces in India, that, "in connection with the consideration which His Majesty's Government have recently given to the defence problems of India, we suggest that it would be of the greatest assistance to both Governments if an authoritative body of enquiry could be formed and sent to India at the earliest opportunity to investigate the military and financial aspects of the problem on the spot and submit a report to His Majesty's Government which would form the bases of further negotiation between the two Governments."[137]

Further, the Viceroy suggested that "having regard to the increased cost of modern equipment, to the desirability of organising, equipping and maintaining the forces in India in accordance with modern requirements in the light of experience gained by the British re-armament programme and to the limited resources available in India for defence expenditure, to examine and report how these resources can be used to the best advantages, to what extent these resources will require to be supplemented, and to make recommendations."[138] He further suggested that "the enquiry not be called a

Commission, which word has unfortunate association out here (India) and the use of which word would undoubtedly lead to a demand for the appointment of one or more Indian members; we suggest under all circumstances the body be described as an 'Expert Committee'.[139]" In order to retain the imperial hegemony over the defence forces of India and to avoid the Indian participation in the 'Commission', the British decided to call the 'Commission' an 'Expert Committee'.

The Chatfield Committee (The Expert Committee on the Defence of India, 1938–1939) was appointed by His Majesty's Government in September 1938 to look into the development/expansion of the Defence Force in India, with the terms of reference as "In the light of the recent Report by the Chiefs of Staffs, and of Reports of the Cabinet Committee on the Defence of India, and having regard to the increased cost of modern armament, to the desirability of organising, equipping and maintaining the Forces in India in accordance with modern requirements, and to the limited resources available in India for defence expenditure, to examine and report, in the light of experience gained in executing the British rearmament programme, how these resources can be used to the best advantage, and to make recommendations."[140]

The task before the Chatfield Committee was thus one of evolving such recommendations as would best serve to provide "the minimum assurance" against the twin problems of attack on India's ports and attack on her sea supply lines – nor did it approach this task with an entirely free hand. Its hands were tied first (but to an extent which could have been modified) by the 1938 agreement between His Majesty's Government and the Government of India, and secondly and by far the more serious, by the niggardly extent of expenditure permitted by the Government of India upon defence as a whole. This latter element was to prove to be the most serious trouble throughout the Committee's deliberations on all aspects of defence; in the case of maritime defence, the small proportion of the whole which the RIN was able to claim proved a limitation almost insuperable if an efficient answer to defence by sea were to be provided.

The Chatfield Committee did not accept the distinction drawn in the Garran Report of 1933 between the 'Major' and 'Minor' danger as a valid or practical criterion.[141] The general principle that the Committee put forward in its place was that the forces maintained in India should be adequate not merely for the narrower purposes of purely local defence, but also should assist in ensuring her security against the external threats and further that India should acknowledge that her responsibility cannot in her own interests be safely limited to the local defence of her land frontiers and coasts. The Committee did not suggest that the forces in India should, or could, be made self-sufficient for these wider purposes and India should necessarily bear the entire financial burden of the armed forces kept in India at any time. But the Committee recommended the joint responsibility for the external security of India.[142] The principle of joint responsibility was stated in a somewhat different form in the Pownall Sub-Committee's Report as "the changed strategic situation throughout the world and the development of modern armaments, particularly air forces, have brought into prominence the need for India, in her own interest, to play a more important part in the defence of the vital areas on our Imperial communications in the Middle and far East."[143]

In this connection the concern of the Sub-Committee was to find the most advantageous disposition of the total forces that could be made available in the East. For this purpose the Committee recommended the unconditional allocation of one division to the British Government as a strategic reserve for use wherever and whenever required. The Pownall Sub-Committee recommended that its allocation should be unconditional, and the Chiefs of Staff laid special stress on this proposal in paragraph 15 of their report. The Cabinet finally endorsed the conclusion that "the degree of obligation on the Government of India to place these troops at the disposal of the Home Government should be made somewhat more definite, and expressed more precisely than is at present the case with reinforcements from India, but should fall short of an unconditional obligation."[144] The Chatfield Committee discussed the joint responsibilities and obligations and were of the opinion that "in any case the hypothesis of a conditional obligation is somewhat unreal, since in a major crisis the Government of India would naturally strain every nerve to help and in theory could be ordered to do so. Nevertheless, so long as the obligation remains in form conditional; there is great practical difficulty in making effective plans in advance."[145] The Committee had the opinion that India normally has, over and above the forces regarded as the minimum necessary for keeping her frontiers and coasts intact and ensuring internal security, forces available for the external defence of India as a matter of common and direct concern to both Governments. According to the Committee, the obligation on the Government of India was no longer a contract to perform something outside the sphere of their normal duties and it would become an integral part of those duties. The Committee further recommended that "both the Governments would collaborate in preparing plans which, as regards India, would take account not only of India's local defence and internal security, but also of the threats external to, and perhaps not even localised near, her frontiers and coasts, instead of treating them in isolation."[146]

Recommendations of the Chatfield Committee

The Committee advocated joint responsibility so far as the external security of India is concerned and the sharing of the financial burden. At the same time the Committee was well aware that it was impossible to evaluate in terms of the actual costs the degree to which each party should at any time contribute to the common cause. For the Committee, in accordance with the principles on which the relations between the Governments of Britain and India had been based, the Government of India must be responsible for the administration of all defence forces situated in India for her local defence and for purposes covered by the joint responsibility, and India must therefore have full financial control over expenditure necessary for the maintenance of its defence forces. As far as the financial contribution is concerned, the Committee had the opinion that in the situation of a joint responsibility, the Government of Britain should make a contribution to India.[147] It was recommended that, in accordance with the principle of joint responsibility and having regard to the strength and composition of the forces proposed, the subsidy (then) paid by the British Government to India under the Garran Award should be continued at the higher level of £2 million a year.[148]

Further the Committee recommended that "if forces held in India for the purposes covered by the joint responsibility are used outside India in an emergency affecting India's external security, their ordinary maintenance charges should continue to be borne by India. The apportionment between Imperial and Indian funds of the extraordinary or extra cost of such forces while so employed should be a matter for agreement by the two Governments at the time having regard to all the circumstances of the emergency."[149] As far as the war plans were concerned, it was recommended that "the plans for the use of armed forces in the defence of India in War should as a matter of course be the subject of the closest consultation between the authorities in India and the Committee of Imperial Defence before the approval of the two Governments."[150]

The Committee recommended a timetabled modernisation of the armed forces in India with minor variations that would not affect the general level of efficiency. To this end a thoroughgoing scheme of re-equipment and modernisation was recommended with a time frame for completion of five years.[151] The withdrawal of certain British units, like 1 Cavalry regiment, 3 Royal Horse Artillery Batteries, 1 Field Artillery Regiment, 1 Medium Artillery Regiment and 2 Infantry Battalions, was recommended, to home establishment and the reductions in number of Indian units, like 3 Indian Cavalry Regiment, 4 Companies of Sappers and Miners, and 14 Indian Infantry battalions, as they held that with increased efficiency and mobility afforded by modernisation it was possible to provide an equal measure of security with a smaller number of modernised troops.[152] Further, it recommended the re-equipment of the Air Squadrons maintained in India of the Royal Indian Navy and the Local Defence Troops. As far as modernisation was concerned, the committee recommended the modernisation of the coast defence and the reorganisation and expansion of Ordnance factories in India.[153]

On his return to England, Lord Chatfield became the Minister for coordination of defence in the British Cabinet, which undoubtedly helped in the approval of his proposals by both the Government of India and that of the United Kingdom.[154]

Priority to local naval defence

The Chatfield Committee, with reference to the Royal Indian Navy, regarding India's maritime defence, concluded in its report that "first in priority was placed the provision of adequate Local Naval Defence." The Chatfield Committee was not the first body to reach such a conclusion. Adequate local naval defence was called for as the first essential by the Committee of Imperial Defence (memo No. 509 M) in 1923; the provision of suitable local naval defence in India had been one of the two conditions on which HM Government had agreed to forgo (by the agreement of January 1938) the annual subvention of £100,00 by the Government of India towards the upkeep of the Royal Navy, and it had been one of the most important aspects of the Nine-Year Plan submitted by the Flag Officer Commanding, Royal Indian Navy in 1938 to implement the above agreement.

The reason for this emphasis upon Local Naval Defence was not far to seek. Both for India's own internal security and defence and as a vital link in the Imperial war effort, protection of India's great ports – Bombay, Karachi, Calcutta, Madras, Cochin and Vishakhapatnam – was an obvious essential. Bombay, as well as being the base of the RIN itself, housed the main repair facilities available to the British and Allied war vessels serving on the East Indies Station. In addition, all these ports would, on the outbreak of war, assume major importance (and become proportionately desirable targets for enemy attack) as convoy assembly ports, emerging routing ports, ports of refuge for merchant ships, centres for the fitting out of armed merchant cruisers and the defensive armament of merchantmen, and military embarkation and debarkation and supply ports whose efficient and unimpeded functioning would be a sine qua non of all military plans for land defence or offence.

Measuring the 'scale of attack'

The main aim of the Chatfield Committee was to ascertain "the minimum assurance which it was essential to provide," and accordingly it was necessary to define first the scale and type of attack which might be anticipated on India's coastline. The Committee agreed that the "risk of attack from seaward can be particularised with reference to the scale of attack" laid down by the Committee of Imperial Defence in regard to Indian Ports during war with Japan and/or one or more Western powers, viz:

1 Attack by cruisers or armed merchant vessels

    a By gunfire
    b By mine laying in the approaches to ports.

2   Attack by submarines
    a   By gunfire at moderate and close ranges.
    b   By mine or torpedo on shipping in the harbour or immediate approaches.
3   Attack by air by light seaborne forces.

Elaborating upon this suggested scale of attack, the Committee pointed out that such raids "could inflict much material damage and cause serious alarm among the civilian population" – the obvious precedent was the bombardment of Madras by the Emden in 1914.[155]

Strong naval force against 'major' dangers

While placing local naval defence first in order of priority, the Committee had to look to the other great danger to India from seawards – that of interruption of her vital sea communications by either hostile naval or air forces. This was the second main problem to be met; it was pointed out that such "risks emanate not only from Japan but also from Italy in the event of a World War in which Italy was engaged against the Empire."

The Committee's preoccupation with this aspect of India's defence can be seen not only in the naval section of their Report, but as recurring throughout the army sections also. It was this same consideration which in the previous year had given rise to the first provision of the 1938 agreement – that India should maintain an oceangoing squadron of not fewer than six modern escort vessels which should be available to operate with the Royal Navy on the outbreak of war. The Commander-in-Chief, East Indies Station, pointed out to the Chatfield Committee that (on the outbreak of hostilities) until Reserve Fleet Cruisers arrived on his station, he would have to rely on station resources alone, including India's six escort vessels.

Details of the original Nine Year Plan were submitted by the Flag Officer Commanding, Royal Indian Navy, and they were discussed by the Chatfield Committee. The final decisions of the Chatfield Committee were as follows:[156]

1   The construction of four Bittern class escort vessels to replace *Cornwallis*, *Lawrence* and *Clive* (to be scrapped); the first pair to be ordered in 1939–1940 and completed in 1941–1942; the second pair to be ordered in 1942–1943 and completed in 1943–1944.
2   The construction of 4 Mastiff class trawlers to be ordered in 1945–1946 and completed in 1946–1947.
3   The loan from the Royal Navy of four Halcyon class mine-sweepers, the first pair in 1939–1940, and the second pair in 1941–1942.
4   The re-arming of *Indus* and *Hindustan* to meet modern requirements.

5   The provision of depots and instructional equipment and Local Naval Defence equipment as proposed in the Flag Officer Commanding's Nine-Year Plan.

These recommendations all bear directly upon the two problems of defence as formulated above. The construction of the four new sloops and the re-arming of the two already in existence was designed to furnish the required "minimum assurance" for the protection of India's sea communications; thus, it was intended to be co-operate with the Royal Navy at the time of a war. The loan of the four Halcyon class minesweepers from the Royal Navy was designed not merely to assist in keeping India's ports clear and open, but mainly to afford much-needed training facilities for the personnel who would ultimately be required to carry out the full plans approved by the Committee under clause "5" above.

Local naval defence plans

The Nine Year Plan helped in taking up the case for new acquisitions, in the event of war, of 48 merchant vessels, 25 to be fitted out as auxiliary minesweepers, and 23 as auxiliary anti-submarine craft. Division of these among the Defended Ports was as follows: – Karachi – 3 auxiliary M/Ss and 2 auxiliary A/S vessels; Bombay – 4 auxiliary M/Ss and 6 auxiliary A/S vessels; Calcutta – 15 auxiliary M/Ss and 10 auxiliary A/S vessels; and the remaining 8 vessels to be used for these duties at Madras, Cochin, and Vizagapatam.[157] Those vessels on being taken over were to be manned by their peacetime mercantile crews, signed on under the T124 (India) agreement, or by other local personnel, plus Naval Reserve Officers and ratings as and when available.[158] The vessels intended to be used for this purpose were earmarked beforehand and appropriate lists were maintained.

These measures were thus designed to protect the defended ports and their immediate approaches against attack by mine or torpedo. This still left the problem of attack by bombardment unaccounted for; it was not considered that local naval defence vessels could offer effective defence against this form of attack, and as all HM and HMI ships would have other duties to perform, and would therefore not be available for permanent stationing for this purpose, the only remaining alternative was defence by coastal batteries, with assistance where possible by aircraft.[159] The Chatfield Committee examined the situation in detail and formulated recommendations upon the type and calibre of guns which should be installed at the various ports; sites had been suggested in the respective Port Defence Schemes.

In addition to these active measures to prepare for projected hostile attack, a number of standardised precautionary measures were laid down to be taken at ports in respect to control of shipping, entry into the ports, etc. Thus, arrangements were made for the immediate operation of an

Examination Service functioning under a Chief Examining Officer, the work in each port to be carried out by members of the local Pilotage Service in addition to their normal duties, assisted by the personnel and craft of the respective Port Trusts. This service was naturally to work in close co-operation with the Examination Battery at each port, and with the assistance of the Port War Signal Station. Examination anchorage had been defined. Uniform regulations governing the conduct of the Examination Service, procedure regarding the detention of ships and cargos and "Droit de Prince" had been laid down in CB 1618(R) (*Handbook on the Examination Service and Issue of Local Traffic Regulations*, 1938) and the DOI 1935 (Detaining Officers' War Instructions India 1935), whilst the regulations governing the entry of British and Allied warships, and British, Allied and neutral merchantmen into Indian ports, and the functioning, duties and procedure of Port War Signals Stations were tabulated in CB 1618Q (Instructions for Entry into British Defended Ports, 1938).

For the protection of the ports of India, the Chatfield Committee recommended the utilisation of two Bomber Squadrons of the Air Force in undertaking the dual role of duties on the 'frontier' and for 'coast defence'.[160] It was also proposed that five flights of aircraft be raised on a volunteer basis to assist in defence of the ports. The employment of aircraft for coast defence afforded a measure of insurance against direct bombardment of the ports by ships. The installation of counter-bombardment artillery was another line of defence since the attack would be launched from outside the range of coast defence.

The extra forces required, therefore, had to be largely obtained by expanding the forces in India. The Chatfield Committee of 1939 summed up: "the arena of India's defence against aggression should therefore now be regarded as covering not only primarily her North-Western land frontier but also to an increasing extent her sea communications in Eastern waters and the strategic points which are vital to their security."[161] The Committee had recommended that "the defence forces maintained in India should be adequate not merely for the narrower purposes of purely local defence, but also to assist in ensuring her security against the external threats, and, further, that India should acknowledge that her responsibility cannot in her own interests be safely limited to the local defence of her land frontiers and coasts."[162] The Committee did not recommend self-sufficient defence forces in India for wider purposes. Further it recommended that "India should not be solely responsible for her external defence, and she should not necessarily bear the entire financial burden of the armed forces kept in India at any time. And the financial arrangements between the two Governments should be based is that India should bear some share in a joint responsibility for her external security."[163] As per the recommendations of the Committee, the forces held in India for the purposes covered by the joint responsibility that would be used outside India in an emergency affecting India's external security would have their ordinary maintenance charges borne by India.[164] The apportionment between Imperial and Indian funds of the extraordinary or 'extra' cost of such forces while so employed was a matter for agreement by the two Governments at the time, considering all the circumstances of the emergency.

Reorganization of Royal Indian Navy

The Chatfield Committee recommended the reorganisation of the Royal Indian Navy based on the agreement reached by the British and Indian Governments in January 1938.[165] Under this agreement His Majesty's Government consented to forgo the Government of India paying an annual subvention of £100,000 and miscellaneous annual charges valued at an amount £15,000–20,000 on condition that the Government of India maintained a seagoing squadron of not fewer than six modern escort vessels, which would be free to co-operate with the Royal Navy for the defence of India, and, in addition, that they would fulfil India's responsibility for the local naval defence of Indian ports.[166] The contributions accordingly ceased as on 1 April 1938.[167]

The Flag Officer Commanding RIN and the Commander-in-Chief, East Indies Station were not in favour of the Fleetwood class escort vessel due to its slow speed of 15 knots. The primary duty of the escort vessels was that of close escort of troop ships conveying reinforcement, and the secondary assignment was that of assisting in the protection of the trade routes. For the former duties a 19-knot ship was required, and in support of that argument, the Admiralty decided to acquire the new British India Company ships with a speed of 16.5 knots for wartime. The Chatfield Committee recommended the construction of four new escort vessels in replacement of old *Cornwallis, Lawrence* and *Clive*' and for the re-armament of *Indus* and *Hindustan*.[168] As regards the type, the Committee agreed with the view that the cost of the Black Swan (Rs.55 lakhs) class was prohibitive and recommended the construction of Britten (Rs.47 lakhs) class. As per the recommendations of the Committee the first pair was to be ordered in 1939–1940 and completed in 1941–1942, the second pair to be ordered in 1942–1943 and completed in 1944–1945.[169]

The Chatfield Committee recommended the construction of four Mastiff class trawlers, to be ordered in 1945–1946 and completed in 1946–1947. The Committee recommended the loan of four Halcyon class trawlers to RIN, the first pair in 1939–1940 and the second pair in 1941–1942, and it was agreed that consideration should be given to India being relieved of a portion of the maintenance expenditure.[170] The Admiralty has agreed to provide four Halcyon class minesweepers on loan to the RIN to cater for the training requirement in peacetime on the condition that on the outbreak of war, these vessels would be immediately required elsewhere and would not be available for the local naval defence of the major ports of India.[171]

Further recommendations were re-arming with H.A./L.A. guns of HMIS *Indus* and HMIS *Hindustan* and the provision of depots and instructional establishments and of local naval defence equipment.[172]

The Commander-in-Chief submitted the proposals for the reorganisation and modernisation of the land, air and naval forces required for the local defence of India to the Chatfield Committee, along with the detailed estimates of the capital cost of the proposals and of the future maintenance charges of the reorganised forces. These estimates were subsequently revised to give effect to the alterations of the original proposals made during the course of the Committee's enquiry by the Commander-in-Chief.[173] Rough estimates of the capital cost of modernisation and of the annual maintenance costs of the defence forces reorganised as proposed by the Chatfield Committee[174] are in Table 2.1:

Table 2.1 Net capital cost in lakhs of rupees

	1st Year	2nd Year	3rd Year	4th Year	5th Year	After 5th Year (Saving)	Total
Army	586	824	805	848	93	142	2,964
Army (External Defence Troops)	331	331	–	–	–	–	662
Air Force	337	76	49	–	–	–	462
Air Force (External Defence Troops)	11	145	3	–	–	–	159
Navy	10	45	46	43	44	74	362
Total	1,225	1,421	903	891	137	(Net Saving) 68	4,509

Source: Expert Committee Report (The Chatfield Committee Report), 1939, T 162/993, The National Archives, Kew

In the figures showing the estimated net capital cost, no deduction had been made for the contribution provisionally offered by His Majesty's Government towards the cost of modernisation. There is, necessarily, considerable uncertainty as regards a very large number of detailed estimates and the assumption underlying them; and many of them from their nature contain a sub-critical element of conjecture and speculation. Time had not permitted any critical examination of the estimates as a whole by the Military Finance Branch. On the basis of the estimate prepared, as the Chatfield Committee explained, the *net total capital cost*[175] is given in Table 2.2.

On the assumption referred by the Report as to (1) the length of time which would be required to complete the work of equipping the forces, and

Table 2.2 Net total capital cost

	Crores of rupees	Million £
Army	36.26	27.20
Air Force	6.21	4.66
Navy	2.62	1.96
Total	45.09	33.82

Source: Expert Committee Report (The Chatfield Committee Report), 1939, T 162/993, The National Archives, Kew

Table 2.3 Net total capital cost year by year

	Crores of rupees	Million £
1st year	12.25	9.19
2nd year	14.21	10.66
3rd year	9.03	6.77
4th year	8.91	6.68
5th year	1.37	1.03
Total	45.77	34.33

Source: Expert Committee Report (The Chatfield Committee Report), 1939, T 162/993, The National Archives, Kew

Table 2.4 Annual recurring cost of maintaining the Forces in crores of rupees

	Army	Air Force	Navy	Total
1st year	40.91	2.25	0.83	43.99
2nd year	40.46	3.70	0.83	44.99
3rd year	40.64	3.84	0.85	45.33
4th year	40.68	3.90	0.91	49.49
5th year	40.85	3.82	0.95	45.62
Total				225.42

Source: Expert Committee Report (The Chatfield Committee Report), 1939, T 162/993, The National Archives, Kew

(2) the spread of the expenditure over this period, due regard being had to the co-relation of the several operations, it is estimated that the net capital cost would be incurred year by year[176] as set out in Table 2.3.

In years immediately following the fifth year, net capital savings amounting to Rs. 18 lakhs (£510,000) would accrue, reducing the total to Rs. 45.09 crores (£33.82 million). The annual recurring cost of maintaining the forces during the five years in which modernisation was being carried out[177] is estimated in Table 2.4.

These figures give an average estimated annual cost for the first five years of Rs. 45.08 crores (£33.81 million). After the fifth year, when the reorganisation would be practically completed, the estimated costs rose to an average of Rs. 46.46 crores (£34.84 million) a year for 10 years and thereafter dropped to Rs. 45.81 crores (£34.36 million). These increases were mainly due to heavy charges averaging Rs. 3 crores (£250,000) a year for renewals and replacements for which provision has been made in the estimates.

After deducting the contribution from His Majesty's Government under the Garran Award, India's defence expenditure for the year 1938–1939 was at the rate of Rs.46.15 crores (£34,612,500) per annum, an excess over the budget provision of the year of Rs.97 Lakhs (£727,500). The total of 46.15 crores was made up of Army expenditure Rs.43.27 crores (£32.45 million), Air Force 2.05 Crores (£1.54 million) and Navy Rs.83 lakhs (£606,000).[178]

Introduction of War Book (India) 1939

In 1939, a committee consisting of representatives from all departments (including the Under Secretary, Defence Dept. [Navy Branch]) was formed to prepare the War Book (India) 1939, also known as the Defence Scheme, with an object "to provide in a concise and convenient form of a state of peace to a state of war." The principle lay in a system of pre-arranged telegrams sent from the India Office (London) notifying the Government of India of certain of the more important steps taken by the British Government during a time of strained international relations, and designed to ensure simultaneous action throughout the empire.

Two main stages were:

1. Warning Telegrams, denoting that relations had become so strained that the British Government had found it necessary to adopt precautions and initiate preparations for war
2. War Telegrams, denoting the existence of a state of war

There were a number of other pre-arranged telegrams indicating, for example, the calling out of Royal Naval Reserves, imposition of censorship, initiation of the Examination Service in UK Ports, closure of certain ports in the United Kingdom, assumption of control of merchant shipping by the Admiralty, interruption of cable services, etc. Upon the receipt of each telegram, government departments passed on the information to such of their sub-areas, sub-officers, sub-units and subordinate officers as was necessary to ensure the carrying out of the specific and pre-arranged plans for the implementation of precautionary and defence measures.

Insofar as it affected the RIN, the provisions of the Defence Book can be summarised thus:

1. Mobilisation of RIN: The Central Government was to decide on the necessity for mobilising the RIN in the following circumstances: (*a*) when a request was received from the Admiralty or from the Commander-in-Chief, East Indies Station or Eastern Forces, prior to the receipt of the warning or war telegrams, or (*b*) when the Naval Reserves telegram (indicating the calling out of Reserves for the Royal Navy) was received. The Central Government was subsequently to inform the Flag Officer Commanding, Royal Indian Navy, of its decision.

    Mobilisation was to take place automatically upon receipt of either the warning or war telegrams. The India Office was to arrange for the immediate return to India of all retired RIN personnel liable to recall, all RIN personnel on leave in Europe and all officers undergoing courses in the United Kingdom except officers undergoing Royal Navy courses conducted by the Admiralty.

2. Disposition of RIN Vessels: On receipt of the warning telegram, escort vessels of the RIN with their crews were to be automatically placed under the orders of the Naval Commander-in-Chief, East Indies Station. If a request was received from the India Office prior to the receipt of the warning telegram, the approval of the Governor General's Council was to be obtained before the vessels were placed under the orders of the Commander-in-Chief, East Indies Station.

3. Fitting Out of Auxiliary Craft: On receipt of the warning telegram, all merchant vessels previously earmarked for requisitioning and equipping as auxiliary M/S and A/S craft were to be immediately taken up and fitted out.

4. Port War Signal Stations: On receipt of the warning telegram, communications (if not laid in peacetime) were to be laid, and all personnel detailed for duty at Port War Signal Station to be warned. On receipt of the examination service telegram from the United Kingdom, Port War Signal Stations were to be brought into operation. (This affected the RIN only in the case of Bombay, as the army was then responsible for Port War Signals Stations at other defended ports.)

5. Examination Service: On receipt of the India Office Examination Service telegram, the pre-arranged examination service was to be brought into operation at each of the defended ports.

6. Closure of Ports: On receipt of the information from the India Office regarding closure of pre-arranged ports in the United Kingdom, the Defence Department (Navy Branch) was to consult with the Naval Commander-in-Chief, East Indies Station and the Commerce and Communications Department regarding the desirability of such action in India.

7   Naval Intelligence: On receipt of the Warning Telegram, the Defence Department (Navy Branch) was to instruct all naval reporting officers to put into force the War System of Naval Intelligence as laid down in a Confidential Memorandum of 1938.

The Royal Indian Navy War Organisation said that "The Flag Officer Commanding, Royal Indian Navy, will cooperate with the Commander-in-Chief, East Indies or Eastern Forces. He will continue to carry out the duties of Principal Sea Transport Officer, India, and to deal with all administrative matters in connection with the Royal Indian Navy. He will be responsible for the execution of the local naval defence arrangements for the harbours and coasts of INDIA. He will be responsible for expanding his staff and the staffs at the defended ports to meet war requirements."[179] The British had given importance to the Local Naval Defence, especially the defence of Bombay due to a naval strategic point of view. The anticipated Local Naval Defence plans for Bombay were: -

1   A M/S Flotilla of four Auxiliary M/Ss, their duty being to maintain a swept channel (as defined by Admiralty instructions) marked by buoys. This was to be in two sections of 24 miles.
2   An A/S Flotilla of six auxiliary vessels whose duties were to provide

  (a) An Inner Patrol by day to seaward of a Line Prong's Point to Thal Shoal, and by night from a line half to southward of Prong's Buoy bearing 110°.
  (b) An outer Patrol as an escort in the searched channel and for reconnaissance seaward.

3   A Harbour Patrol of two launches or motorboats covering the area within the harbour limits. These were to be armed with Lewis or machine guns and were to patrol the harbour by day to see that no country craft were under way without a pass, and to keep a lookout on all vessels at anchor, and by night to maintain a specific patrol on the eastern side of the harbour.

All the measures became operative on receipt of the warning telegram. During peacetime, the Naval authorities in Bombay were responsible for the following:

1   To keep the naval portion of the Port Defence Scheme up to date in accordance with local and Admiralty requirements.
2   To maintain specimen copies of all telegrams, letters, written orders, notices and other communications to be brought into force at the precautionary stage of the scheme.

ORIGIN AND DEVELOPMENT OF RIN

3   To provide and keep in complete readiness all materials required for Local Naval Defence and minesweeping.
4   To maintain lists of all earmarked vessels required for the precautionary and war stages, and of all equipment and stores to be provided.
5   To prepare plans for the engagement of additional civilian labour necessary for the precautionary and war stages.
6   To arrange for the passive air defence of the RIN dockyard.
7   To arrange for periodic tests of the Examination Service.

During the precautionary and war stages, the Naval Officer-in-Charge, Bombay, and his staff were responsible:

1   To request the Central Government to authorize the requisitioning of all vessels required for Local Naval Defence duties.
2   To arrange to fit out and equip such vessels.
3   To request the Bombay Government to take steps to keep secret the movements of HM and merchant ships.
4   To apply to the Bombay Government for authority to requisition accommodation required.
5   To request the Bombay Government to instruct marine engineering and shipbuilding firms that the Naval Officer-in-Charge had a prior claim to their services.
6   To arrange to engage civilian personnel to assist in coding and cyphering until such times as Volunteer Reserve personnel were detailed for these duties.
7   To put in hand arrangements for buoying the searched channel.
8   To inform the Port War Signal Station of the expected time of arrival of ships supplied with the 'private' signal, and also of the current reply.

Organisation and detailed plans at other ports were of a similar nature, differing mainly in degree and in local requirements. Thus at Calcutta, an integral part of the port defence scheme lay in shifting the positions of the normal navigation buoys; it was considered that in view of the great navigational difficulties presented by the Hooghli, this in itself was a considerable measure of defence, though the Flag Officer Commanding, Royal Indian Navy, opined that too great reliance should not be placed on this fact.

At Karachi, the officer responsible for making the necessary defence arrangements during peacetime and during the precautionary and initial war stages was the Sea Transport Officer; at Calcutta, the Principal Officer, Mercantile Marine Department in each case, upon mobilization of the RIN being decided upon, these officers assumed the duties of Naval Officer-in-Charge at their respective ports.

6. Conclusion

In the pre-war period, the British did not find any threat to the British Empire in the Indian Ocean. The colonial government kept the navy in India as a reserve force, as in the case of Royal Naval Reserve,[180] for local naval defence and for any emergency. The officers of the Royal Indian Marine were not given the King's Commission, which made them subordinate to the Royal Navy officers. During wartime the officers of RIM, who were serving onboard Royal Navy vessels, were given temporary commissions. In the post–First World War era the Royal Indian Marine again went back to a non-combatant role. During this era the British did not want to develop a combat Navy for the protection of colonial India.

The post-war period witnessed a drastic curtailing in defence expenditure, especially on RIM, on the basis of the recommendations of the Inchcape Committee. The Commission virtually reduced the RIM into a Marine Survey Unit and a yacht squadron for the benefit of senior Government officials wishing to travel by sea. More than that, from 1925 to 1930 not a single Executive Officer was recruited. The gap in seniority thus created became, later in the 1940s, advanced to the middle of the list of Lt Commanders, and moreover it created the lack of experienced officers during wartime.

Unfortunately, the years between 1928 and the outbreak of the war were years of financial depression in India, and all proposals for expansion were blocked by the Government of India on the grounds of financial stringency. And the Army dominance over the financial matters of other services was a serious obstacle to the expansion of the RIM.

In the beginning of the 1930s Britain, was well aware of the possibility of another world war and anticipated that the war would seriously affect her colonies too. It was essential to develop fully fledged defence forces in her colonies to protect her imperial interests through the deployment of defence forces on colonial lands. The Imperial Government had given more priorities to the Army and Air Force in the case of development of defence forces in India. The role of Armed Forces defined defence of India as protection against external aggression and the maintenance of internal peace.[181] "The military commitments of the Army and Air Force of India were defined as the defence of her land frontiers against aggression by a second class power; initial operations with available forces, and pending the arrival of Imperial reinforcements, against aggression by a first class power; the close defence of her coastline against seaborne aggression; the support of the civil power in the maintenance of internal law and order; and if the situation in India permits, the provision in an emergency of some assistance to the Imperial forces outside India."[182] The forces maintained were not intended to repel external attack by a major military power, though the duties of these forces might include initial resistance to such an attack pending the arrival of Imperial reinforcements or the exercise elsewhere by Imperial forces of pressure which would relieve the situation. Because of this reason, the RIN was restricted to local naval defence. The main reason behind the expansion of defence forces in India, especially in the case of the Army, was to place them under the disposal of the British for overseas deployments.[183] The colonial defence forces under the British fought against her enemies around the world for the protection of the British imperialistic interests.

Many committees were formed to look into the development of defence forces of colonial India in the post–World War I period. The Imperial Government wanted most of these committees exclusively handled by the British. In order to avoid Indian participation, the Imperial Government called the Commission an 'Expert Committee', under Lord Chatfield. The Chatfield Committee made the position clear by emphasising the concept of 'joint responsibility'. The Committee Report stated that "the fact remains that the Government of India have neither claimed nor admitted any responsibility in this connection beyond that of deciding whether forces can be spared from India in the circumstances. In any case the hypothesis of a conditional obligation is somewhat unreal, since in a major crisis the Government of India would naturally strain every nerve to help and in theory could be ordered to do so. Nevertheless, so long as the obligation remains in form conditional, there is great practical difficulty in making effective plans in advance."[184]

A nine year plan of expansion and conversion was, however, advanced by the RIN, and, after several disappointments and delays, was presented to the Chatfield Committee in 1938. This plan, condensed into a five year plan, was approved by the Chatfield Committee, and the £1,00,000 annual payment to the Admiralty was abolished. The Committee's report was not published until the spring of 1939, barely six months before war broke out, and as a result, all expansion had to be undertaken under the stress of wartime conditions. The highest credit goes to the small nucleus of RIN officers whose work had made the expansion possible, and to the Reserves, hastily trained and many of them without any previous naval experience, who formed about 89% of the total officer strength of the RIN.

The inadequacy is closely linked up with the question of finance. In view of India's great need with her 3,000 miles of coastline vulnerable to attack, and her far-flung sea supply lines for efficient naval defence, the proportion of expenditure as recommended by the Chatfield Committee on naval defence was not sufficient. The total net capital cost of the Committee's recommendations was estimated at 45.09 crores of rupees; the Royal Indian Navy's allocation was 2.62 crores, or 5.8% of the whole, representing only one-third of the expenditure recommended for the Indian Air Force and about one-fourteenth part of that recommended for the Army. "The policy for expansion was essentially one of opportunism and improvisation to meet immediate needs."[185] Plans and recommendations for a Navy capable of large scale operations were abandoned, and the emphasis shifted to an enhanced local naval defence force within the general framework of

ORIGIN AND DEVELOPMENT OF RIN

imperial strategy. The Committee did not pay any heed to the future aspects of naval defence of India. Because It had no concern for any attack by a 'major' naval power; when British forces might not be available to assist in India's defence, then the results might be very grave indeed.

Notes

1. Esher Committee Report, CAB/24/112, The National Archives, Kew, UK, 1920, p. 93.
2. Ibid.
3. File titled 'Conversion of Royal Indian Marine into Royal Indian Navy', ADM 1/8797, The National Archives, Kew Gardens, UK.
4. Ibid.
5. Ibid.
6. Esher Committee Report, CAB/24/112, The National Archives, Kew, UK, 1920, p. 93.
7. Ibid.
8. Ibid.
9. Ibid.
10. *Story of the Pakistan Navy: 1947–72*, Compiled by Pakistan Navy History Section, History Section, Naval Headquarters, Islamabad, 1991, p. 22 and Nicholas Tracy, *The Collective Naval Defence of the Empire, 1900–1940*, The Navy Records Society, London, 1997, p. xxxiv.
11. Len Barnett, *The Honourable East India Company (1600–1857): A Realistic Guide to What Is Available to Those Looking into the Careers of Seagoing Servants (1600–1834)*, www.barnettmaritime.co.uk/mainbombay.htm.
12. Captain Sir E. J. Headlam, 'The History of the Royal Indian Marine', *Journal of the Royal Society of Arts*, 5 April 1929, p. 534.
13. Ibid.
14. Ibid.
15. Rear Admiral K. Sridharan, *A Maritime History of India*, Publication Division, Government of India, New Delhi, 1982, p. 216.
16. Rear Admiral Satyindra Singh, *Under Two Ensigns: The Indian Navy 1945–50*, Oxford University Press, New Delhi, 1986, p. 19.
17. Report of the Mesopotamian Commission, 1917, Naval Historical Branch, Portsmouth, UK.
18. Esher Committee Report, CAB/24/112, The National Archives, Kew, UK, 1920, p. 94.
19. Ibid.
20. Report of Viscount Jellicoe's Naval Mission, 1919, Cab 11/159, The National Archives, Kew, UK.
21. Ibid. and Admiral A. K. Chatterji, 'The Indian Navy-How Army Dominance Inhibited Its Development', *Indo-British Review*, Vol. 16, No. 1, March 1989, p. 20.
22. Admiral A. K. Chatterji, 'The Indian Navy-How Army Dominance Inhibited Its Development', *Indo-British Review*, Vol. 16, No. 1, March 1989, p. 20.
23. Ibid.
24. Ibid.
25. Ibid.
26. Esher Committee Report, CAB/24/112, The National Archives, Kew, UK, 1920, p. 94.

27 Report of the Mesopotamian Commission, 1917, Naval Historical Branch, Portsmouth, UK. The Mesopotamian Commission recommended reorganization of the Royal Indian Marine, with a view to giving the Director, RIM a higher status and a staff adequate to his work. Part XII Section B, Para. 33 of the recommendations.
28 Esher Committee Report, CAB/24/112, The National Archives, Kew, UK, 1920, p. 94.
29 Ibid.
30 Ibid.
31 Ibid.
32 Ibid.
33 Ibid., p. 95.
34 File noting of Commander-in-Chief, entitled 'Defence Policy – India', in Response to the Defence Secretary's Note, dated 02 October 1937, p. 1, Naval Headquarters, New Delhi.
35 Bisheshwar Prasad, *Defence of India: Policy and Plans*, MoD History Division, New Delhi, 1963, p. 53.
36 Ibid.
37 File noting of Commander-in-Chief, entitled 'Defence Policy – India', in Response to the Defence Secretary's Note, dated 02 October 1937.
38 Ibid.
39 Garran Tribunal Report of 1933, WO 32/3864, The National Archives, Kew, UK.
40 Expert Committee Report (The Chatfield Committee Report), T 162/993, The National Archives, Kew, UK, 1939.
41 Changes in the International Situation Affecting India's Defence Policy and Commitments, Secret Document, Submitted by the GOI to the Secretary of State, dated 04 November 1937, p. 5.
42 Ibid.
43 Ibid.
44 Defence Policy of India 1936–37, General Staff paper entitled 'Memorandum on the Defence Forces', 1936, Most Secret Document, MoD History Division, New Delhi, p. 8.
45 Ibid., p. 1.
46 Ibid., p. 3.
47 Ibid., p. 5.
48 Expert Committee Report (The Chatfield Committee Report), T 162/993, The National Archives, Kew, UK, 1939, p. 18.
49 Ibid., p. 9.
50 Ibid., p. 10.
51 Defence Policy of India 1936–37, General Staff paper entitled 'Memorandum on the Defence Forces', 1936, Most Secret Document, MoD History Division, New Delhi, p. 6.
52 Official History of the Indian Armed Forces in the Second World War, p. 48.
53 Defence Policy of India 1936–37, General Staff paper entitled 'Memorandum on the Defence Forces', 1936, Most Secret Document, MoD History Division, New Delhi, p. 7.
54 Ibid.
55 Expert Committee Report (The Chatfield Committee Report), T 162/993, The National Archives, Kew, UK, 1939, p. 4 and Official History of the Indian Armed Forces in the Second World War, MoD History Division, New Delhi, p. 47.

ORIGIN AND DEVELOPMENT OF RIN

56 Defence Policy of India 1936–37, General Staff paper entitled 'Memorandum on the Defence Forces', Most Secret Document, MoD History Division, New Delhi, Had Concluded the Same in 1936.
57 Ibid., p. 8.
58 Rear Admiral Satyindra Singh, *Blueprint to Bluewater: The Indian Navy 1951–65*, Lancer International, New Delhi, 1992, and Rear Admiral K. Sridharan, *A Maritime History of India*, Publication Division, MoI&B, GOI, New Delhi, 1982, p. 251.
59 Report of the Mesopotamian Commission, 1917, Naval Historical Branch, Portsmouth, UK.
60 Ibid.
61 Papers of Commander G. E. Walker, RINVR, 'File of Historical Notes', 1944, RIN/16/2, Caird Library, National Maritime Museum, Greenwich, UK.
62 Rear Admiral K. Sridharan, *A Maritime History of India*, Publication Division, Government of India, New Delhi, 1982, p. 266.
63 Ibid.
64 'Empire Naval Policy and Co-Operation', Letter from Charles Walker, Deputy Admiralty Secretary to Hankey, the Secretary of the Committee of Imperial Defence, dated 25 May 1921. Source: Publications of the Navy Records Society, Vol. 136, *The Collective Naval Defence of the Empire, 1900–1940*, pp. xli, 286.
65 Inchape Committee Report, CAB/24/133, The National Archives, Kew, UK. The committee is generally known as 'Indian Retrenchment Committee 1922–23'.
66 Admiral A. K. Chatterji, 'The Indian Navy-How Army Dominance Inhibited Its Development', *Indo-British Review*, Vol. 16, No. 1, March 1989, p. 21.
67 The Inchcape Committee Report.
68 Papers of Commander G. E. Walker, RINVR, 'File of Historical Notes', 1944, RIN/16/2 (2), Caird Library, National Maritime Museum, Greenwich, UK, p. 5.
69 J. H. Godfrey Report, India: 1943–46, Vol. 2, GOD/42, Caird Library, National Maritime Museum, Greenwich, UK.
70 Defence Policy of India 1936–37, General Staff paper entitled 'Memorandum on the Defence Forces', Most Secret Document, MoD History Division, New Delhi, p. 11.
71 Papers of Commander G. E. Walker, RINVR, 'File of Historical Notes', 1944, RIN/16/2 (2), Caird Library, National Maritime Museum, Greenwich, UK, p. 13.
72 Ibid.
73 Defence Policy of India 1936–37, General Staff paper entitled 'Memorandum on the Defence Forces', Most Secret Document, MoD History Division, New Delhi, p. 11.
74 Reserves were the defence personnel, who were not in active service, but were trained and kept for emergency needs. The retired defence personnel were also kept in the Reserve List.
75 Committee of Imperial Defence Memorandum by the Secretary of State for India (W. Wedgwood Benn), 'Control of Royal Indian Marine in War', December 1931.
76 Memorandum by the Marine Department of the Government of India, Simla, 08 September 1932, Naval Headquarters, New Delhi.
77 Colonel G. L. Pepys, Staff Officer Attached to the Military Department, India Office, to the Admiralty, 13 January 1933.

78 Rear Admiral K. Sridharan, *A Maritime History of India*, Publication Division, Government of India, New Delhi, 1982, p. 266.
79 Rawlinson Committee Report, 1922, CAB /23/39, The National Archives, Kew, UK, The Committee Was Known as Rawlinson Committee.
80 Rawlinson Committee Report, 'Re-Organisation of the Royal Indian Marine, Report of the Departmental Committee', March 1925, Naval Historical Branch, Portsmouth, UK.
81 Ibid., p. 2.
82 Ibid.
83 Ibid., p. 6.
84 Papers of Commander G. E. Walker, RINVR, 'File of Historical Notes', 1944, RIN/16/2 (2), Caird Library, National Maritime Museum, Greenwich, UK, p. 7.
85 'White Ensign' was the recognized flag of the naval fighting force of the British Empire.
86 Yastur H. Malik, *Story of the Pakistan Navy: 1947–1972*, Pakistan Navy History Section, Lahore, 1991, p. 30.
87 Papers of Commander G. E. Walker, RINVR, 'File of Historical Notes', 1944, RIN/16/2 (2), Caird Library, National Maritime Museum, Greenwich, UK, p. 8.
88 Press release, Information Officer, India Office, 'The Indian Navy (Discipline) Bill', 05 September 1934 and Minutes of Brown to the Under Secretary of State for India, 07 October 1934, quoted by Yastur H. Malik, *Story of the Pakistan Navy: 1947–1972*, Pakistan Navy History Section, Lahore, 1991, p. 30.
89 Colonel Sir Clive Wigram, Private Secretary to the King to Samuel Hoare, Secretary of State for India, 15 September 1934, Decipher of Telegram from Government of India, Army Department, to Secretary of State for India, 20 September 1934 and J. A. Simpson, Deputy Clerk of the Council of India and Principal Officer, Military Department, India Office, to the Secretary of the Admiralty, 14 December 1934.
90 Papers of Commander G. E. Walker, RINVR, 'File of Historical Notes', 1944, RIN/16/2 (2), Caird Library, National Maritime Museum, Greenwich, UK, p. 8.
91 Ibid.
92 Defence Policy of India 1936–37, General Staff paper entitled 'Memorandum on the Defence Forces', Most Secret Document, MoD History Division, New Delhi, p. 1.
93 Ibid.
94 Ibid.
95 File titled 'Conversion of Royal Indian Marine into Royal Indian Navy', ADM 1/8797, The National Archives, Kew Gardens, UK. It says that "... it is now the intention to legalise this state of affairs by means of Indian Legislation. Otherwise of course, the employment of the Indian Marine is strictly intended for use within Indian waters."
96 Bisheshwar Prasad (Ed.), *Indian War Economy (Supply, Industry & Finance)*, MoD History Division, New Delhi, 1962, p. 299.
97 Garran Tribunal Report of 1933, WO 32/3864, The National Archives, Kew, UK.
98 Ibid., The terms of reference of the Garran Tribunal.
99 Ibid., Para 19 of the Garran Report.
100 Bisheshwar Prasad (Ed.), *Indian War Economy (Supply, Industry & Finance)*, MoD History Division, New Delhi, 1962, p. 300.
101 Ibid., p. 301.

102 Ibid.
103 Government of India proposal. George Stanley, Governor of Madras; Field Marshal Sir P. W. Chetwode, Commander-in-Chief India: Khan B. M. Fazl-i-Husain, Vice President Governor General's Executive Council, and Others to Sir Samuel Hoare, Secretary of State for India, dated 14 June 1934 quoted by Nicholas Tracy, *The Collective Naval Defence of the Empire, 1900–1940*, Ashgate, The Navy Records Society, London, 1997, pp. 487–492.
104 Ibid., p. 487.
105 Ibid.
106 Ibid., p. 490.
107 Ibid.
108 Ibid., p. 491.
109 Neville Chamberlain, Chancellor of the Exchequer, to the Marquis of Zetland, Secretary of State for India, 30 September 1935, Nicholas Tracy, *The Collective Naval Defence of the Empire, 1900–1940*, Ashgate, The Navy Records Society, London, 1997, pp. xliii and 517–519.
110 Ibid.
111 Vice Admiral Arthur Bedford to Little, September 1935. Nicholas Tracy, *The Collective Naval Defence of the Empire, 1900–1940*, Ashgate, The Navy Records Society, London, 1997, p. 516.
112 Ibid., p. 517.
113 Murray, Admiralty Secretary, to J. A. Barlow of Treasury, October 1935. *The Collective Naval Defence of the Empire, 1900–1940*, Ashgate, The Navy Records Society, London, 1997, p. 519.
114 Ibid.
115 Ibid., p. 520.
116 *The Collective Naval Defence of the Empire, 1900–1940*, Ashgate, The Navy Records Society, London, 1997, p. xliii.
117 Murray to J. A. Barlow dated 08 November 1935, *The Collective Naval Defence of the Empire, 1900–1940*, Ashgate, The Navy Records Society, London, 1997, p. 520.
118 Neville Chamberlin to Zetland, dated 03 January 1936, *The Collective Naval Defence of the Empire, 1900–1940*, Ashgate, The Navy Records Society, London, 1997, p. 521.
119 Commander D. J. Hastings, *The Royal Indian Navy, 1612–1950*, McFarland & Company, Inc., Publishers, London, 1988, p. 89.
120 Defence Policy of India 1936–37, General Staff paper entitled 'Memorandum on the Defence Forces', Most Secret Document, MoD History Division, New Delhi, had concluded the same in 1936. p. 8, The first Phase was the provision of Local Naval Defence, i.e, protection of shipping in the immediate approaches to ports from submarines and mines. The second Phase was the Acquisition of a few seagoing ships and development of training and repair facilities. The third Phase was the Formation of a seagoing squadron and the fourth Phase was the Provision, in addition to local naval defence, of squadrons or Capital ships to take part in the general scheme of naval defence of the Empire.
121 Defence Policy of India 1936–37, General Staff paper entitled 'Memorandum on the Defence Forces', 1936, Most Secret Document, MoD History Division, New Delhi, p. 9.
122 Ibid., p. 15.
123 Retired or about to retire sailors.
124 General Staff Memorandum entitled 'India's Defence Commitments and Her Ability to Implement Them', dated 24 March 1937, Submitted by the Defence Department, Government of India, p. 16.

ORIGIN AND DEVELOPMENT OF RIN

125 Defence Policy of India 1936–37, General Staff Paper, 'Memorandum on the Defence Forces', 1936, p. 9.
126 Summary of the General Staff Memorandum entitled 'India's Defence Commitments and Her Ability to Implement Them', dated 24 March 1937, Submitted by the Defence Department, Government of India, p. 1.
127 Ibid., pp. 2–3.
128 Minute by J. A. Simpson to General Wilson and Rear Admiral Herbert Fitz Herbert, Commander-in-Chief, Royal Indian Navy, 16 April 1937, Naval Headquarters, New Delhi.
129 Secret letter from A. Duff Cooper, First Lord, to Simon, dated 1 July 1937, Naval Headquarters, New Delhi.
130 Simon to Zetland dated 26 July 1937, Zetland to Simon dated 03 August 1937 and Private and Personal Telegram from Marquis of Linlithgow, the Viceroy of India, to Zetland, Received on 06 September 1937, Naval Headquarters, New Delhi.
131 The RIN Enquiry Commission Report, 1946, Naval Headquarters, New Delhi, p. 4.
132 Expert Committee Report (The Chatfield Committee Report), T 162/993, The National Archives, Kew, UK, 1939, p. 46 and RIN Enquiry Commission Report, 1946, Naval Headquarters, New Delhi, p. 4.
133 Expert Committee Report (The Chatfield Committee Report), T 162/993, The National Archives, Kew, UK, 1939, p. 46.
134 Ibid.
135 Chatterji, 'The Indian Navy-How Army Dominance Inhibited Its Development', *Indo-British Review*, Vol. 16, No. 1, March 1989, p. 21.
136 Expert Committee Report (The Chatfield Committee Report), T 162/993, The National Archives, Kew, UK, 1939, p. 22.
137 General Robert Cassels's Correspondence & Telegram between the Viceroy and Secretary of State for India dated 24 August 1938 Dealing with Defence Expenditure Matters, File No. 601/7478/H, MoD History Division, New Delhi, p. 2.
138 Ibid.
139 Ibid., pp. 2–3.
140 Expert Committee Report (The Chatfield Committee Report), T 162/993, The National Archives, Kew, UK, 1939, p. 4.
141 Ibid., p. 18.
142 Ibid. The report said that "But quite clearly in our view, the principle on which the financial arrangements between the two Governments should be based is that India should bear some share in a joint responsibility for her external security."
143 Pownall Sub-Committee's Report, Para 61, quoted in the Chatfield Committee Report, p. 18.
144 Second Report of the Cabinet Committee, dated 29 July 1938, CID Paper No.198-D, Para 5–7.
145 Expert Committee Report (The Chatfield Committee Report), T 162/993, The National Archives, Kew, UK, 1939, p. 19.
146 Ibid., p. 20.
147 Ibid., The Chatfield Committee opinioned that "If at any time there are forces held for the purposes covered by the joint responsibility, a contribution should, in our opinion, be made by the British Government to India, and the method of the Garran Award offers, we think the possible solution", p. 20.
148 Ibid., p. 61.
149 Ibid., p. 20.

150 Ibid., p. 61.
151 Ibid., p. 63.
152 Ibid., p. 62.
153 Ibid., p. 63.
154 Admiral A. K. Chatterji, 'The Indian Navy-How Army Dominance Inhibited Its Development', *Indo-British Review*, Vol. 16, No. 1, March 1989, p. 21.
155 During the First World War, the German light cruiser *Emden* bombarded the oil installations at the Madras harbour on 22 September 1914 (2130 Hrs). Even though the attack resulted in little casualty, it was a shame for the British Empire.
156 Expert Committee Report (The Chatfield Committee Report), T 162/993, The National Archives, Kew, UK, 1939, pp. 5-7.
157 A/S stands for Anti Submarine and M/S for Minesweeper.
158 T. 124 Revised Agreement, MT 40/ 154, The National Archives, Kew Gardens, UK.
159 Coastal Batteries are the armed defence units at major coastal areas to defend seaborne threats.
160 Expert Committee Report (The Chatfield Committee Report), T 162/993, The National Archives, Kew, UK, 1939, p. 49.
161 Ibid., p. 10.
162 Ibid., p. 18.
163 Ibid.
164 Ibid., p. 20.
165 Ibid., p. 64.
166 Ibid., p. 46.
167 Ibid.
168 Ibid., p. 48.
169 Ibid.
170 Ibid.
171 Ibid.
172 Ibid.
173 Ibid., p. 54.
174 Ibid., p. 91.
175 Ibid., p. 55.
176 Ibid., p. 56.
177 Ibid.
178 Ibid.
179 Royal Indian Navy War Organisation, 1938, ADM 1/9829, The National Archives, Kew Gardens, UK.
180 Report of Mesopotamian Commission, 1917, Naval Historical Branch, Portsmouth, UK.
181 File noting of Commander-in-Chief, entitled 'Defence Policy – India', in Response to the Defence Secretary's Note, dated 02 October 1937, p. 1.
182 Ibid., pp. 1-2.
183 Ibid.
184 Expert Committee Report (The Chatfield Committee Report), T 162/993, The National Archives, Kew, UK, 1939, para 72.
185 James Goldrick, *No Easy Answers: The Development of the Navies of India, Pakistan, Bangladesh and Sri Lanka, 1945-1996*, Lancer, New Delhi, 1997, p. 6.

3

MANPOWER AND RECRUITMENT IN THE RIN DURING THE WAR

1. Introduction

On 3 September 1939 Britain declared her entry into the war. Subsequently Lord Linlithgow, the Viceroy, announced India's participation in the war without consulting the Indian leaders. The Congress and the League decided to support the British in the war on condition that India would be given independence immediately after the war. Due to post–First World War defence policies and reduction of its role into an auxiliary force, RIN was inadequately prepared at the outbreak of the war. Britain's entry into the war necessitated the expansion of the navy in India for the defence of coasts, harbours and seaborne trade. Manpower became the cardinal issue in the Royal Indian Navy during the war.

Recruitment was the greatest problem faced by the colonial government in India, where enlistment was entirely voluntary. In connection with the recruitment admiral Godfrey, FOCRIN has said that,

> From 1940 onwards energetic steps were taken to persuade the Government of India to embark on a planned expansion of the Service coupled with a shipbuilding programme. Dilatoriness in arriving at a decision strangled the growth of the Service and when the decision was finally taken it presented the Navy with the almost impossible problem as regards recruitment and training of the numbers required.
>
> With the comparatively slow expansion of the Service between 1939 and 1941 there is no doubt that the Army had a clear field for recruitment and secured the cream of the population; this was particularly the case in northern India. To obtain the numbers required in later years it became necessary to open up recruitment on an India – wide scale, large numbers of ratings from Bengal and Southern India were enrolled together with a comparatively large number from the cities as opposed to the villages of India.[1]

MANPOWER AND RECRUITMENT DURING THE WAR

2. State at the outbreak of the war

The total sanctioned strength of officers and ratings prior to the outbreak of war, including those undergoing specialist courses in the United Kingdom, training with the East Indies squadron of the Royal Navy and leave reserves, are summarised as follows:[2]

(a) **Officers**

Executive	72
Engineer	37
Total	**109**

(b) **Warrant Officers**

Gunners and Boatswains	19
Signal Boatswains	4
Warrant telegraphists	11
Warrant mechanicians	2
Warrant schoolmasters	6
Warrant writers	11
Assistant Surgeons	10
Total	**63**

(c) **Ratings**

Seaman Branch	482
Engine room branch	401
Communication Branch	
Signalman	136
Telegraphists	103
Artificers and Artisan Branch	54
Accountant Branch	41
Domestic branch	232
Medical branch	21
Instructional branch	12
Miscellaneous	1
Total ratings	**1,483**
Deduct those borne at Admiralty expense	40
Total RIN ratings	**1,443**

In addition the strength of the reserves was as follows:[3]

RINR	None borne
RINVR Executive officers	21
Accountant officers	13
RIFR	none borne

On 3 September 1939, when the war broke out, the RIN consisted of 198 officers and 1,475 ratings. Five years later, on 3 September 1944, the number of officers and ratings in RIN had risen to 2,750 (including RINR – 319; RINVR – 1995; and Warrant Officers – 224) and 24,543 respectively.[4] The permanent cadre of ratings at the outbreak of war was 1,723 men. This consisted of the following:[5]

Non artificers branches
Chief Petty Officer	85
Petty Officer	219
Leading	289
Able Seaman (A.B.)/Ordinary Seaman (O.D.)	1,025
Total	**1,618**
Chief Artificer Rate	18
Other Artificer Rates	87
Total	**1,723**

At the outbreak of the war there were 985 continuous servicemen in the RIN, but with the subsequent attainment of man's rate through the medium of boy and apprentice entry, this number stood at 2,104 at the end of the war. The borne strength[6] composition equivalent to the above cadre breakdown was as follows:[7]

Non-artificers branches
Chief Petty Officer	373
Petty Officer	561
Leading	328
A.B./O.D.	740
Total	**2,002**

Artificers branches
Chief Artificer Rate	24
Other Artificer Rates	78
Total	**2,104***

* Excluding 151 pre-war men on non-continuous service agreement.

By 31 December 1939, the numbers of both officers and men was almost exactly doubled. The additional officers came from the Merchant Service and civil life from a variety of trades and professions. Initially the ratings came almost entirely from the Merchant Service but for various reasons both financial and religious, the best men remained in the Merchant Service.[8] Throughout the war, the higher ranks of the Service and the key positions were held by Europeans.[9]

In general, since the outbreak of war, the RIN expanded piecemeal, filling vacancies haphazardly as they arose. One planned scheme for expansion, however, was prepared in 1940 for the manning of the service. In order to plan the requirements of personnel to meet material expansion up to October 1941, a committee consisting of the Commanding Officer Depot, the Staff Officer (Plans), the Registrar of Reserves, and the Squadron Engineer Officer met at Bombay and prepared the report.[10] Their report was submitted to the Flag Officer Commanding Royal Indian Navy (FOCRIN) on 9 November 1940, covering expansion ashore and afloat.[11]

3. Selection of Officers

Up to 1924, selection of Officers of the Regular RIN was made from officers of the RNR (Royal Navy Reserve) who had obtained at least a second mate's certificate. There were one or two exceptions to this.[12] Post-1924, officers entered as cadets and were trained as special entry cadets with the Royal Navy before joining for Service in India. There were a number of exceptions to this and the necessary numbers were filled from officers joining from the RNR or Merchant Navy.[13] Regular officers of the RIN were sent to the United Kingdom each year to specialise in the full long course at the various Specialist Establishments, and promotion was similar to that of the Royal Navy.

The grant of Commission to Indian candidates in the RIN began in 1932; prior to that the entire officer cadre was filled by British and Europeans. One-third of the vacancies were reserved for the Indian candidates and out of these one was usually reserved for cadets of the IMMTS (Indian Mercantile Marine Training Ship) *Dufferin*.[14] The vacancies were filled by competitive examinations conducted by the Federal Public Service Commission annually, in October, at Delhi for general candidates and at Bombay for the cadets of the IMMTS *Dufferin*.[15] The senior rank which was attainable in the RIN in 1943 was Commodore 1st Class.[16] The Flag Officer Commanding RIN had always been an officer lent from the Royal Navy.[17] However the Indianisation of the officer cadre came at a slow pace. There were only 40 Indian officers in the RIN at the outbreak of the war.[18] The British believed in the inadequacy of suitable potential officers in India; this was put forth as a justification for maintaining the numerical preponderance of British personnel in the armed forces.[19]

At the outbreak of the war the position was most favourable in respect of voluntary recruitment of European officers to the RIN Reserves. "Unfortunately the enthusiasm and inherent love of the sea of the cream of the European British community in India and of the best type of businessmen, was thrown away. The Navy's hands were tied by the thinness of the dribble of official sanctions for vacancies, it could open only a little wicket gate to the spate of valuable personnel volunteering for enlistment."[20] Due to the slow issue of the Government sanctions in the Navy with the Army suffering no such delay, volunteers released from civil employment preferred to join the Army. RIN suffered a big loss of gentlemen with yachting experience and technical and engineering qualifications when each officer joined the Army.[21]

The naval recruiting organisation

Recruiting of officers, originally carried out by the Registrar of Reserves and the Drafting Officer, became the concern of a committee acting as a selection board in April 1940. By this time the functions of Commanding Officer Depot and Registrar of Reserves, previously carried out by one officer, were separated, and the title Registrar of Reserves became that of Director of Reserves.[22] These officers, with the small committee of co-opted members, linked up with the organisation of National Service Advisory Committees, carried out the final selection of candidates for recruitment, both from volunteers and those taken up by the committee.[23] The Registration (Emergency Powers) Act (I of 1940) was subsequently re-enacted as the National Service (European British Subjects) Act (XVIII of 1940), when it was amended to make compulsory the voluntary provisions of the earlier act.[24]

The system now worked in this manner: In accordance with the National Service (European British Subjects) Act, the military district command called up any European British subject between the ages of 18 and 50 for interview by the National Service Advisory Committee, in order that the committee might pronounce upon his availability for military service and enquire into his qualifications and preferences.[25] If the Committee considered the individual available for calling up, he would then receive a calling-up notice from the military command. The calling-up notice was a compulsory summons, but subject to a right of appeal by either the individual himself or his employer to a tribunal appointed by the Central Government and consisting of one Government servant (Indian Civil Service (ICS)), one military officer and one representative of trade and industry.[26] As this tribunal had the final power of decision, when the National Service Advisory Committee had decided that an individual was not available for service, in doubtful cases the military command would still issue a calling-up notice to force an appeal to the tribunal.[27] In practice the Committee made a list of firms in their area, called up the leave reserves of a firm's strength unless they had already volunteered, and then heads of firms were called upon to provide a quota of the remainder, balanced against each other's sacrifices, or show cause to the contrary. Tea and coffee plantations released their three men (RIN Reserves) out of every four against the return of retired men over military age.[28]

In order to avoid a dead period of three months of initial training, it was suggested that every European British subject should be recruited to take three months' military training on the outbreak of the war, and then be permitted to return to his civil employment until he was called up.[29]

In practice the naval situation in respect to recruitment under this Act showed various disadvantages. The loss of valuable material by lack of sanctioned appointments has been mentioned earlier. A large number of marine engineers employed in jute mills were taken by the Army. The Navy's requirement of trained marine engineers, internal combustion experts and electrical officers could not meet as they had already been absorbed elsewhere.[30] The National Service Advisory Committee, with no naval representation, had given priorities to military requirements.[31] This was visible particularly in Central and Northern India, where candidates were frequently not asked their choice of service as the Navy was ignored. As a result 98% of reserve officers came from the coastal towns.[32] "The volunteers were not lacking; it was the system which tied the Navy's hand."[33]

Recruitment of Indian officers

Indian British Subjects were recruited directly, at first by the Commanding Officer, Depot, acting as Registrar of Reserves, and the Drafting Officer, subsequently by the Director of Reserves and a selection committee.

Indian officers of the Mercantile Marine, most of whom had been cadets of the IMMTS *Dufferin* came as volunteers for the Royal Indian Navy Reserve (RINR).[34] Royal Indian Navy Volunteer Reserve (RINVR) had a strong representation of the Parsi community in Bombay.[35] The best Indian officer candidates opted to join the Army rather than Navy, the reason being that promotion in the RIN was not by shore qualifications but by the length of service, and there was more rapid promotion in the Army.[36] Other reasons were that naval service required hard work over long hours in uncomfortable surroundings and separation from families. "In general the standards of education in India were low, which was a serious handicap to a service with standards as high as those of the Navy must be, where technical training in all branches must be rapidly absorbed."[37] Other discouraging factors were that the early training establishments were not attractive to recruits. Furthermore, the individual civil disobedience movement, the war news and of the Japanese entry into the war had serious effects on recruitment.[38]

The Royal Indian Navy selection board and the Recruiting Directorate of the Adjutant General's Branch

In the spring of 1941, the board previously consisting of the Director of Reserves with co-opted members was re-constituted with the Commanding Officer, and a retired Indian civil servant with experience of the Federal Public Services Commission.[39] In January 1942, the recruiting was reorganised with the centralisation of the recruiting for all three services in the

Recruiting Directorate of the Adjutant General's Branch, General Headquarters, India.[40] This consisted of a Director of Recruiting, responsible to the Adjutant General, with five sections, dealing with:

1. Non-technical recruiting for all services
2. Technical recruiting for all services
3. Indian Officer Recruiting for all services
4. British Officer recruiting under the National Service Act
5. All recruiting propaganda and publicity

The Navy was represented on the Directorate by the Assistant Adjutant General (Recruiting), who was responsible for all matters connected with naval recruitment and also for sections 3, 4 and 5.[41] This system covered the whole of India, working through 12 Recruiting Officers, each in charge of a district for non-technical recruitment and with his assistant Recruiting Officers in charge of sub-districts, and through four Technical Recruiting officers whose organisation was parallel.[42]

The Naval Selection Board

The Naval Selection Board later became the final authority for selection of commissioned ranks and midshipmen for the Navy, and reconstituted of naval officers only. Candidates appearing before it were required to undergo both educational and medical examinations.[43] "The recruitment in India of European British subjects was almost confined to those previously under 18 and therefore ineligible under the National Service Act, as India had been nearly milked dry of available persons between the ages of 18 and 50."[44] Under this Directorate any person called up under the Act could express a preference for a particular service, when the case would be passed to the Selection of Personnel Directorate. In the case of persons suitable for the Navy, information was then passed to the Recruiting Directorate, who would arrange for an interview at Bombay by the Naval Selection Board, who would make the final decision. If more than one service claimed any one individual, the case was settled by negotiation among the Chiefs of Staff, but it was accepted that possession of Board of Trade Master's or First Class Engineer's Certificates gave the Navy prior claim to the individual concerned.[45]

Indian officers

Indian candidates applied for recruitment in the armed forces through District Magistrates or other civil authorities to the Provincial Selection Board in their area.[46] Those over the age of 35 were treated as direct applicants, and they were sent to Bombay if suitable for the Navy. Those between the ages of 17 and 35 were weeded out by Provincial Selection Boards, those

MANPOWER AND RECRUITMENT DURING THE WAR

Table 3.1 Recruitment status in 1942

	Executive	*Engineer*	*Accountant*	*Electrical*
British	183	38	32	5
Indian	146	10	54	3
Total	329	48	86	8

Source: General State of RIN on outbreak of war in 1939 & RIN Expansion, OSD/C10/ii, History Division, Ministry of Defence, New Delhi, p. 35

passed going thence to Central Interview Boards, and thence, in the case of the Navy, to Bombay.[47] Indian officer recruitment on the whole was below requirements under this system for the same reasons as mentioned previously.

During the period 1942–1943, to increase recruiting to the desired figure, permission was obtained from the Adjutant General to canvas Officers' Training Schools for volunteers to transfer to the Navy. This method provided a large percentage of recruitment, but objection was taken by the War Office in the case of European cadets and so far as these were concerned, this door was now closed. Volunteers were called for from the Royal Naval Reserve (RNR) and the Royal Naval Volunteer Reserve (RNVR) in the United Kingdom, and special arrangements were made to recruit on the beach from the batches of evacuees arriving in India from Malaya and Burma.[48] Under the order of the Director of Reserves in consultation with the Adjutant General's Branch, direct interview was arranged with the Naval Selection Board, and this also assisted in increasing recruitment. A total of 471 were recruited in 1942 and the Indian representation was only 5%, because "the educational standard in India is so low."[49] Recruitment figures during 1942 are given in Table 3.1:[50]

Warrant officers

The position of the naval warrant officers was not strictly comparable with that of the military warrant officer, as in the Navy the term refers to an officer, not a rating or other rank. A warrant officer was promoted from the lower deck (rating) after long service and in face of keen competition, with the result that his long experience of work and his emergence out of the heavy competition give him exceptional value.[51] In the Royal Indian Navy, as the educational and professional standards, required for a rating were not realised, there were comparatively few men of the standard necessary for promotion to warrant rank. The warrant officer was eligible for promotion to commissioned rank, and a case occurred of entry from the lower deck leading to flag rank by this road. With time, when naval schools produced the material, it was hoped that the paucity of warrant officers would be

Table 3.2 Warrant Officers sanctioned and borne as on 30 September 1943[52]

	Sanctioned RIN	Borne RIN	Borne Landing Craft Wing (LCW)	Total Borne	Lent by RN (deduct)
Gunners	46	26	1	27	10
Gunners (Torpedo)	4	7*	–	7	7
Boatswains	13	5	–	5	–
Boatswains (A/S)	2	1	–	1	–
Signal Boatswains	9	6	–	6	1
Warrant Telegraphist	28	17	–	17	7
Warrant Engineer	96	103**	8	111	–
Warrant Electrician	8	3	1	4	3
Warrant Writer	25	16	–	16	–
Warrant Shipwright	2	–	2	2	1
Warrant Schoolmaster	40	20	1	21	–
Assistant Surgeon	33	–***	–	–	–
Warrant Master at Arms	9	–	–	–	–
Total	315	204	13	217	29

Source: General State of RIN on outbreak of War in 1939 & RIN Expansion, OSD/C10/ii, History Division, Ministry of Defence, New Delhi, p. 35

*Excess borne in lieu of Lieutenants.
**99 Warrant Engineers, RINR (T124X [I] agreement) 4 Warrant Mechanicians
***Commissioned officers, Indian Medical Service (I.M.S.) and Indian Medical Department (I.M.D.) borne in lieu

overcome. The naval warrant officer ranks with but senior to a conductor, Royal Army Ordnance Corps (RAOC) a master gunner 1st class or a 1st class Staff Sergeant Major, all British Army. A midshipman ranks with these but junior to them all. 1st class officers, British Army, or all warrant officers 1st class, Indian Army are junior to the warrant officer and midshipman (see Table 3.2).

RINR & RINVR

In early 1939, a reserve cadre was constituted to grant commission to both Indians and Europeans in two categories, Royal Indian Navy Reserve (RINR) and Royal Indian Navy Volunteer Reserve (RINVR). RINR and RINVR were at one in that they were bodies of men who underwent periodic training in peacetime and were available for mobilisation in time of war without being part of these standing establishments.[53] RINR consisted of professional seamen and marine engineers who were officers and warrant officers of the Merchant Marine Service. The RINVR officers were directly recruited from the civilians, and had no previous experience at sea.[54] The first proposals for the creation of Reserves were made in 1930 and were

MANPOWER AND RECRUITMENT DURING THE WAR

incorporated in each subsequent scheme for expansion.[55] Provisional regulations for the RINVR were forwarded in 1937 and the form in which they were sanctioned by the Government on 1 October 1938, and recruiting was ordered by the FOCRIN in January 1939.[56] The first entries took place in March 1939. Provision was originally made for both permanent and temporary commissions, the recruitment and training of Executive and Accountant officers. The first sanction for recruitment on 23 January 1939 sanctioned 10 Executive and 10 Accountant officers; the second sanction on 28 April 1939 was for 12 Executive and 8 Accountant officers.[57] The reserve was to recruit Indian and British Officers in equal numbers so that at any stage it would be half Indian and half European.[58]

Professional regulations for the RINR were similar with the addition of qualification of training in mercantile marine training establishments, the possession of seagoing certificates of competency and sea service according to class.[59] Officers were to be of Executive and Engineering Branches; Ratings of deck, Engine room and writer branches.[60] At the commencement of the war no recruitment had taken place either for officers or ratings.[61] In respect of ratings, the reason for this was the low standard of education among mercantile marine ratings had been found to render them unsuitable material for technical duties they would be needed to carry out; in respect of officers there was firstly the fact that most suitable material had already been taken by the RNR, and secondly the IMMTS *Dufferin* took her first cadets at the end of November 1927, with the result that Indian Merchant Ships were mainly officered by Europeans for the years necessary for these cadets to complete their training and obtain their certificate. The first entries took place on the outbreak of the war. The earlier plan of granting permanent commission to the RINR and RINVR officers were withdrawn at the outbreak of the war and they were given temporary commissions during the war.[62]

As fast as merchant ships were taken over according to size of the vessel. Of the mercantile marine officers serving in these ships, about nine in every ten dock officers were Portuguese, usually from Daman, with the result that, out of all the officers thrown out of employment, only five could be recruited on T 124 (India) agreement into the RINR.[63] The engineer officers were mainly British Subjects and were recruited easily enough, but they were on different rates of pay according to their company and had to be brought to a uniform and acceptable scale.[64]

Royal Indian Navy Fleet Reserve (RINFR)

Royal Indian Navy Fleet Reserve was the body of ratings retired from active service who were at call in an emergency and who underwent periodic training.[65] Draft regulations for this Reserve were submitted to the Government in November 1937, and finally issued in Squadron Order dated 28 July 1938.[66] By these regulations all ratings joining the service after 1 April 1934

Table 3.3 Increase in the reserves

RINR Officers	Executive	46
	Engineer	2
Warrant Officers	Executive	5
	Engineer	64
RINVR Officers	Executive	36
	Engineer	25
Total		**178**

Source: General State of RIN on outbreak of War in 1939 & RIN Expansion, p. 7

were required to serve in the reserve, and all joining prior to that date were invited to do so, but no man had a right to join the reserve. Only ratings of the rate of able seamen, its equivalence or higher rates were eligible; men not of good character or of low efficiency or over 42 years of age were not to be drafted into the reserve.[67] Ratings were to be taken from men who had completed a period of enrolment but had not qualified for a pension, and from those in receipt of pensions other than disability pensions.[68] Reservists were to reside in India but service in the mercantile marine in British or Indian ships calling regularly at Indian ports was provided for. Enrolment was for 10 years with certain exceptions as to classes and in some cases discharge at 47 years of age.[69] In certain cases re-enrolment was possible. This reserve provided a body of men at call in time of war for expansion to proceed upon a firm core of trained and experienced men of high value in stiffening new entry expansion, provided always that time permitted the proper growth of the reserve.[70] To man the vessels and staff the ports, transfer of active service officers were made, and a leap in reserves took place, shown by the figures in Table 3.3 on 10 November 1939:[71]

4. Recruitment of ratings

The army had permanent recruiting officers stationed all over northern India. Prior to the war, a recruitment team consisting of a Naval officer and a small party used to go on a recruitment campaign twice or thrice a year to the Muree Hills and the Salt Range, mainly with the object of recruiting boys for the slow but sound method of imbuing landsmen with the spirit of the sea.[72] The RIN officials used to inform the army recruiting official about the visit of the naval recruiting party in their district on a certain date. The army recruiting team used to provide all assistance to the RIN team. As a result of the publicity given by the Army for the RIN, hundreds of young men used to turn up as volunteers in each district to join the navy, and about 2% of them were finally selected. The boys stood in a long line and the recruiting officer and medical officer walked down the line, rejecting about 50% of the boys out of hand. Commander G. E. Walker says that "On one occasion the officer thought the line was rather long and he found that as the boys were rejected and told to fall out and go home they crept along to the end of the line and fell in again. To get over this difficulty the medical officer stamped the eligibilities on their backs with a rubber officer stamp. Even this was no good as the boys managed to transfer the still wet ink from one back to another with the palm of their hands."[73] It clearly shows that socio-economic conditions prevailed in the Indian villages forced the young Indians to become volunteers for the defence forces and serve the British.

In 1925, all ratings of the Royal Indian Marine were Musalman; 75% of the ratings were recruited from the principal recruiting places, Punjab and North Western Frontier Provinces (NWFP). The remaining 25% were from the Konkan coast, especially from Ratnagiri, about 250 miles south of Bombay.[74] Even though the Punjabi men were 1,000 miles far from the sea and had no seafaring tradition, the British officials had given priority to the men from Punjab because they had very fine physiques, were intelligent and above all very keen and loyal to the core.[75] Especially the Punjabi Musalman, they were considered better than the ratings from Ratnagiri, who lived by and on the sea, because of better IQ and courage.[76]

This clearly shows that despite the fact that Punjabis and people from the North West Frontier Provinces were thousands of miles away from the sea and had no knowledge of seafaring, still they were given preference over the recruits from other parts of the country. Hence it is very much evident that British applied the 'martial race' theory in the RIN on similar lines of the Indian Army. However the British never accepted that they were the inventors of the martial theory. "The 'martial races' were certain categories of people from the subcontinent whom the British considered to be particularly suited, physically and mentally, for inclusion in the Indian Army."[77] "[T]the British officialdom for much of the nineteenth and early twentieth centuries actually believed that certain Indian ethnic groups were more suited to military life than others."[78] According to Philip Mason, "The division of the people into 'martial' and 'non-martial' was not an invention of the British; it was the recognition of something already implicit in the Indian social system."[79] He further says that "The idea that some people will make soldiers and some will not is of course much older than the British. It is implicit in the Hindu caste system; no raja would have paid the money lender or the trader caste to bear arms. But was the British who after the mutiny, step by step, formulated and codified the principal, turning what had been a matter of practical choice into a dogma proclaimed with theological rancour."[80] However, Anirudh Deshpande has a different perception of it. Deshpande says that "As late as 1932, officially the most important 'ethnic types' represented in the Indian Army were the Punjabi Musalmans, Gurkhas, Sikhs,

MANPOWER AND RECRUITMENT DURING THE WAR

Dogras, Rajputs, Pathans, Marathas, Garwalis and Kumaonis."[81] According to Deshpande, the popular literature on recruitment reflects this bias.[82]

Categories of ratings

Ratings of RIN were divided into two cadres: permanent and temporary.

Permanent cadre

The permanent cadre was the number of sanctioned personnel at the outbreak of war, with the addition of the regular intake of boys and apprentices.[83] In this, the limitation was a safeguard against the accumulation of a body of men surplus to requirements after the war, for whom no employment could be found but whose terms of enrolment prevented their discharge or transfer to the RIFR.[84] They fell into two categories: Continuous and Non-continuous service.

1. **Continuous Service Ratings.** Continuous Service ratings were the normal recruitment of the Navy except for domestic rates, and entered as boys or apprentices according to their branch. They served for 10 years from the date on which they were advanced to a man's rate, and were then drafted into the RIFR for a future 10 years. Until the outbreak of the war, where the entry of boys was not sufficient for requirements, the RIN could recruit men directly into this category. In this case the date of enrolment was that of the commencement of their service. Direct entry into continuous service was suspended on the outbreak of the war to prevent a swollen cadre, but where requirement did not cover wastage or where it was insufficient for requirements, special service ratings were selected for transfer to continuous service.
2. **Non-Continuous Service Ratings.** Non-Continuous Service Ratings were the domestic branches, Cook, Steward and Topass[85] recruited directly as men and serving for three years from the date of entry. They might have been required to transfer to the RIFR.

Temporary cadre

The temporary cadre was divided into two categories, Special Service and Hostilities Only ratings.

1. **Special Service Ratings**
   The Special Service Ratings were entered directly to men's rates. They were first recruited in 1938 under a regulation permitting the Flag Officer Commanding to authorise direct recruitment in the seaman, stoker, and communication branches, to meet deficiencies which the Boys'

Training Establishment (BTE) was unable to fulfil.[86] Their term of service was 10 years, originally five years or fewer on Active Service and the remainder in the RIFR, but it was altered by the Extension of Services Act of 1940, to as long as might be required upon active service. As Special Service ratings did not go through the Boys' or Apprentices' courses, but through the shorter courses designed for men, they provided material for rapid expansion, and at the same time their shorter and more elastic terms of service enabled the retrenchment of Active Service personnel and strengthening of the RIFR to take place more rapidly.[87] A Special Service scheme stabilizing this category of ratings was approved in April 1940.[88]

2 **Hostilities Only Ratings**

Government sanction for the recruitment of Hostilities Only (HO) Ratings was obtained in August 1939, on the very eve of the outbreak of the war.[89] Hostilities Only ratings were seamen, stokers, etc., from the mercantile marine, signed on articles for naval service in the same way as for the merchant service, who were used for ordinary deck and similar duties for which their experience suited them.[90] The Hostilities Only ratings were recruited and borne as an emergency measure to replace an active service rating, in order to relieve trained naval ratings for more technical duties.[91] They were available at government shipping offices for immediate recruitment and were subject to immediate discharge when their service was no longer required. Practically, the Hostilities Only ratings were a valuable means of filling emergency gaps which RIN training establishments would take time to overtake.

Active service ratings

The Active Service included continuous, non-continuous, and special service ratings, and the hostilities only ratings.[92]

Recruitment from mercantile marine

When the RIN took over the command of merchant vessels, the problem in respect of recruitment of ratings of these merchant vessels was no easier. "Deck crews from Daman were Portuguese subjects and could not be recruited, while the remainder of the deck crews were usually Hindus, not willing to serve in a service mainly Mohameden, as it was at that time."[93] In consequence entirely new crews had to be found and signed on at the Shipping Masters Officer in Bombay and Calcutta. These sailors refused to engage at coastal rates of pay, and would serve only on deep sea rates plus a war bonus.[94] At this time the mercantile rates of pay were increasing rapidly under the stimulus of competition between companies for the services of

Table 3.4 Borne strengths of active service ratings at the outbreak of war and on 31 December 1939

Branch	Sept. 1939	Dec. 1939	Increase
Seaman (including Gunners)	480	554	74
	(20)	(20)	–
Signalmen	70	105	35
Telegraphists	52	82	30
Stokers	336	338	2
Artificers & Artisans	64	64	–
Writers	41	41	–
Domestics	238	36	–2
Sick berth Attendants	19	21	2
Schoolmasters	10	10	–
Electrical W/T rates	3	3	–
Totals	1,313	1,454	141

Source: General State of RIN on outbreak of War in 1939 & RIN Expansion, p. 15

men who were insufficient in number for all the berths available. The battle of the rates became a tug of war with the mercantile marine winning hands down, taking the seaman and leaving the beach rates for the navy.[95]

Engine room ratings, who were mainly Muslims, usually stayed by their ships except for a small proportion of Portuguese subjects. As a result of this 'rate war', the HO recruits who presented themselves were of exceptionally low physical standard, so low that men selected on their continuous discharge certificate were rejected by the Medical Officer to a proportion of more than two-thirds of each batch sent for medical check-up, and this was in spite of lowering the standards of physical fitness in an endeavour to speed manning by reducing the heavy burden of reselection.[96] The number of rejects even under the lower standards was still so high than the men were discouraged from presenting themselves for enlistment.[97] As a result, the burden of manning was cumulative in its difficulties.

The original agreement T 124 (I), upon which these warrant officers and ratings were signed, was similar to the merchant shipping agreement in that it was made between each ship and her own crew for 12 months.[98] This technically did not admit of drafting from ship to ship, and also necessitated renewal of the agreement every 12 months. As the rate continued to exist between the shipping companies, the pay and terms of service of HO ratings change was renewed on the lapse of the previous agreement.[99] In this way the second year of war commenced with some 'three months' work in renewing agreements where possible, and recruiting all over again to make good the losses by refusals to re-sign. To meet this particular difficulty on the 30 May 1942, a new agreement, T 124 X (I) was introduced, an individual agreement between each man and the government of India for the duration of the war.[100] By this agreement the man could not claim release as a right, but government could discharge him at 24 hours' notice.[101] At the same time a new rate of pay was assigned.

Recruitment from the common

The RIN selected the ratings to various branches of the RIN through a common entry, due to lack of seafaring tradition in the Northern provinces. The boys selected their branch after the completion of the six months ab initio training. The next 18 months they specialised in whichever branch they selected, after which they did 6 months sea time (posting onboard ships) before being examined for the post of ordinary seaman. Till 1940 there was no promotion to the commissioned rank from the ratings, but the rating had the chance to become Warrant rank. The Indian ratings were known for their high intelligence and efficiency in the communication branch. When Lord Jellicoe was on his world cruise in 1919, he was so impressed with the signalmen that he took 12 of them to Australia in his flagship, the *New Zealand*.[102] See Figure 3.1.

The process of recruitment of ratings was successful in that the quality of the sailors turned out to be good. But the quantity was totally inadequate to

Figure 3.1 New recruits at the RIN Entry Camp
Source: Naval History Division, Indian Navy, New Delhi

meet the needs of the war. On the basis of this experience, the Naval Headquarters decided that the recruitment field need not be contiguous with the seacoast. In late 1937, headquarters decided to introduce direct recruitment of men, and a recruitment drive was made with the hope that the seafaring communities might be able to supply the needs of the Navy. Even though an adequate number of boys from the coastal area joined, the general quantity was far below anything which could be usefully employed in a modern Naval Service.[103] Even then no organised recruitment measures were introduced until the end of 1941, and during the early years of the war, recruitment was carried out mainly in Bombay. Most of the time, the recruitment team carried on their search in the heart of the Army recruitment fields, which caused distress and despair to the military authorities.[104] Finally in 1941, General Sir Claude Auchinleck, the Commander-in-Chief, came up with a policy of an all-India Recruiting Organisation, but neither the Navy nor the Air Force could spare any personnel for this task, and the whole responsibility fell on the Army. One of the major limitations in the recruitment was that the recruitment drives during 1940s largely depended upon the agricultural activities and seasonal epidemics like plague, malaria and cholera.[105] These epidemics often restricted the movement of the recruitment team between different areas.[106]

Accordingly in 1942 the Inter-services Recruiting Organisation, the Manpower Recruitment Directorate in the Adjutant General's Branch of the War Department, Government of India, commenced to function and conducted the entire recruitment of service personnel.[107] In the work of the Directorate in relation to naval recruitment, RIN Officers were associated but not in sufficient numbers to impart knowledge of or acquaintance with the conditions and requirements of naval service to the recruiting staff all over the country. This insufficiency was due to the dearth of officers who could be spared.[108] In 1942 the only Naval Recruiting Officer made available was done among the officers who had held the appointment of Permanent Recruiting Officer before the amalgamation.[109] Two more officers joined early in 1943, and this number was increased later. Naval School Masters (Warrant Officers) were detailed to the Regional Recruitment Centres (RRCs) at Jhelum, Meerut, Poona and Bangalore.[110] As naval representation increased, the tendency was more and more for Army AROs and ATROs to make a preliminary selection of potential recruits for the Navy and to despatch those selected to RRCs. Here final selection was made by naval personnel attached to the RRCs and special educational tests applied by the Schoolmasters. All recruits for the RIN were passed to the Naval section of the RRC and held there until called forward to HMIS *Akbar* for naval training.[111]

Post-creation of the Manpower Recruitment Directorate, the Chiefs of Staff (India) Committee appointed a Manpower Subcommittee for the purpose of examining the requirements of each Service and potential manpower available and make recommendations in regard to control and allocation.

From the point of view of the RIN, the most important aspect of this Sub-committee was the allotment of recruiting priorities in favour of whichever Service was considered to be most in need of a particular category or type of man.[112] Although this priority system was occasionally felt by some to be invidious in a country where enlistment to the services was entirely voluntary, it proved to the Navy to be of considerable value.[113] The RIN's demands for a certain type of educated men were very small by comparison with the other services, and psychologically the pressure brought upon recruiting officers in general by this system had its marked effect on the meeting of these demands.

When the priority system was first introduced, it was used very conservatively, and the granting of a priority in a particular zone was the exception rather than the rule. Later the system was applied rather more extensively, the tendency being for each service to be granted a degree of priority within each zone, either first, second or third.[114] Naval Headquarters rather felt that by this extension the force of the priority was less effective. Had conscription existed, it would have been a very necessary measure, but when priority was effected by persuasion tactics, it inclined to lose its meaning.

The war period can be divided into two as regards recruiting. The first period covers from the beginning of the war up to 31 December 1941 and the second from 1 January 1942 up to the cessation of hostilities. The cardinal reason for this was that during the first period recruitment was undertaken solely by the RIN, whilst the Inter Service Recruiting Organisation took over from the beginning of 1942.[115] Certain direct recruitment continued after this date but was very limited.

The time the Recruiting Directorate of Adjutant General's Branch commenced, it was tasked with the maintenance of an establishment 4,396 strong, and the making up of a deficiency of 5,728 and its consequential maintenance.[116] The borne strength quoted comprises only Active Service Ratings, all the Directorate was called on to maintain, but the deficiency provided for an intake sufficient to replace HO men. Table 3.5 shows the progress made year by year up to the end of the war.

Upon the introduction of the Landing Craft Wing[117] in 1942, RIN's largest manpower problem was created. Not only was the aspect so difficult as regards quality, but the speed with which acquisition and training had to be carried out if the wing was to be used to the best operational advantage. The dilution within general service of trained technical ratings meant that their replacement was of great urgency, particularly because RIN's deficiencies were at that time very large and new construction promised early delivery of ships to be manned. Increased demands, priorities and a special recruiting effort by the Recruiting Directorate produced good results for a time, but very soon it became apparent that within particularly the matriculation zone (communication branches) RIN's demands could not be met. This meant that delay in producing requirements in full had to be accepted.

Table 3.5 Manpower status during the war

Position as on	Active Service Borne strength	Gross Deficiency in Target	HO Borne in lieu	Net Working Deficiency
1.1.1942	4,396	5,728	2,056	3,672
1.1.1943	9,256	6,929	3,506	3,423
1.1.1944	1,6745	8,529	4,783	3,746
1.1.1945	20,445	8,079	4,698	3,391
15.8.1945	23,567	4,140	4,084	56

Source: RIN Man-Power situation 1939–1945 (Secret), Monograph Approved by FOCRIN, 10 October 1945

At the same time, however, RIN's primary objective was attained and the Landing Craft Wing was able to go well ahead.[118] A certain degree of disappointment was later felt that despite these supreme efforts, the wing was not called upon operationally for long.

In the first three years, there was no appreciable change in the deficiency, despite the fact that in addition to the special service intake a further 2,642 HO men had been signed on, recruited by the RIN. The intake demanded was controlled by training facilities available, and demands were never met. The primary reason for the failure to eliminate the deficiency was heavy wastage incurred (desertion, not completing training, etc.) and the extreme increases in the target numbers. It was only when the target had been severely controlled and restricted that progress was made towards wiping out the deficiency. The rate of recruitment prior to August 1942 was quite inadequate to meet the service requirements, but from August 1942 onwards such strides were made and as a result, in certain branches of the Service, target figures were practically reached by April 1943. The rate of recruitment whilst based on the requirements of the particular branch of the Navy was restricted to a large extent by the availability of the training facilities and accommodation.[119] During the monsoon period it was necessary to slightly curtail the intake for reasons of limited accommodation. This had set back the RIN considerably in 1943. With restricted intake, high wastage, increase in shore establishment's complements and the necessity to transfer a large number of ratings to the Landing Craft Wing to meet Combined Operations requirements, shortages were such that a high level of recruitment for several months was necessary for the new ships to be manned.

Prior to 1942 direct recruitment produced 7,193 men, and from then until the end of the war a total of 8,476 were recruited.[120] From its inception until the end of the war the Recruiting Directorate recruited 25,090 men.[121] In addition 2,306 men were transferred directly from the Indian Army to the Landing Craft Wing.[122] The RIN found that through the Recruiting Organisation, 58% of RIN manpower was obtained, and through other sources,

Table 3.6 Number of HO ratings recruited between the outbreak of war and 31 December 1939

Seamen	540
Stokers	605
Artificers & Artisans	49
Domestics	206
Total	1,400

Source: General State of RIN on outbreak of War in 1939 & RIN Expansion, p. 15

mostly direct RIN recruitment, was 42%.[123] Average monthly direct recruitment through the war (excluding Army transferees) was approximately 220. A major portion of this figure covers HO ratings. The monthly average number of Special Service men received through the Recruiting Directorate was almost 600. In the later stages Special Service men were being recruited to replace the HO men recruited earlier in the war, so that in effect a certain amount of duplication of effort was expended during the course of the entire war.

The RIN had undergone great expansion during the war. The total number of RIN Special Service ratings was roughly equivalent to the Special Service ratings in the Royal Navy and the HO ratings in the RIN was approximately equivalent to the T 124 ratings in the Royal Navy.[124] But the manpower position (General Service) was struggling to meet the requirements. Of the officers borne in General Service as on 30 September 1943, 38.8% were Indian or of Indian domicile, and in the Landing Craft Wing it was 16.6%.[125] The shortage of ratings was met temporarily by the employment of HO ratings and account branch ratings by civilian clerks.[126] Even though the RIN had faced an acute shortage of manpower, it took the policy of consolidation rather than expansion, with extensive concentration upon training.[127]

In the earlier days of the Inter Service Recruiting Directorate, the periodic normal recruitment plans prepared by the RIN were somewhat haphazard in their calculation. The controlling factor being the capacity of the RIN training establishments, both as regards accommodation and instructional staffs, intake in those days bore little or no relation to the actual manning situation.[128] In the majority of the branches of RIN, deficiencies of Special Service men were so large that it was a matter of obtaining as many men of the required standard as could be provided and trained. Most of the RIN Training Establishments were too small in size to accommodate the required intake to enable the RIN to produce the required manpower to man the new ships.[129]

Thus expansion of almost all Training Establishments was essential. As soon as this was accomplished, this enabled RIN to increase Navy recruiting demands. Unfortunately, however, by the time this increase was possible, manpower resources had become drained of a large portion of the best material particularly in the higher educational zones. As the other services also required these educated men, RIN was never subsequently able to realise their demand in full.

Demands were normally calculated on the basis of ensuing 12 months' requirements. The basis figure in each category and branch was the deficiency of trained men against total requirements (target). To this was added the anticipated wastage of trained men during the following 12 months, and in addition such wastage for the period of initial training thereafter. Expected variations in target were next taken into account. There might be either increases or reductions. The result was the gross requirement of trained men at the end of the ensuing year.

Manpower supply

This subject, although very closely connected with the general problem of intake discussed in the previous paragraphs, is worthy of separate consideration. Manpower resources were classified into five zones as follows:[130]

Zone I	Matriculation
Zone II	Clerical
Zone III	Semi-educated
Zone IV	Literate in own language
Zone V	Miscellaneous

By wartime standards these zones comprise, in general terms, men within the following branches of the RIN:

Zone I	Communications
Zone II	Supply, Secretariat
Zone III	Seamen, Stokers, Sick Berth Attendants (S.B.As)
Zone IV	Cooks (Officers), Stewards
Zone V	Cooks (Sailors), Topasses

During the war it was necessary in many instances to compromise both educational and physical standards in order to obtain sufficient men to meet war commitments.[131] The question of reservation of the higher branches applicable to future intake was taken up at the end of the war, and it was intended to apply to new recruits when recruitment re-opened in May 1946.[132] Consequent to the ceasefire the recruitment of Special Service Ratings was suspended in 1945 while the boys' entry continued, as this method ensured continuity within the permanent element of the service.

MANPOWER AND RECRUITMENT DURING THE WAR

The RIN considered the Royal Indian Air Force as a competitor for Zone I recruits, as the strength of the RIAF comprised a very high proportion of matriculates.[133] Demands within the zone, though never met in full, were comparatively well satisfied; the RIN's average receipts being in the region of 60%. In this zone, from 1943 onwards, RIN had a fair share of priority, firstly, to replace trained communications ratings transferred immediately to the Landing Craft Wing (whose operational role was assumed to be imminent) and, secondly, to meet the revised commitments on re-organisation of the branches later in 1943.

For the RIN, availability of Zone II manpower resources was the most difficult problem of all. The deficiencies were large and on a percentage establishment basis RIN was consistently worse off than the other services.[134] In actual numbers, however, the Indian Army's position was far more serious. There was such a large demand for this class of men from industrial and commercial concerns, in many cases involved in war work, that the services could never acquire an adequate representation.[135]

Within Zone III, RIN never faced any real difficulty. It was, however, found that a large number of recruits were not entirely suitable for, or adaptable to, naval life, and wastage assumed at times serious proportions. Competition in this zone came primarily from the Army, though their requirements were not large except for medical orderlies during times of imminent operations.

Figure 3.2 Issue of uniform kit to new recruits
Source: Naval History Division, Indian Navy, New Delhi

It is doubtful whether the standard implied by Zone IV was high enough to be applied to officers' cooks and stewards, and the general quality within these branches was at times rather low. Cooks in particular were difficult to find, and in both branches the service depended to a great extent on the HO rating. In Zone V RIN met with little difficulty regarding sailors' cooks, but topasses[136] were always extremely hard to find in sufficient numbers. In consequence, deficiencies had to be met by an increasing number of HO ratings and civilian sweepers. See Figure 3.2 for a photograph of new recruits.

5. Relaxation in medical examination

Before 1941 the RIN recruits had to go through only a preliminary medical examination by a RIN medical officer of the recruit touring team. The recruits who passed the medical examination were sent to the RIN Depot, Bombay, or in the case of boys, to the Boys' Training Centre, Karachi. There the recruits were finally medically examined, and those unfit for service were rejected. Post-amalgamation of 1941, the RIN recruits were examined by a military Regimental Medical Officer (RMO) or a civilian doctor appointed for the medical examination. Later, as a result of the introduction of the 'filter scheme', the Commanding Officer of the Recruiting Centre or an officer appointed by him, a naval officer if available, inspected the recruits and those recruits found to be below prescribed physical standards were sent to the Filter Medical Officer for medical examination.[137] All recruits proceeded from Recruiting Centres to the RIN Depot, where they were given a thorough medical examination and those found unfit were recommended for rejection. Certain recruits with minor condonable defects were retained provided there was a reasonable prospect of their becoming fit and attaining the prescribed physical standard.[138] The Commanding Officer, RIN Depot, was vested with the authority to take a decision on whether to retain or discharge a recruit on medical grounds.[139] A final medical examination was conducted at the base depot to avoid the wastage during the training of those who should not have been recruited at all. Prior to the war, the minimum physical standards of the RIN recruits to the Boys' Training Establishment appear in Table 3.7.:

Table 3.7 Minimum physical standards of the RIN recruits prior to the war

Age	Height	Weight	Chest	Vision	Hearing	Colour Vision
15–17	5' 1"	100 lbs	30"	6/6 both eyes	Normal	Normal

Source: B. L. Raina, *Official History of the Indian Armed Forces in the Second World War 1939–1945: Medical Services, Administration*, Combined Inter Services Historical Section, India & Pakistan, 1953, p. 140

MANPOWER AND RECRUITMENT DURING THE WAR

During wartime RIN had to compromise the physical and medical standard to meet the manpower demands. The modified wartime standards for boys' entry appear in Table 3.8.:

Table 3.8 Modified physical standards of the RIN recruits during the war

Age	Height	Weight	Chest	Vision	Hearing	Colour Vision
15–17.5	5'	90 lbs	28"–29"	6/6 both eyes	Normal	Normal

Source: Official History of the Indian Armed Forces in the Second World War 1939–1945: Medical Services, p. 141

During the war men between the ages of 18 and 30 were recruited, and in certain branches the age limit went up to 35. The direct entry recruits had to meet the required physical standards, and no relaxation was granted. The physical standards appear in Table 3.9.:

Table 3.9 Physical standards of the direct entry recruits

Height	Weight	Chest	Vision	Hearing	Colour Vision
5' 2"	105 lbs	30"	6/6 both eyes	Normal	Normal

Source: Official History of the Indian Armed Forces in the Second World War 1939–1945: Medical Services, p. 141

However, to meet the wartime requirement, physical standards were modified as follows:[140]

Table 3.10 Modified physical standards of the direct entry recruits

Height	Weight	Chest	Vision	Hearing	Colour Vision
5'	94 lbs	29"	Not less than 6/12 in both eyes after correction with glasses	Normal	Minor defects accepted

Source: Official History of the Indian Armed Forces in the Second World War 1939–1945: Medical Services, p. 141

"Defects of colour vision and other minor disabilities did not constitute a bar if the recruit was otherwise fit for the duties for which he was recruited."[141]

6. Pay and allowances

HO ratings

At the outbreak of war, an ordinary seaman in the Merchant Service and his counterpart in the RIN both received Rs.20/- a month with certain allowances. On 4 September 1939, the shipping companies agreed to allow a war bonus of 25%.[142] A week later, approval was given for a similar increase in the pay of HO ratings. The pay of ordinary seamen then became:[143]

Merchant Service	Rs.25/-
RIN (Hostilities Only)	Rs.25/-
RIN (Active Service)	Rs.20/-

On 31 December 1939, an increase in the Merchant Service basis rate was made and the rates then were:[144]

Merchant Service	Rs.30/-
RIN (Hostilities Only)	Rs.25/-
RIN (Active Service)	Rs.20/-

This process continued. The HO ratings lagged behind the Merchant Service (from which they had been recruited) and consequently the best type of man naturally remained in the Merchant Service and those who could not obtain jobs in it joined the RIN. There are, of course, exceptions to this generalisation. The difference in pay between Merchant Service and HO ratings must have led to dissatisfaction among the latter.[145]

Active service ratings

In 1941–1942 recruiting difficulties necessitated an increase in the Active Service rates of pay. The Director of Recruiting formed the opinion that unless the Naval rates of pay were increased to compare more favourably with those offered to technical recruits in the Army, all naval recruitment would come to a standstill.[146] The scales were accordingly revised for the Seaman, Stoker, Communication and Writer branches. These increases led to repercussions on other branches and a subsequent increase still did not prove satisfactory, so a further revision was made, improving the scales of pay of all existing branches.[147] All this took place in 1942, and before the year was out another increase in the pay of Artificers and Artisans was made at the instance of the recruiting authorities.[148]

In 1944 a general revision of pay was undertaken, recruiting again being the main reason for it. Emphasis was laid on improving the pay of junior ratings in order to attract recruits. The pay of senior ratings was also increased but not by so much proportionally.[149] As an example, Tables 3.11 and 3.12

Table 3.11 Pay of seaman branch ratings

	Pre-war and up to 31–01–1942	01–01–1942 to 30–04–1942	01–05–1942 to 30–11–1944	01–12–1944 onwards
First 12 months	15	15	15	15
Boy (Remaining 6 months	15	15	15	20
Boy Seagoing	–	–	25	30
Ordinary Seaman	20	30	40	40
Able Seaman	25	35	45	45
Leading Seaman	34	45	60	60
Petty Officer	50	65	80	85
Chief Petty Officer	70	80	90	110

Source: RIN Mutiny Enquiry Report, Naval Headquarters, New Delhi

Table 3.12 Pay of communication branch ratings

	Pre-War and up to 31–01–1942	01–01–1942 to 30–04–1942	01–05–1942 to 30–11–1944	01–12–1944 onwards
Boy (First 12 months)	15	–	–	15
Boy (Remaining 6 months)	15	–	–	20
Boy Tel* or Signal Boy (Seagoing)	–	–	25	30
Ordinary Sig or Ordinary Tel	26	60	60	60
Signal or Tel	34	65	65	65
Leading Signal/Tel	44	70	70	70
Yeomen Signal or Petty Officer Tel	55	80	80	95
Chief Yeomen Signal or Chief Petty Officer Tel	80	95	95	115

Source: RIN Mutiny Enquiry Report, Naval Headquarters, New Delhi

* Tel = Telegraphist

show the rates of pay of the Seaman and Communication Branches as the war progressed. Only the rate of pay of each rating is shown. In most cases there is an annual increment.[150]

7. Recruitment publicity

As regards the Viceroy's Commissioned Officers (VCO), the need for qualified (officer-like qualities) men was paramount at the beginning of the war.[151] During the war, the British started wide publicity regarding the recruitments for the post of VCOs, ratings and Women's Royal Indian Navy Service. During the conference held at General Headquarters in March 1942, regarding using military personnel for propaganda purposes, the Attorney General recommended the use of spare trained soldiers for this particular task.[152]

As mentioned earlier, in the later stages of war the recruitment for the tri-services was taken over by the Central Recruitment Organisation, which was predominantly handled by the Indian Army. During the conference[153] Commander Streatfield James raised the issue of why naval recruits were not taken from the coastal districts and from among populations used to the sea. The British considered that for the use of modern equipment in modern ships a high degree of education and intelligence was required and the RIN accordingly found it necessary to recruit from the upper provinces in an attempt to secure the proper material. Prior to the war the RIN used to recruit boys, but in the later stages of war they started to recruit men to increase the numbers.[154] The British believed that the response would be very much greater if more was known about the Navy in the upper provinces. In relation with the publicity and recruitment, sundry recruiting parties were essential for the RIN, but in the circumstances owing to the heavy call placed upon the Navy during the war, it was very difficult to arrange this as they were short of men. In 1942, a total of three officers and men toured the country for the purpose of publicity and recruitment.[155]

The common men in India were unaware of the functions and duties of the RIN, because of India's geographical location. In the later stages of the war, the British wanted to introduce a subject on India's seaborne trade and the maintenance of sea defence in the school syllabus to motivate the youth to have a liking for the Naval Service.[156]

Many boys applied for a Commission or a Viceroy's Commission in the Army, and if they could not get the commission, hung about in the hope that the standard would go down and they would eventually be successful. In the meantime RIN was urgently in need of educated men. Prospects were in the Navy were just as good, if not better, than in the Army. The pay was as good and feeding and clothing better. There was a demand for higher class recruitment for signalmen, wireless operators etc. but response had been most disappointing. The age limits were from 17.5 to 24 years, and recruits were required to be not below the 6th standard for seamen and stokers, and up to the 9th standard for signalmen, wireless operators and other technicians.

During the conference,[157] Mr. Stubbs, District Collector, emphasised the need for immediate recruitment of boys expressing a wish to become Naval Officers.[158] The Attorney General recommended that "special arrangements can always be made to send down to provinces to select candidates direct provided a reasonable number are forthcoming for interview."[159] The Navy was a closed book to most people living inland and for the same reason, it was decided to plan visits of representatives from provincial Governments to RIN Depots to help potential recruits understand the Navy and its functioning. It was expected that, on their return, they would be in a position to visit schools and the educational institutions and advise boys on actual conditions in the

Navy. Commander Streatfield James, on behalf of the RIN, agreed that the Navy could make arrangements for parties to visit Bombay for this purpose.

At the same time the Air Force too had considerable difficulties in finding suitable recruits for air crews. This was partly due to the high physical and educational standards which were necessary, but it was due more to the reluctance of candidates to join the flying training.[160] At the beginning of the war, the British had experienced difficulty in finding the right boys for the Royal Air Force from the United Kingdom. The youngsters were often discouraged by both schoolmasters and parents from joining the RAF.[161]

Because the British could offer no assured permanent employment after the war, they had difficulty in finding educated Indians for the defence services. During the Conference the matter of giving some assurance of employment was discussed, especially in the case of RIAF.[162] During the war, for increasing the recruitment, the colonial Government adopted a policy of appeasement towards the provinces and local supporters. Civil and courtesy titles and sanads[163] to those helping in recruitment, offers of granting of honorary rank to the recruits, and one month pay as bonus to the recruits to induce them to enrol, were common during wartime.[164] In the early stage of the war, the British even thought about the introduction of rewards including remission of land revenue to attract Indian youth to join defence forces.[165] But after the Conference of August 1941, with members of NWFP, Punjab and UP Governments, the plan had not been pursued further. For getting better response from the Indian youth, the British introduced publicity campaigns, using films, posters, booklets, pamphlets and advertisements during the peak of war. The information on defence forces, job opportunities, pay and allowances in booklet form was available everywhere, but the need for oral propaganda was vital. Without an explanatory agency, these measures were of little value to the Indian masses. The method of showing films was much too advanced for the ordinary Indian villager, and the shots were so quick that nobody could follow the sequence or intentions of the film.[166] Even the educated Indians were not aware of the role, function and duties of defence forces, pay, allowances and career prospects.

The British Government had used all means and ways, like the press, posters, booklets, leaflets, films, cinema slides etc. for the wide publicity of the recruiting message throughout the length and breadth of India. Between March 1942 to November 1943, the largest single press campaign was carried out for the Royal Indian Air Force (RIAF), spending Rs. 54,200.[167] A total of 68 newspapers, both English and vernacular, were used, and each paper inserted six advertisements over a period of six weeks. These advertisements were specifically addressed to the civilians to join the RIAF as technicians and indicated the advantages which a technical training in the RIAF would give to the civilian in the postwar era. Contrasting to the above-mentioned recruitment drives, the advertisements for RIAF pilots were written and designed with an entirely new angle to 'glamourise' the RIAF.[168]

MANPOWER AND RECRUITMENT DURING THE WAR

In the case of the Indian Army, press advertisements were concentrated on the Specialist Services. Advertisements through press campaigns, posters and leaflets were launched for the Indian Army Medical Corps, Indian Army Ordnance Corps (IAOC)/Indian Electrical and Mechanical Engineers (IEME), Indian Army Veterinary Corps, Auxiliary Nursing Service, Indian Military Nursing Services (T) and Women's Auxiliary Corps (India). By 1942, the writing and production of publicity films for recruiting had been undertaken by Adjutant General 2 (e) (A.G. 2(e)) in conjunction with Information Films of India and the Army Film Centre. Four of such films were as follows:

1 *Young India Goes to Sea* - Royal Indian Navy
2 *India's Navy* - Royal Indian Navy
3 *Aiming High* - Royal Indian Air Force
4 *Behind the Wings* - Royal Indian Air Force

Efforts were made to spread knowledge about the RIN in India as a whole and to recruit up to the numbers required. There were considerable difficulties such as insufficient staff and adverse war news, which had their effect on the number and type of recruits.[169] By 1943, a new series of radio advertisements were started through various All India Radio Stations. At the end of 1943, an intensive publicity campaign was launched. Press advertising concentrated on the vernacular papers and naval goodwill parties visited the Punjab and NWFP, to contact the relatives of serving ratings.[170] Senior RIN officers used to visit the recruitment centres very often to evaluate the situation (Figure 3.3).

Figure 3.3 Visit of FOCRIN to the Recruitment Centre
Source: Naval History Division, Indian Navy, New Delhi

MANPOWER AND RECRUITMENT DURING THE WAR

The Flag Officer Commanding Royal Indian Navy (FOCRIN), also visited the abovementioned provinces and toured other recruiting areas of Bombay and Ratnagiri. The British used these tactics as a confidence building measure to attract the youth to join the RIN. The details of advertisements and other steps taken by the RIN for better recruits up to 1942 are detailed in Tables 3.13, 3.14, 3.15, 3.16 and 3.17.:

Table 3.13 Wartime advertisements: posters

Card No.	No. of Jobs	Quantity
38	1	50,000
39	2	50,000
50	1	50,000
62	1	50,000
1	9	45,000
144	1	Cancelled
278	1	50,000
279	1	Suspended
397	1	150
402	1	50,000
Total	**19**	**345,150**

Source: Proceedings of a Conference Held at General Headquarters on the 19, 20 and 21tMarch 1942 to Consider Methods of Enhancing India's Recruiting Effort, History Division (MoD), New Delhi

Table 3.14 Wartime advertisements: booklets

Card No.	No. of Jobs	Quantity
13	1	20,000
14	1	20,000
17	1	60,000
18	1	10,000
41	1	15,000
46	1	2,000
225	1	Abeyance
292	1	10,000
Total	**8**	**137,000**

Source: Proceedings of a Conference Held at General Headquarters on the 19, 20 and 21 March 1942 to Consider Methods of Enhancing India's Recruiting Effort, History Division (MoD), New Delhi.

Table 3.15 Wartime advertisements: folders, leaflets, etc.

Card No.	No. of Jobs	Quantity
15	2	10,000
81	1	40,000
102	6	15,000
172	1	20,000
28	6	360,000
173	1	15,000
273	1	100,000
308	1	10,000
324	1	15,000
327	5	?
329	1	21,000
355	1	45,000
401	1	?
Total	28	651,000

Source: Proceedings of a conference held at General Headquarters on the 19, 20 and 21 March 1942 to Consider Methods of Enhancing India's Recruiting Effort, History Division (MoD), New Delhi.

Table 3.16 Wartime advertisements: press schemes

Card No.	No. of Advertisements	No. of Papers
8	1	15
8	6	55
8	1	5
30	1	7
36	2	28
37	6	52
59	1	44
60	1	41
121	3	22
132	1	11
133	1	30
152	2	26
52	3	28
55	3	31
56	1	32
122	1	23
123	1	8
134	1	43

(*Continued*)

Table 3.16 (Continued)

Card No.	No. of Advertisements	No. of Papers
135	1	43
256	1	35
262	1	25
318	1	40
330	1	42
335	3	28
338	6	49
339	1	27
343	1	30
384	1	?
Total	**53**	**820**

Source: Proceedings of a conference held at General Headquarters on the 19, 20 and 21 March 1942 to Consider Methods of Enhancing India's Recruiting Effort, History Division (MoD), New Delhi.

Table 3.17 Wartime advertisements: cinema slides

	No. of Jobs	Quantity
RIN	4	24
	4	24
	1	6
	1	333
	18	738
	6	246
IILF	1	100
Women's Auxiliary Corps	2	–
(India) (WAC(I))	2	186
RIAF	2	12
	1	333
	16	688
3 Services	4	572
	1	3
	3	261
Others	5	98
	4	288
Total	**75**	**3,912**

Source: Proceedings of a Conference Held at General Headquarters on the 19, 20 and 21 March 1942 to Consider Methods of Enhancing India's Recruiting Effort, History Division (MoD), New Delhi.

In October 1943, the Naval Headquarters reviewed the recruiting situation and the attendant difficulties. Accordingly, steps and remedies were planned to overcome the difficulties in recruitment and training. The inadequacy of the existing naval recruiting staff and inability to provide proper naval representation in all areas were met by the appointment of a Captain, RIN, as Deputy Director of Recruiting (Navy) in the Recruiting Directorate and increase in the sanctioned number of Assistant Recruiting Officers from 12 to 25. This placed the RIN on a proportional basis with the RIAF, and by the end of May 1944 recruiting improved in areas where additional officers had been posted.[171] To educate the Army Recruiting Officers on naval matters like conditions and service requirements, five parties of Assistant Recruiting Officers were sent on tour to Bombay and Karachi naval establishments in early 1942. The Chief of Staff Committee allotted priority inductions of 80 writers and 250 communication ratings monthly, and for the recruitment of 200 motor engineers II–IV Class. These priorities produced immediate results and intake rose substantially. During the war, the medical and physical examinations of the recruiting candidates were not carried out properly due to the general shortage of medical officers and the deployment elsewhere of the best of them.[172] Later on, in the beginning of 1944, the Naval Headquarters decided to circulate comprehensive data of physical requirements and disqualifying defects of the candidates to the recruiting authorities to use it as a standard guideline in the absence of a medical officer.[173]

The service conditions were also not in favour of the youth joining the RIN. The feeling, particularly amongst the pre-war service classes, was that senior RIN ratings were inferior to equivalent Army ranks. This was especially true in the case of CPOs (Chief Petty Officers) vis-à-vis VCOs (Viceroy's Commissioned Officers). The promotion to the commissioned ranks from the lower decks[174] in the RIN compared unfavourably with other services. There was only one promotion vacancy a year, and this had never been filled.[175] The lack of promotion opportunities had occasioned public comment and very definitely affected the RIN recruiting to the advantage of the other services. Comparatively less pay, allowances and promotion in the RIN attracted the youth towards the other services. The other services and the civil labour market competed keenly for men of the high standard required. Service at sea was not popular, and the opportunities for promotion were greater in the other services since the promotion in the RIN depended largely on length of service. In early 1944, the Naval Headquarters carried out a comparative study on the pay structures in the Indian Army, Air Force, Royal Navy, British Royal Naval Volunteer Reserve and Ceylon Royal Naval Volunteer Reserve and recommended to the Government of India an equitable basis of pay for the RIN with other services in May 1944.[176]

As the war progressed, as per the recommendations of the Chatfield Committee report, the number of training establishments was increased. By the end of 1943, two Boys' Training Schools at Karachi and Specialist Schools in signal, anti-submarine, tactical and gunnery were commissioned. HMIS *Feroze*, the Officers Training School, was commissioned in December 1943 and followed by HMIS *Akbar*, a New Entry Ratings Disciplinary Training School and Seamanship Training School in January 1944. The British created these establishments in haste and it resulted in overcrowding and lack of suitable accommodation and training equipment. Worst of all, the RIN faced the lack of trained officers and senior ratings as instructors. The worst lack was that of a Reserve Officers Training School, and all Reserve Officers taken into service up to the end of 1943 were sent for more training, then four months' technical courses during working hours in Bombay, and had no disciplinary training and no corporate service life; many officers frequently never even completed these courses. Thus the majority of Reserve officers lacked that initial disciplinary training which was the basis of an officer's duties.[177]

When the expansion started, the Navy had inadequate training facilities for the number recruited, and the short time which recruits could spend in the training establishment was devoted to technical training at the expense of disciplinary training. The Communication Branch has been pointed out as a glaring example of this. Some of the training establishments became overcrowded and the training staff was inadequate. For example, 300 men were sent for training to the Radar School, which was only designed to take 120. The cooking arrangements in new entry establishments and supplies of clothing did not keep pace with the rate of expansion.[178] Although the planned expansion stopped in 1943, the numbers borne were considerably below the target figures. The shortages were fairly large, as shown by Tables 3.18 and 3.19, which give the position for May 1943:

Table 3.18 Shortage of officers

Branch	Target	Borne
Executive	1,598	1,276
Engineers	229	224
Electrical	52	43
Accountants	200	181
Medical	58	54
Warrant Officers	310	181

Source: RIN Enquiry Report, Naval Headquarters, New Delhi, p. 12

Table 3.19 Shortage of ratings

Branch	Target	Borne
Seamen	7,817	6,478
Communication	3,629	2,939
Engine Room Artificer (E.R.A)	391	165
Stokers	2,611	1,723
Shipwrights	186	75
Accountants	841	488
Stewards	794	667
Cooks	1,417	911
Topasses	920	371
Regulating	232	56

Source: RIN Enquiry Report, Naval Headquarters, New Delhi, p. 12

At the beginning of the war, all training matters were dealt with at Naval Headquarters by the Director of Personnel Services (DOP), along with a very small staff. By the last stages of the war, on 26 July 1945, Naval Headquarters was reorganised as per the directives of the Admiralty, and a Director of Training, assisted by six staff officers, was appointed.[179] Technical Staff Officers at NHQ were responsible to the Director of Training for Technical Training questions, but equally the Director of Training was responsible for the co-ordination and implementation of all training matters of all branches. However the responsibility for the training of the Account Branch was vested with the Director Account Department since 1943 and the training of Medical Branch was with the Principal Medical Officer. The reorganisation and the increased number of staff at Naval Headquarters helped the fruition of previously laid plans and an increase in supply of equipment. The Director of Training was given the responsibility for Disciplinary, Technical and Tactical training.

During the peak of the war, there was a close collaboration between the Directorate of Recruiting, SP Directorate (both of these were located at Meerut) and Naval Headquarters, concerning the application of SP methods and selection of both officers and ratings of the Royal Indian Navy, to ensure better quality of candidates for the service. However, a fundamental weakness in the system of entry of officers remained. Unlike the Indian Air Force and Indian Army, officer candidates for the Royal Indian Navy entered directly as officers, and once in, there were no penalties attaching to failure in their course, and the service was committed to retaining these officers, unless cause could be shown to the Governor General-in-Council why they should be discharged.[180]

Formation of reserve cadre

Prior to 1939, there were no reserve Officers in the RIN, but with the threat of war both Royal Indian Navy Reserve (RINR) and Royal Indian Navy Volunteer Reserve (RINVR) were formed,[181] on similar lines to the those in the United Kingdom, the RINVR Officers being those who have seafaring experience and at least a 2nd Mate's certificate.[182] The training of these officers presented a severe problem, for new facilities existed but there was a great shortage of instructors. Instruction started in late 1939, all courses being of three weeks duration, with the exception of anti-gas course, which was one week. In May 1943, all courses with the exception of divisional and anti-gas were increased to four weeks. A divisional course for reserve officers and instruction in seamanship, navigation and anti-gas was carried out in the RIN Depot, Castle Barracks under the supervision of a reserve training officer. Instruction in signals, gunnery and asdic was given at the Specialist Schools. Seamanship and navigation classes could each accommodate 32 officers. Mess facilities for Reserve Officers were limited. Junior officers were accommodated in Bombay in a block of flats known as Dhanraj Mahal and the Old 'Admirals House' became a mess for senior officers.

Formation of reserves for the RIN was undertaken before the war. The Royal Indian Naval Reserve comprised serving officers of the Indian Mercantile Marine and had two branches, executive and accountant, to which the engineering branch was also added at the outbreak of the war. The RINVR was constituted by inducting qualified members of the general public as commissioned officers and giving them six months' intensive training at Bombay. This was also done for sailors, called ratings at that time.

In addition to the regular service ratings, special service ratings were recruited who served for five years before being transferred to the Fleet Reserve for 10 years. These ratings belonged to the cadre of Royal Indian Fleet Reserve (RIFR). Personnel from the merchant marine were also recruited as 'Hostilities Only' ratings for service during the war. The personnel strength of the RIN on 1 October 1939 was 114 officers and 1,732 ratings with only 16 officers manning the Naval Headquarters which was located inside the Naval Dockyard at Bombay.[183]

8. Induction of women in RIN

At the outbreak of the war in 1939, the RIN decided to employ a number of wives of serving RIN officers to assist in the code and cipher departments. This experiment started in Bombay, and later on was extended to other ports. At the beginning of 1941 it was decided to expand this organisation by accepting European civilian women. It was not till the beginning of 1943 that the need for a properly organised women's service to work with the RIN was felt. Even then the British never visualised that India would become an important base of operations and that the Corps would have to expand to over 1,000 officers and ratings.

Women Auxiliary Corps (India), (WAC [I]) personnel were first employed in the RIN at Bombay in June 1943, the appointment of 6 cipher officers and 239 auxiliaries having been sanctioned. The experiment proved most successful, and thereafter members of the WAC (I) were employed at all naval ports to meet communications commitments and to carry out other duties.

By November 1943 the manpower target was 78 officers and 713 auxiliaries against a borne strength of 19 officers and 125 auxiliaries. Recruiting was then almost at a standstill. The manning of the communications organisation was an urgent matter and had received a high operational priority. Accordingly, to attract recruits, the WAC (I) Naval Wing, with its own distinctive unit form, was formed early in 1944. Courses for signals auxiliaries were arranged at HMIS Talwar, and a hostel for officers and auxiliaries were opened at Chittagong, Visakhapatnam, Cochin and Bombay. The Women's Royal Indian Naval Service (WRINS) continued to expand. The sanctioned and borne strength of officers and WRINS in 1945 is illustrated in Table 3.20.

In 1945, when the war hostilities were almost finished, the target figure was reached and certain restrictions were made. The direct recruitment of officers was curtailed and the transfer of Army wing personnel to commissioned rank in the WRINS was stopped, except in exceptional cases[184] The overriding priority in recruitment accorded to WRINS was cancelled, and the selection of communication officers by shortened selection boards were abolished.[185] From 1945 onwards all candidates for officer cadre had to appear before full selection boards. As British women were repatriated in increasing numbers, their places were taken by Indian women and the representation of Indian women became 38% by 1945 (see Figure 3.4).[186]

To meet the demands of WRINS personnel, six additional WRINS recruiting officers had been appointed in 1945. Further Inter-Services recruiting drives were conducted at Karachi and central India.[187] The Inter-Services

Table 3.20 Strength of officers and Women's Royal Indian Naval Service (WRINS)

		Sanctioned	Borne
Officers	March 1945	318	251
	April 1945	289	261
	May 1945	290	269
WRINS	March 1945	802	679
	April 1945	736	723
	May 1945	739	718

Source: Report on the Royal Indian Navy, January–June 1945, Naval Headquarters, New Delhi, 1946, p. 7, ADM 1/19413, The National Archives, Kew, United Kingdom.

Figure 3.4 WRINS Officers

Source: Naval History Division, Indian Navy, New Delhi

Recruits Centre in Ahmednagar was moved to Bangalore. A WRIN officer was appointed as selection personnel officer of the centre and 223 recruits passed through in the first half of 1945.[188] Sixty-six officers completed the Divisional Course in HMIS *Feroze* during April to June 1945, 27 of whom were subsequently trained as cypher officers. During the same period, 64 WRINS passed through HMIS *Talwar* and 33 WRINS passed out of the supply and secretariat establishment.[189] In 1945, four WRINS underwent a three-month course at the Army School of Cookery, Poona, and were appointed as mess Petty Officers.

Chief Officer M. L. Cooper and Second Officers P. Cunningham and K. Sen were sent to the United Kingdom on deputation in early April 1945 and returned in July.[190] They were attached to the Woman's Royal Naval Service and visited several A.T.S. establishments and were given a course of instruction in WRNS methods of administration and training.[191] The knowledge and the experience they gained in the United Kingdom during this visit helped to carry out efficient administration of the WRINS in India.[192]

9. Inter-provincial and communal development

The recruitment of Special Service Ratings by the Inter Service Recruiting Organisation in 1942 opened up a very wide field not only numerically but geographically. Provinces, districts and areas which had hitherto been virtually untouched were thrown open through the vast organisation at RIN's disposal.[193] The result of this was that the Inter Provincial balance of the service changed very considerably during the course of the war, and from having a very great predominance from the North at the beginning, it finished the war with a majority from the South. India was divided into four zones, North, South, East and West and the comparative strength of each zone is shown in Table 3.21.

Most of the ratings were recruited from Punjab in pre-war days and bore the brunt of supplying the Indian Army in the early years of the war.[194] By RIN's own recruiting efforts, RIN managed to acquire a fair proportion from Punjab though not so plentifully as later through the Recruiting Organisation. Bombay Presidency,[195] which was after Punjab in the pre-war composition, fell off very considerably after a steady start.[196] Ratnagiri district continued a fair supply, but recruitment from other areas was disappointing. However, this province supplied a large majority of HO ratings and thus the contribution towards wartime manning was significant.

The main support in the form of manpower came from the South, which contributed very largely to the Communication and Supply and Secretariat branches and later to the Domestic branches.[197] The standard of education in the South was generally higher than in the North, and was more widespread. "The men were inclined to be more adaptable where brain takes precedence over brawn, but lacked on the whole the physical attributes which go into the making of an ideal naval rating."[198]

Table 3.21 Zone-wise manpower representation

Zone	As on 03.9.1939	As on 15.8.1945
Northern Zone (Punjab, NWFP, UP, Kashmir, Rajputana, Baluchistan & Delhi)	685	8,176
Western Zone (Sind, Bombay, Central Province, Hyderabad & Goa)	541	3,178
Southern Zone (Madras, Travancore, Cochin & Mysore)	75	8,812
Eastern Zone (Bengal, Bihar, Orissa & Assam)	12	3,401
Total	1,313*	23,567*

Source: RIN Man-Power situation 1939–1945 (Secret), Monograph Approved by FOCRIN, 10 October 1945

*These figures exclude HO Ratings.

The effect of this provincial development was reflected in the communal composition. At the outbreak of the war, the strength consisted of almost two-thirds Muslims, whereas at the end of the war nearly one-half were Hindus and only one-third Muslim.[199] This was the natural consequence of the intake from the South, where the states are predominantly Hindu (see Table 3.22).

The percentage of each class of rating in the RIN in 1939 and 1945 is illustrated in Table 3.23.

The percentage and numbers from each locality are given in Tables 3.24 and 3.25.

Initially the HO ratings recruited were of Merchant Service origin, but as the war went on, many other types of men were enrolled on T124X (India) agreement and filled the serious gap caused by the lack of Special Service recruits. Particularly this was so in the case of Artificers and Engine Room

Table 3.22 Communal development – Communication (C.S) & Supply and Secretariat (S.S) ratings

Religion	As on 03.09.1939	As on 15.08.1945
Hindu	96	9448
Muslims	963	7,843
Christians	180	4,548
Pathans	19	475
Rajputs	10	347
Sikhs	4	342
Anglo-Indians	33	307
Maharattas	–	202
Parsees	5	26
Buddhists	–	17
Jews	3	7
Gurkhas	–	5
Total	1,313	23,567

Source: Monograph Approved by FOCRIN on the RIN Man-Power situation 1939–1945 (Secret) dated 10 October 1945, p. 30

Table 3.23 Communal representation in the RIN – ratings

Religion	1939	1945
Hindus	9.25%	42.50%
Muslims	75.00%	35.00%
Christians	13.00%	19.50%
Sikhs	0.25%	1.50%
Anglo-Indians	2.00%	1.25%
Miscellaneous	0.50%	0.25%

Source: RIN Enquiry Report, Naval Headquarters, New Delhi, p. 8

Table 3.24 Locality-wise representation – ratings

Region	1939	1945
Kashmir	0.50%	1.25%
NWFP	3.25%	3.00%
Punjab	44.75%	21.25%
Delhi	0.25%	0.50%
Sind	0.25%	0.25%
Rajputana & CI	0.25%	3.25%
U.P	3.25%	7.25%
Bombay	38.00%	8.25%
Madras	4.25%	25.25%
Travancore	0.25%	9.00%
Cochin	0.25%	1.50%
Hyderabad } Mysore		
Bihar & Orissa	9.00%	1.75%
Bengal	0.50%	11.50%
Assam	0.25%	1.00%
Others	–	3.00%
Goa & Portuguese India	2.25%	0.75%

Source: RIN Enquiry Report, Naval Headquarters, New Delhi, p. 8

*These percentage do not add up to 100% as they are only shown to the nearest 0.25%

Table 3.25 Development area-wise – C.S & S.S ratings

State	Strength as on	
	03.09.39	15.08.1945
Punjab	586	4,990
Bombay	498	1,890
Madras	55	5,888
Goa & Portuguese India	33	178
NWFP	44	693
United Province	41	1,687
Travancore	18	2,152
CP & Bevar	6	295
Bengal	7	2,668
Kashmir	7	292
Rajputana	4	208
Sind	3	75
Assam	3	282
Delhi	3	150
Bihar & Orissa	2	430
Cochin	2	493
Hyderabad	1	340
Mysore	–	187
Others	–	669
Total	1,313	23,567

Sources: Monograph Approved by FOCRIN on the RIN Man-Power situation 1939–1945 (Secret) dated 10 October 1945

personnel, but at a later stage, due to an increase in target, the Domestic Branches became almost equally reliant on these men.

10. Desertion

The initial reception of recruits at their first training centres too gave a bad picture about the RIN to the Indian youth. The recruits had widespread complaints of harsh discipline, bad food and unsympathetic treatment.[200] The adverse inputs sent home by recruits had affected recruiting in some areas whence the complaints came. The leave on completion of training was given in the Army and RIAF but had not been the rule in the RIN till 1944. The matter was also important from the desertion aspect. During the peak of the war, the rate of desertion became almost 25% of the average monthly intake, and in December 1943 desertion became 253, which exceeded the intake of 226.[201] The majority of the desertions were amongst recruits. The posters, pamphlets and booklets circulated to attract the recruits were misleading and tended to represent to the recruits that the Navy offered a permanent career, a happy life, good and ample food and clothing, liberal pay plus many allowances, quick promotion and sympathetic and helpful officers.[202]

Wastage by desertion was a very serious matter and from a third to a half of recruits were lost to the Service as a result. In some months the wastage from all causes actually exceeded the intake. As one means of reducing the number of desertions, serious consideration was given to improving the initial reception of recruits at their first training establishments. This was also designed to have its effect on recruiting because, as mentioned above, bad reports sent home by ratings during their first weeks had a very adverse effect on recruiting. Other matters which were considered with a view to improving recruiting were the granting of leave on completion of training (as was done in the Indian Army and Royal Indian Air Force) and additional promotions from the lower deck to the commission rank. In 1944, an improved scale of rations was introduced which might have helped to encourage recruiting.[203]

The recruiting system, which after December 1941 was common to all Indian Services, included an agreement whereby local agents were employed who were paid a per capita grant for each recruit they produced. Posters were issued to attract recruits, and in their efforts to obtain men, recruiting officers drew a rosy picture of life in the RIN. It undoubtedly led to a great deal of discontent in the Service, and many of the desertions were directly attributable to it.[204]

During the war period many recruits deserted. The home life of an Indian rating was always well to the fore in his mind, and it was to his credit that the sanctity of the home and all that it meant was of so great importance. From the service point of view, however, it has been proved that healthy and congenial surroundings had gone a long way to counteract the recruit's natural feeling of homesickness which, under less favourable conditions,

MANPOWER AND RECRUITMENT DURING THE WAR

tempted him to desert. Such desertion had an adverse effect on recruitment as it readily produced hostile and subversive propaganda.

During the course of the war over 9,000 HO men were recruited. Though continuous wastage claimed approximately 4,600 of this figure, there were over 1,800 desertions, the remainder being by discharge and death. The desertions took place mainly at times when Merchant Service rates of pay were increased. Actually this desertion ratio, when considered in the light of the entire war, was in effect higher, as during 1943, about 500 class V motor engineers were enrolled for service in the Landing Craft Wing, but were quickly discharged and replaced by Special Service Stokers from General Service. Thus incidental wastage desertion accounted for nearly 45%, an incredibly high figure for the RIN.

Finally, following stabilisation of the target in 1944, and after acquiring a steady intake of Special Service men, it was found possible to commence their replacement in May 1945. Replacement continued steadily until the end of the war. See Table 3.26 for recruitment and wastage

Table 3.26 Recruitment and wastage during the war – active service ratings

	Recruitment	*Discharges*	*Desertions*	*Total Wastage*	*Borne Strength*
31–12–1939	125	29	9	38	1,451
31–03–1940	166	25	10	35	1,612
30–06–1940	278	43	23	66	1,852
30–09–1940	263	75	14	89	2,058
31–12–1940	261	50	19	69	2,253
31–03–1941	785	72	37	109	2,953
30–06–1941	446	126	28	154	3,277
30–09–1941	843	112	44	156	3,967
31–12–1941	556	112	66	178	4,397
31–03–1942	1,153	63	37	100	5,463
30–06–1942	664	77	117	194	6,072
30–09–1942	1,619	134	190	324	7,375
31–12–1942	2,145	134	291	425	9,258
31–03–1943	2,765	128	354	482	1,1671
30–06–1943	1,923	305	396	701	13,033
30–09–1943	1,770	388	790	1,178	13,777
31–12–1943	1,790	481	690	1,171	14,697
31–03–1944	2,085	384	544	928	16,041
30–06–1944	2,483	574	402	976	17,707
30–09–1944	1,876	1,179	528	1,707	18,068
31–12–1944	1,701	772	563	1,335	18,668
31–03–1945	1,677	339	675	1,014	19,595
30–06–1945	2,078	380	400	780	21,202
30–09–1945	2,110	302	563	1,365	2,2291

Source: RIN Enquiry Report, Naval Headquarters, New Delhi, p. 13

Table 3.27 Manpower status of Hostilities Only ratings during the war

	Recruitment	Discharges	Desertions	Total Wastage	Borne Strength
31–12–1939	1,183	120	9	129	1,104
31–03–1940	228	158	10	168	1,167
30–06–1940	86	101	7	108	1,095
30–09–1940	453	342	13	355	1,333
31–12–1940	425	268	11	279	1,408
31–03–1941	217	72	18	90	1,535
30–06–1941	267	111	47	158	1,644
30–09–1941	349	129	23	152	1,846
31–12–1941	355	102	23	125	2,044
31–03–1942	527	153	55	208	2,331
30–06–1942	556	139	303	442	2,590
30–09–1942	915	58	77	135	3,153
31–12–1942	539	64	143	207	3,506
31–03–1943	910	129	136	265	4,158
30–06–1943	255	160	112	272	4,228
30–09–1943	610	130	94	224	4,606
31–12–1943	507	62	42	104	4,783
31–03–1944	268	78	63	141	4,926
30–06–1944	105	87	135	222	4,822
30–09–1944	100	80	107	187	4,760
31–12–1944	62	58	106	164	4,698
31–03–1945	137	51	141	192	4,650
30–06–1945	21	81	82	163	4,549
30–09–1945	5	1093	55	1148	3,437

Source: RIN Enquiry Report, Naval Headquarters, New Delhi, pp. 14–15

during the war. See Table 3.27 for manpower status of hostilities only ratings during the war.

Rate prevailing – January 1944:

1	No. of men under initial training 1.2.1944	3,200
2	No. of recruits received between 1.2.1944 to 1.2.1945	7,000
3	Total	10,200
4	Actual no. of trainees deserted or discharged between 1.2.1944 to 1.2.1945	2,200
5	Percentage rate of wastage	21.53%

MANPOWER AND RECRUITMENT DURING THE WAR

Rate prevailing – January 1945

1	Borne strength 1.2.1944	15,000
2	Borne strength 1.2.1945	19,000
	Average	17,000
3	Actual no. of trained men deserted or discharged between 1.2.1944 to 1.2.1945	1,400
4	Percentage rate of wastage	8.23%

Towards the end of the war the target had almost been achieved: 27,651 men were borne against a target of 27,706. To attain that strength a total of over 43,000 men had to be recruited.[205]

11. Progress of manpower situation

All officers (including Warrant Officers) on active list on the 10 November 1939 were as follows: (See Table 3.28 for manning progress during the war.)[206]

Royal Indian Navy	165
Royal Indian Naval Reserve & Royal Indian Naval Volunteer Reserve	178

Figures for all ratings borne on 31 December 1939 are appended below:[207]

Active Service	1,454
Hostilities only	1,400

Table 3.28 Manning Progress of RIN during the war

Year	Period	Target	Borne Strength	Deficiency
1939	Outbreak of war	1,722	1,476	247
	31 December	2,954	2,349	105
1940	30 June	3,460	3,340	120
	31 December	5,316	3,716	1,600
1941	30 June	6,486	4,950	1,536
	31 December	10,124	6,452	3,672
1942	30 June	13,661	8,661	5,000
	31 December	16,185	12,762	3,423
1943	30 June	23,745	1,9176	4,569
	31 December	25,274	21,528	3,746
1944	30 June	29,081	24,828	4,853
	31 December	28,534	25,143	3,391
1945	30 June	28,448	27,434	1,014
	End of War 15 August	29,706	27,651	2,055
	30 September	27,933	26,532	1401

Source: General State of RIN on outbreak of War in 1939 & RIN Expansion, OSD/ C10/ii, History Division, Ministry of Defence, New Delhi, pp. 15

The Tables 3.29, 3.30. 3.31, 3.32 and 3.33 show the increase in the strength of officers and ratings from the beginning of the war to the end of the war.[208]

Table 3.29 Increase in the strength of officers during the war

As on	RIN*	RINR	RINVR	Total
September 1939	114	9	29	152
December 1939	117	65	52	234
December 1940	132	108	163	403
December 1941	161	155	387	703
December 1942	170	261	880	1,311
December 1943	220	301	1,671	2,192
December 1944	241	335	2,104	2,680
December 1945	269	250	1,919	2,438

Source: RIN Enquiry Report, Naval Headquarters, New Delhi, p. 7

*Includes Midshipman and Cadets and RN, RNR and RNVR officers on loan.

Table 3.30 Increase in the strength of warrant officers during the war

As on	RIN	On loan from RN	Total
September 1939	35	11	46
December 1939	125	12	137
December 1940	141	9	150
December 1941	151	21	172
December 1942	180	23	203
December 1943	181	25	206
December 1944	187	34	221
December 1945	198	16	214

Source: RIN Enquiry Report, Naval Headquarters, New Delhi, pp. 7–8

Table 3.31 Increase in the strength of ratings during the war

As on	Continuous Service Non-Continuous Service and Special Service Ratings	Hostility Only Ratings	Transferred from Army	Total
September 1939	1,313	162	–	1,475
December 1939	1,449	1,400	–	2,849
December 1940	2,253	1,463	–	3,716
December 1941	4,396	2,056	–	6,452
December 1942	9,258	3,506	–	12,764
December 1943	14,679	4,783	2,089	21,551
December 1944	18,668	4,698	1,779	25,145
December 1945	18,610	1,678	905	21,193

Source: RIN Enquiry Report, Naval Headquarters, New Delhi, pp. 8–10

* In 1941 about 2,400 Special Service ratings were recruited.

Table 3.32 Number of RIN officers of different nationalities

As on	British	Indian	Anglo-Indian	Others*	Total
1939 Sept to Dec	57	29	4	1	91
1940	165	42	4	1	212
1941	240	77	17	10	344
1942	309	168	45	26	548
1943	430	233	99	21	783
1944	140	280	48	8	476
1945	36	120	39	3	198

Source: RIN Mutiny Enquiry Report, Naval Headquarters, New Delhi, p. 7

* The 'others' were of many different nationalities.

11. Conclusion

Many committees and plans recommended the expansion of the RIN since 1928, but the British government never implemented those recommendations due to 'stringent financial conditions'. However, the colonial government had given more priorities to the Army over the Navy. The sudden outbreak of the war made the British Government realise that the expansion of the RIN was indispensable for the protection of the Indian coasts, harbours and shipping. Manpower became the most crucial factor in the expansion of the Navy to manage the newly built ships and shore establishments. Officers recruited to the RIN were mainly British, Indian and Anglo-Indian, but a small number came from several other countries. "Their ethnic, religious, linguistic and cultural backgrounds varied which is an indication of the urgency that prompted into a Service that was basically Indian though under foreign rule."[209] The manpower was practically unlimited in India. The most important consideration was the fact that only a minute portion of the large population was literate. This small portion had thrust upon it the burden of supplying industry and commerce, in addition to the tremendous requirements of the services during a major war. Thus during the early years a fair degree of selection was possible, but as time went on, the market rapidly became drained of its best material. During the early years of the war each service carried out its own recruitment, and whilst the potential was still large and the end of the war was still fairly remote, this was not unsatisfactory. As soon as the full impact of war came to India it was evident that an effort of the greatest magnitude only could satisfy the demands of the defence services. It is clear from these figures that the strength of the RIN was doubled between the outbreak of war and 31 December 1939.

Prior to the war, like the Army, the Navy had followed the racial theory in recruiting the ratings. At the outbreak of the war 82% of ratings were recruited from the Punjab and Ratnagiri district of Bombay. Most

Table 3.33 Manpower development (sailors) during the war

Year	Period	Continuous & Non-Continuous Service Ratings	Special Service Ratings	HO Ratings	Ex-Army Personnel in Landing Craft Wing (Special Service)	Boys	Apprentices	Total
1939	Out Break of war	984	329	162	–	233	–	1,708
	31 December	1,089	360	1,400	–	248	50	3,147
1940	31 March	1,150	472	1,511	–	314	49	3,496
	30 June	1,178	674	1,488	–	327	72	3,739
	30 September	1,211	847	1,510	–	404	67	4,039
	31 December	1,213	1,040	1,463	–	537	89	4,342
1941	31 March	1,238	1,713	1,570	–	516	88	5,125
	30 June	1,273	2,004	1,673	–	561	88	5,599
	30 September	1,275	2,691	1,853	–	675	123	6,617
	31 December	1,327	3,069	2,056	–	617	121	7,190
1942	31 March	1,387	4,075	2,351	–	717	120	8,650
	30 June	1,534	4,537	2,590	–	658	3	9,322
	30 September	1,578	5,846	3,161	–	828	27	11,440
	31 December	1,692	7,564	3,506	–	805	75	13,642
1943	31 March	1,781	9,482	4,158	905	911	77	17,312
	30 June	1,876	11,551	4,228	1,521	872	82	20,130
	30 September	1,857	11,923	4,421	1,982	297	92	21,172
	31 December	1959	12,697	4,783	2,089	800	116	22,444
1944	31 March	2,043	13,973	4,926	1,925	847	104	23,818
	30 June	2,057	15,549	4,822	1,800	908	120	25,256
	30 September	1,908	16,059	4,760	1,799	900	114	25,540
	31 December	1,974	16,687	4,698	1,784	904	126	26,173
1945	31 March	2,040	17,460	4,650	1,775	971	125	27,021
	30 June	2,132	18,986	4,549	1,767	967	125	28,526
	30 September	2,255	19,587	4,084	1,725	1,048	130	28,829
	31 December	2,202	19,961	2,900	1,469	1,086	134	27,752

Source: RIN Mutiny Enquiry Report, Naval Headquarters, New Delhi

of the recruiting camps were conducted in northern India, especially for the Musalmans and Pathans from Punjab, Karachi and the North Western Frontier Provinces. The RIN was predominantly manned by Muslims; they constituted 75% of the force in 1939. These ratings became the groomed, trained and experienced sailors by the end of the war. These senior sailors opted for Pakistan during Partition, and the Indian Navy was left with a few Hindu trained sailors.

In 1942, when the recruitment Directorate was created, manned by the Army, the Navy started losing good recruits because the best among the recruits were recommended for the Army. Subsequent advertisements by the Navy and the campaigns by the recruitment agents which gave a rosy picture of the naval service and false promises like a better life, better food, accommodation, pay and allowances and quick promotion, etc. created dissatisfaction and led to desertion by recruits; later they became one of the reasons behind the RIN Revolt of 1946. The later stage of the war saw the shifting of recruitment towards the English educated youth of the southern part of India. Thus the number of Hindu ratings increased to near 43% at the end of the war.

The socio-economic situation of India at the outbreak of the war forced the Indian educated youth to join the Armed Forces under the British Raj and serve the colonial master. The enlistment in the armed forces was on a volunteer basis, and the Indian rating was not merely a mercenary of the colonial government. Prior to the war, the RIN followed the 'martial' theory and concentrated recruitment in the Punjab region and Ratnagiri district in Bombay. "A shift in recruitment from Ratnagiri Muslims, traditionally sailors on the Konkan coast, to Punjabi Muslims, one of the 'higher martial races' in the Indian Army. This was because 'as a gunnery . . . specialist the Punjabi Mussalman was way ahead of the Ratnagiri',"[210] who possessed 'few natural martial qualities',[211] while it was the Punjabi's 'guts which count'.[212] But during the peak of the war, when the scarcity for manpower became acute, RIN had to leave the so-called martial theory and to compromise on the educational, physical and medical standards of the Indian recruits. Later "the political pressure, and the requirement for a better-educated technical skill base to operate more sophisticated warships, forced the RIN into recruiting more Hindus from South India."[213] A memorandum by the Secretary of State for India states that "A great difficulty has also been encountered in the provision of Viceroy's Commissioned and Non-Commissioned officers for these new units. Recruiting from the 'Martial classes' recruited in the pre-war Indian Army is now gradually drying up, and the monthly intake of these classes is only just sufficient to maintain existing units. All further expansion has now to be carried out with Madrassis (Southern Indian classes), who were only recruited to a very small extent before the war."[214]

Notes

1. RIN Enquiry Report, Naval Headquarters, New Delhi, p. 11.
2. General State of RIN on outbreak of War in 1939 & RIN Expansion, OSD/C10/ii, History Division, Ministry of Defence, New Delhi, pp. 10–11.
3. Ibid., p. 11.
4. Report on Progress in Training in Royal Indian Navy, 26th July 1943 to 30th September 1944, Report by the Flag Officer Commanding Royal Indian Navy, Secret Document, 1944, MoD History Division, New Delhi, p. 1.
5. Monograph Approved by FOCRIN on the RIN Man-Power situation 1939–1945 (Secret), dated 10 October 1945, MoD History Division, New Delhi.
6. Borne Strength is the total number of personnel in a unit/ship/establishment.
7. Ibid.
8. RIN Enquiry Report, Naval Headquarters, New Delhi, p. 7.
9. Ibid.
10. General State of RIN on Outbreak of War in 1939 & RIN Expansion, OSD/C10/ii, History Division, Ministry of Defence, New Delhi, p. 23.
11. Ibid.
12. Composition and State of Training of the Royal Indian Navy, 30 September 1943, NHQ, New Delhi, p. 5.
13. Ibid., p. 8.
14. RIN Recruitment Publicity booklet titled 'How to Become an Officer in the Royal Indian Navy', Prepared by the RIN, Government of India Press, Calcutta, 1938, p. 21, Naval Historical Branch, Portsmouth, UK.
15. Ibid.
16. Composition and State of Training of the Royal Indian Navy, 30 September 1943, NHQ, New Delhi, p. 8.
17. Ibid.
18. File titled 'Commissioned Officers', 601/12160/H, MoD History Division, New Delhi, p. 3.
19. Bisheshwar Prasad (Ed.), *Expansion of the Armed Forces and Defence Organisation 1939–45*, Ministry of Defence, History Division, New Delhi, Pentagon Press, 2012, p. 52.
20. General State of RIN on Outbreak of War in 1939 & RIN Expansion, OSD/C10/ii, History Division, Ministry of Defence, New Delhi, p. 31.
21. Ibid.
22. Ibid.
23. Ibid.
24. Ibid.
25. Ibid., p. 32.
26. Ibid.
27. Ibid.
28. Ibid.
29. Ibid., p. 33.
30. Ibid.
31. Ibid.
32. Ibid.
33. Ibid.
34. Ibid., p. 34, IMMTS (Indian Mercantile Marine Training Ship).
35. Ibid.
36. Ibid. As the Government of India had not approved grant of rank of Lieutenant Commander or above on entry, except in the case of the Special Branch.

Advantage could not be taken of the Royal Navy rule whereby the Naval Commander-in-Chief of a station, or the Admiralty, could grant temporary commissions in the Royal Naval Reserve, in the rank deemed by him or the, appropriate to an appointment for which an individual may possess special qualifications.

37 Ibid.
38 Ibid.
39 Ibid.
40 Ibid.
41 Ibid., p. 35.
42 Ibid.
43 Ibid.
44 Ibid.
45 Ibid.
46 Ibid.
47 Ibid.
48 Ibid.
49 Ibid.
50 Ibid.
51 Ibid.
52 Sanctioned Strength is the approved manpower and Borne Strength is the actual manpower available.
53 General State of RIN on outbreak of War in 1939 & RIN Expansion, OSD/C10/ii, History Division, Ministry of Defence, New Delhi, p. 6.
54 *Recruitment for the Defence Services in India*, History Division, Ministry of Defence, New Delhi, p. 20.
55 General State of RIN on Outbreak of War in 1939 & RIN Expansion, p. 6.
56 Ibid.
57 Ibid.
58 Ibid.
59 Ibid., p. 7.
60 Ibid.
61 Ibid.
62 *Recruitment for the Defence Services in India*, History Division, Ministry of Defence, New Delhi, p. 20.
63 General State of RIN on outbreak of War in 1939 & RIN Expansion, p. 17.
64 Ibid.
65 Ibid., p. 7.
66 Ibid.
67 Ibid.
68 Ibid.
69 Ibid.
70 Ibid.
71 Ibid., p. 14.
72 James, Commander E. C. Stratfield, *In the Wake: The Birth of the Indian and Pakistan Navies*, Charles Skilton Ltd, Edinburgh, 1983, p. 130.
73 Papers of Commander G. E. Walker, RINVR, 'File of Historical Notes', 1944, RIN/16/2, Caird Library, National Maritime Museum, Greenwich, UK, p. 13.
74 Ibid.
75 Ibid.
76 Royal Indian Navy, F.O.C.R.I.N. Letters: 1943–46, GOD/34, Caird Library, National Maritime Museum, Greenwich, UK, p. 2.

77 Pardeep P. Barua, *Gentlemen of the Raj: The Indian Army Officer Corps, 1817–1949*, Pentagon Press, London, 2008, p. 1.
78 Ibid., p. 2.
79 Philip Mason, *Matter of Honour: An Account of the Indian Army, Its Officers and Men*, Natraj Publishers, New Delhi, 2004, p. 24.
80 Ibid., p. 349.
81 Anirudh Deshpande, *British Military Policy in India, 1900–1945: Colonial Constraints and Declining Power*, Manohar, New Delhi, 2005, p. 143.
82 Ibid., p. 147.
83 General State of RIN on outbreak of War in 1939 & RIN Expansion, p. 38.
84 Ibid.
85 Topass Branch Ratings are to maintain the Hygiene of Ships and Units.
86 General State of RIN on outbreak of War in 1939 & RIN Expansion, p. 39.
87 Ibid.
88 Ibid.
89 Ibid., p. 9.
90 Ibid., pp. 9 and 39.
91 Ibid., p. 39.
92 Ibid.
93 Ibid., p. 16.
94 Ibid.
95 Ibid.
96 Ibid., p. 17.
97 Ibid.
98 Ibid.
99 Ibid.
100 Ibid.
101 Ibid.
102 Papers of Commander G. E. Walker, RINVR, 'File of Historical Notes', 1944, RIN/16/2, Caird Library, National Maritime Museum, Greenwich, UK, p. 13.
103 James, Commander E. C. Streatfield, *In the Wake: The Birth of the Indian and Pakistan Navies*, Charles Skilton Ltd, Edinburgh, 1983, p. 130.
104 Ibid.
105 Anirudh Deshpande, *British Military Policy in India, 1900–1945: Colonial Constraints and Declining Power*, Manohar, New Delhi, 2005, p. 150.
106 Ibid.
107 Composition and State of Training of the Royal Indian Navy, 30th September 1943, NHQ, New Delhi, p. 9 and RIN Enquiry Report, Naval Headquarters, New Delhi, p. 135.
108 RIN Enquiry Report, Naval Headquarters, New Delhi, p. 135.
109 Ibid.
110 Ibid., p. 136.
111 Ibid.
112 Composition and State of Training of the Royal Indian Navy, 30th September 1943, NHQ, New Delhi, p. 10.
113 Ibid.
114 Ibid.
115 Ibid., p. 11.
116 Ibid.
117 Landing Craft are used for Amphibious Operations and transportation of troop.

MANPOWER AND RECRUITMENT DURING THE WAR

118 Monograph Approved by FOCRIN on the RIN Man-Power Situation 1939–1945 (Secret), dated 10 October 1945, File No.601/7188/H, MoD History Division, New Delhi, p. 15.
119 Composition and State of Training of the Royal Indian Navy, 30th September 1943, NHQ, New Delhi, p. 1.
120 Ibid., p. 10.
121 Ibid.
122 Ibid.
123 Ibid.
124 Composition and State of Training of the Royal Indian Navy, 30 September 1943, p. 1.
125 Ibid.
126 Ibid.
127 Ibid., pp. 1 and 4.
128 Ibid., p. 10.
129 Ibid.
130 Ibid., p. 13.
131 Ibid.
132 Ibid.
133 Ibid., p. 14.
134 Ibid.
135 Ibid.
136 Sailors belonging to the Topasses Branch were primarily recruited for menial jobs like sanitation, cleaning the ship, and cleaning of officers' toilets and office premises.
137 B. L. Raina, *Official History of the Indian Armed Forces in the Second World War 1939–1945: Medical Services, Administration*, Combined Inter Services Historical Section, India & Pakistan, 1953, New Delhi, p. 140.
138 Ibid.
139 Ibid.
140 Ibid.
141 Ibid.
142 RIN Enquiry Report, Naval Headquarters, New Delhi, p. 10.
143 Ibid.
144 Ibid.
145 Ibid.
146 Ibid.
147 Ibid.
148 Ibid., p. 11.
149 Ibid.
150 Ibid.
151 Proceedings of a Conference held at General Headquarters on the 19th, 20th and 21st March 1942 to Consider Methods of Enhancing India's Recruiting Effort, History Division, MoD, New Delhi, p. 2.
152 Ibid.
153 Ibid.
154 Ibid., p. 4.
155 Ibid.
156 Ibid.
157 Ibid.
158 Ibid., p. 5.
159 Ibid.

160 Ibid.
161 Ibid.
162 Ibid.
163 Sanad was the recognition by the Commander-in-Chief to those helped in recruitment, especially in the case of Indian Army.
164 Proceedings of a Conference held at General Headquarters on the 19th, 20th and 21st March 1942 to Consider Methods of Enhancing India's Recruiting Effort, History Division, MoD, New Delhi, p. 6.
165 Ibid., p. 7.
166 Ibid., p. 8.
167 Ibid.
168 Ibid.
169 RIN Enquiry Report, Naval Headquarters, New Delhi, p. 13.
170 Expansion of the Armed Forces, Naval Headquarters, Secret Document, 1944, MoD History Division, New Delhi, p. 1.
171 Ibid.
172 Ibid.
173 Ibid.
174 The term 'lower deck' refers to sailors (below officer rank).
175 Expansion of the Armed Forces, Naval Headquarters, Secret Document, 1944, MoD History Division, New Delhi, p. 2.
176 Ibid.
177 Report on Progress in Training in Royal Indian Navy, 26th July 1943 to 30th September 1944, Report by the Flag Officer Commanding Royal Indian Navy, Secret Document, 1944, MoD History Division, New Delhi, p. 2.
178 RIN Enquiry Report, Naval Headquarters, New Delhi, p. 12.
179 Report on Progress in Training in Royal Indian Navy, 26th July 1943 to 30th September 1944, Report by the Flag Officer Commanding Royal Indian Navy, p. 3.
180 Ibid., p. 2.
181 Composition and State of Training of the Royal Indian Navy, 30th September 1943, NHQ, New Delhi, p. 5.
182 Ibid.
183 Monograph Approved by FOCRIN on the RIN Man-Power Situation 1939–1945 (Secret), dated 10 October 1945, p. 24, History Division, Ministry of Defence, New Delhi.
184 Report on the Royal Indian Navy, January–June 1945, Naval Headquarters, New Delhi, 1946, p. 7, ADM 1/19413, The National Archives, Kew, UK.
185 Ibid.
186 Ibid.
187 Ibid.
188 Ibid., p. 8.
189 Ibid.
190 Interview with Mrs. M. L. Cooper, Chief Officer WRINS (Retd) at New Delhi, in September 2013.
191 Ibid.
192 Ibid.
193 Monograph Approved by FOCRIN on the RIN Man-Power Situation 1939–1945 (Secret), dated 10 October 1945, p. 24, History Division, Ministry of Defence, New Delhi, pp. 18–19.
194 Ibid., p. 19.
195 During the British time, India was divided in to three Administrative Subdivisions (Presidency), namely Bombay, Calcutta and Madras.

196 Monograph Approved by FOCRIN on the RIN Man-Power Situation 1939–1945 (Secret), dated 10 October 1945, p. 24, History Division, Ministry of Defence, New Delhi, p. 19.
197 Ibid.
198 Ibid.
199 Ibid.
200 Expansion of the Armed Forces, Naval Headquarters, Secret Document, 1944, MoD History Division, New Delhi, p. 2.
201 Ibid.
202 Summary of the Report of the Commission of Enquiry into the R.I.N Mutiny, February 1946, National Archives of India, New Delhi, p. 10.
203 RIN Enquiry Report, Naval Headquarters, New Delhi, p. 13.
204 Ibid.
205 Ibid., p. 15.
206 General State of RIN on Outbreak of War in 1939 & RIN Expansion, OSD/C10/ii, History Division, Ministry of Defence, New Delhi, p. 15.
207 Ibid.
208 RIN Enquiry Report, Naval Headquarters, New Delhi, p. 7.
209 Rear Admiral Satyindra Singh, *Under Two Ensigns: The Indian Navy 1945–1950*, Oxford & IBH Publishing Co., New Delhi, 1986, p. 107.
210 Jefford, GOD/34, MS 80/073, NMM, quoted in Daniel Owen Spence, 'Imperial Transition, Indianisation and Race: Developing National Navies in the Subcontinent, 1947–64', *Journal of South Asian Studies*, Vol. 37, No. 2, 2014, p. 326.
211 Godfrey, quoted in Patrick Beesley, *Very Special Admiral: The Life of Admiral J.H. Godfrey*, Hamish Hamilton, London, 1980, p. 266, quoted in Daniel Owen Spence, 'Imperial Transition, Indianisation and Race: Developing National Navies in the Subcontinent, 1947–64', *Journal of South Asian Studies*, Vol. 37, No. 2, 2014, p. 326.
212 Jefford, GOD/34, MS 80/073, NMM, quoted by Daniel Owen Spence, 'Imperial Transition, Indianisation and Race: Developing National Navies in the Subcontinent, 1947–64', *Journal of South Asian Studies*, Vol. 37, No. 2, 2014, p. 326.
213 Daniel Owen Spence, 'Imperial Transition, Indianisation and Race: Developing National Navies in the Subcontinent, 1947–64', *Journal of South Asian Studies*, Vol. 37, No. 2, 2014, p. 326.
214 India' s War Effort: Memorandum by the Secretary of State for India, dated 01 March 1943, CAB/66/34/39, The National Archives, Kew Gardens, UK, p. 4.

4

EXPANSION OF THE ROYAL INDIAN NAVY

Growth of training and new establishments during the Second World War

1. Introduction

Prior to the Second World War, Britain's Royal Navy was responsible for the overall maritime defence of India. For this purpose, the Royal Navy maintained a fleet based at Trincomalee in Ceylon, a fleet at Singapore and a squadron at Bahrain. The Royal Indian Navy (RIN) was responsible for the coastal defence of India only. It had one naval base at Bombay and training establishments scattered in many regions of India. In September 1939, when the Second World War broke out, the Royal Indian Navy had only five sloops, one trawler, one survey ship and one patrol craft. It had 114 officers and 1,732 ratings. All the six rating training schools were concentrated inside the Naval Dockyard in Bombay – Gunnery, Seamanship, Signals, Anti-submarine, Boys Training Establishment (BTE) and Mechanical Training Establishment (MTE). There were no rating training schools for Torpedo, Electrical or Radar. Officers went to Britain for basic and advanced training in all disciplines. Eighty percent of the rating recruits came from Punjab and Bombay (Konkan area) Presidency, and out of them 75% were Muslims and 9% Hindus.

During the war, the Royal Indian Navy had undergone phenomenal expansion. Thirty one small vessels were immediately requisitioned to serve as minesweepers and patrol craft until newly built ships could enter service. The first Basset class trawler built in Garden Reach Workshop, Calcutta, was commissioned into the Navy in 1941. It was followed by five more. The first Bangor class fleet minesweeper built in India was commissioned into the RIN in 1943. Several other vessels that came from different countries were also inducted into the RIN. Six new sloops came from Britain and were named after Indian rivers. Some Bathurst class minesweepers came from Australia. Numerous minor vessels like motor minesweepers, harbour defence motor launches and landing craft came from Britain, the United States and Australia. In

EXPANSION OF THE ROYAL INDIAN NAVY

order to facilitate the repair facilities, construction of new ships and logistic support, the naval base and naval dockyard at Bombay were modernised. During the period three new branches (Electrical, Educational and Medical) were created as part of wartime expansion of the RIN.

This chapter enumerates the expansion of the Royal Indian Navy in the fields of Vessels, Equipment, Training and Establishments during wartime and how these developments were utilised by the colonial government to the fullest for the protection of the imperial interests. This chapter is based on primary sources and the limitations of my official position do not allow me to quote the source of the material in many places. The facts and figures brought out in this chapter are based on the Report on RIN Training, by the Naval Headquarters in 1944.

2. Composition and strength of the RIN prior to the outbreak of war

Taking the position on 30 June 1939, it may be said that the RIN, except for its six ships and two tenders, was bounded by the walls of the RIN dockyard, with its ordnance in the hands of the Army and with a skeleton sea transport establishment. Its medical staff was provided by the Indian Medical Department, and administered by two part-time officers of the RAMC. Its schoolmaster and accountant staffs were commissioned officers from warrant rank and warrant officers. (See Table 4.1 for an enumeration of warships prior to the war.)

Table 4.1 Warships of RIN prior to the war

HMIS	Class	TONNAGE
Clive	Sloop	2,050
Cornwallis	Sloop	1,290
Hindustan	Sloop	1,190
Indus	Sloop	1,190
Lawrence	Sloop	1,225
Investigator	Surveying ship	1,574
Madras	Steep trawler for target towing 423	423
Pathan		6,95

Source: Composition and state of training of the Royal Indian Navy, 30th September 1943, Naval Headquarters, New Delhi.

*Of these the only two modern ships were HMIS *Indus* and *Hindustan*.

Establishments

Bombay

    Naval Headquarters, RIN Dockyard.
    Depot, with the Naval Barracks, RIN Dockyard
    Signal School, RIN Dockyard
    Gunnery School, RIN Dockyard
    Mechanical training establishment, RIN Dockyard
    Boy's training establishment, RIN Dockyard
    Fort wireless transmitting (W/T) station, RIN Dockyard
    Mahul W/T station, RIN Dockyard
    Office of the Captain Superintendent of the Yard
    The Engineering Department, RIN Dockyard
    The Constructive Department, RIN Dockyard
    The Electrical Engineers Department, RIN Dockyard
    The Naval Stores Office, RIN Dockyard
    The Dockyard Police, RIN Dockyard
    The Dockyard Dispensary, RIN Dockyard
    The Ordnance Depot, Bombay Castle
    The Sea Transport Office, Ballard Estate

Karachi

    Sea Transport Office

Calcutta

    Sea Transport Office

3. Organisational changes

Many administrative and organisational changes also took place in the RIN during the Second World War. The Burma RNVR came under the administrative control of the Flag Officer Commanding Royal Indian Navy and it comprised 34 officers and 261 men. They were distributed between the Landing Craft Wing, Motor Launches and other duties.[1] They had a small Central Headquarters at HMIS *Hilsa* at Mandapam. In 1943, the Royal Navy was considering the transfer of Burma RNVR to the administration of Commanding Chief of the Eastern Fleet.[2]

From the outbreak of the war until March 1941, the Headquarters of the RIN was in Bombay. The expansion of the RIN and the creation of new naval establishments all over India, together with the operational movements of ships on the East coast, forced the FOCRIN to move to a more central position at Delhi. It had the additional advantage of being in close touch with the Government of India and headquarters of the other sister services. Much of the administrative work, however, continued to be done in

Bombay until 1943 when a reorganisation of the Naval Headquarters was undertaken.[3] Intelligence, plans, operation branches and security organisation were brought under the command of the Chief of Staff, who was a Commodore 2nd Class, on post NHQ reorganisation.[4] The post of the Director of Training (Commodore Royal Navy), who was also the Inspector of Training Establishments, was created in July 1943 in order to ensure that the wartime training took place in the quickest possible time.[5] Another Commodore 2nd Class was appointed as Chief of Administration to look after the policy, planning and direction of administrative matters, including the organisation in HMI ships and establishments.[6] He coordinated the work of the following branches:

1   Administration, Planning and Organisation Branch
2   Personnel Directorate
3   Directorate of Equipment
4   Directorate of Engineering
5   Medical Branch
6   Accountant Branch
7   Admiralty Branch

The RIN was divided into three Commands based on the geographical locations. The West coast was under COMCRIN (Commodore, RIN) who was operationally responsible to the FOCRIN for operations on the West coast of India. Simultaneously, Naval Officers-in-Charge (NOIC) were placed at Karachi, Kathiawar Coast, Bombay and Cochin,[7] who were operationally responsible to COMCRIN, but administratively responsible direct to the FOCRIN. Commodore Bay of Bengal (COMBAY) was responsible for operations on the East coast. The Naval Officers-in-Charge at Calcutta, Vizagapatam and Madras were operationally responsible to COMBAY, but administratively responsible directly to the FOCRIN.[8] Areas in Southern India (Tuticorin, Mandapam and Palk Strait) were under the direction of a Naval Officer-in-Charge, Mandapam, who also carried out the duties of the Commanding Officer of HMIS *Hamla*.[9] NOIC Mandapam was directly responsible to FOCRIN for both operations and administration.

4. Training

The training of the wartime rapidly expanding RIN faced many difficulties. At the outbreak of the war in 1939, RIN training establishments consisted only of Seamanship School, Signal School, Gunnery School, Mechanical Training Establishment, Boys' Training Establishment and the Anti-Submarine School. However the training of the officers was carried out in the Royal Navy establishments in the United Kingdom. There were no Torpedo, Electrical or Radar Schools.

As mentioned above, all training establishments were situated within the RIN Dockyard, Bombay. The personnel engaged in instructional duties did not exceed 16 officers and a dozen warrant officers. The main problems in training were the institution of courses not previously undertaken, shortages of instructors and equipment, and the difficult situation originally created by the pre-war policy of centralising all activities within the dockyard area. This problem was by no means solved by the initial removal of training establishments outside the area of the dockyard, nor it was a problem peculiar to training. It involved the Service in general, and in various ways was the cause of many difficulties that had to be overcome.

It has already been stated that at the outbreak of the war all training was carried out in the dockyard area. At that time, however, work had begun on a new RIN Depot (Castle Barracks) at the site of the old Bombay Castle. This depot was expected to meet the wider needs of the Service as envisaged by the recommendations of the Chatfield Committee and was to provide accommodation for 400 petty officers and other ratings. The construction of barracks was completed in January 1941 and subsequent improvisation allowed for the housing of a total of 1,000 ratings. However, it was inadequate for the large wartime needs of the RIN.

Castle Barracks were unable to provide accommodation for all. Considerations of space compelled the transfer of training establishments beyond the confines of the dockyard. Some found a temporary home in the dockyard, whereas others had to be housed elsewhere in makeshift quarters until more permanent schools could be set up.

Training of officers

Up to 1924, selection of Officers of the Regular RIN was made from officers of the RNR (Royal Navy Reserve), who had obtained at least a 2nd Mate's Certificate. There were one or two exceptions to this.[10] Post-1924, officers entered as cadets and were trained as special entry cadets with the Royal Navy before joining the Naval Service in India. There were a number of exceptions to this, and the necessary numbers were filled from officers joining from the RNR or Merchant Navy.[11] Regular Officers of the RIN were sent to the UK each year to specialise in the full long course at the various Specialist Establishments, and promotion was similar to the Royal Navy. The senior rank which was attainable in the RIN in 1943 was Commodore 1st Class.[12] The Flag Officer Commanding RIN had always been an officer lent from the Royal Navy.[13]

Prior to 1939, there were no reserve officers in the RIN, but with the threat of War both RINR (Royal Indian Naval Reserve) and RINVR (Royal Indian Naval Volunteer Reserve) were formed,[14] on similar lines to those in the United Kingdom. The RINVR Officers were those who had seafaring experience and at least a 2nd Mate's Certificate.[15] The training of these officers presented a new and severe problem. Though a few new facilities existed, there was a great

EXPANSION OF THE ROYAL INDIAN NAVY

shortage of instructors. Mess facilities for Reserve Officers were limited. Junior officers were accommodated in Bombay in a block of flats known as Dhanraj Mahal and the Old 'Admirals House' became a mess for senior officers. Instruction started in late 1939. All courses were of three weeks duration, with the exception of Anti-Gas Course, which was just one week. In May 1943, all courses with the exception of Divisional and Anti-Gas were increased to four weeks. A Divisional Course for Reserve Officers and Instruction in Seamanship, Navigation and Anti-Gas was carried out in the RIN Depot, Castle Barracks, under the supervision of a Reserve Training Officer. Instruction in Signals, Gunnery and Asdic was given at the Specialist Schools. Seamanship and Navigation classes could each accommodate 32 officers.

Training of ratings

Special Service Entry for ratings of the Seamen and Stokers Branches of the Royal Indian Navy was introduced in early 1938. Entry under the term of Continuous Service (or Non-continuous Service in the Accountant Branch) was the only form of recruitment to the Royal Indian Navy. Prior to the outbreak of the hostilities the expansion of the Royal Indian Navy was planned on the basis of the recommendations made in the Chatfield Committee's Report.[16] To meet the expansion envisaged in this Report, construction of an RIN Depot on the site of the old Bombay Castle was approved. This Depot, known as HMIS *Dalhousie*, consisted of permanent buildings and was finally completed in January 1941.[17] Originally it was designed to accommodate 400 petty officers and other ratings, but improvisation had since been made allowing for the accommodation over 1,000 ratings. On the outer parapet walls of the original Castle were built the various Depot offices, Drafting offices, Anti-Submarine School, sick quarters, officers mess and classrooms. The major establishment was primarily a barracks for accommodating active service ratings awaiting draft or undergoing training. Included in the buildings were barracks for ratings, mess rooms, storerooms, canteens and a gymnasium cum cinema and concert hall.

The ship HMIS *Dalhousie*, which was built in 1886 in England for Her Majesty's Indian Marine (this service was started in 1892 and became Royal Indian Marine later), became the Depot ship in Bombay in 1922 and later, until 1940, the Boys' Training establishment. The ship, HMIS *Dalhousie*, became the unit for training and examination of new entry Special Service ordinary seamen in seamanship. The course consisted of 12 weeks' instruction in the establishments followed by one week seagoing training. Instruction of Special Service Ratings (Education, Discipline and Professional) started in early 1938. Special facilities did not exist until the mid-1940s, when the Boys' training was transferred from the hulk *Dalhousie* to HMIS *Bahadur*, the new Boys' Training Establishment at Karachi, Sind.[18]

The training of all Special Service Ratings was then carried out at the hulk *Dalhousie*. Subsequent expansions necessitated the transfer of Signalmen, Stokers,

Domestics, etc., to their own training establishments and HMIS *Dalhousie* (Seamanship Training Ship) was converted into the Seamanship School.[19] The last expansion occurred on 10 November 1942, when the first ratings ex HMIS *Khanjar* arrived after the 11 week New Entry Training in the establishment.

5. Growth of training and establishments

Training of seamen

Special service ratings

On the outbreak of the war, recruiting for Continuous Service Ratings ceased. Hostilities Only (HO) ratings were regarded on recruitment as fully trained professional seamen and therefore received no training other than that aboard the ship on being drafted to sea. It was therefore with the training of Special Service ratings and Boys' that they were mainly concerned.

Until the mid-1940s the hulk HMIS *Dalhousie* was the Boys' Training Establishment. When this establishment was moved to Karachi, the hulk was utilised as the training establishment for Special Service ratings. "As Expansion of the Service increased and recruitment gained momentum, Dalhousie was found to be much too small. A position ultimately arose when the intake by recruitment had to be curbed directly by the accommodation situation in the training schools, and this happened at a time when the Service urgently required men. As Castle Barracks were completed the training of Special Service Ratings was moved there, but this afforded only momentary relief, as space there also was extremely limited."[20]

This necessitated a further transfer of the establishment to HMIS *Khanjar*, an area of requisitioned buildings at Varsora, some 18 miles from Bombay. *Khanjar* was admittedly a temporary expedient, pending the construction of a larger and more permanent establishment at Kolshet (HMIS *Akbar*).

At *Khanjar* all Special Service Ratings received their first 11 weeks' training consisting of educational and disciplinary courses. Thereafter seamen were transferred to the hulk *Dalhousie* for a 12-week practical training in seamanship, finally receiving one week seagoing training. The total number of ratings who could be trained at one time at *Khanjar* was as follows:

Seamen	990
Stokers	330
Cooks (Officers)	90
Cooks (Sailors)	90

In 1943 when the intensified campaign of the Recruiting Directorate increased the flow of recruits, *Khanjar* and other training establishments were unable to cope up with the additional numbers and asked for the reduction of recruitment. To avoid such a step, which might have had a permanent adverse effect on recruiting, it was arranged to open Naval Wings at the Recruit Reception Camps at Bangalore and elsewhere. There recruits were held until they could be absorbed by the training establishments.

HMIS *Akbar* was commissioned in January 1944. All new entry training for seamen, cooks, writers, accountants, etc. as well as new entry disciplinary courses for schoolmasters, artificers, stockers, writers, and sick berth attendants was to be undertaken there. The hulk *Dalhousie* and HMIS *Khanjar* ceased to be seamanship and new entry training establishments. While *Akbar* remained incomplete, certain courses for domestic ratings, cooks, etc. were conducted elsewhere, but all these were eventually concentrated at *Akbar*.

Seamanship training at Kolshet comprised a 24-week course at the end of which a rating passed out with the rank of ordinary seaman, although having passed the examination for Able Bodied Seaman. Promotion to the latter rank, however, required one year service, most of the time including four months sea time.

From the middle of 1944 till the end of hostilities, there were no major alterations at HMIS *Akbar*. However considerable improvement was made in the matter of sea training with the formation of the Bombay Training Flotilla consisting of HMI Ships *Cornwallis*, *Clive*, *Dipavati*, *Hira*, *Lal* and *Nilam* in mid-1944. In June 1945 HMIS *Gondwana* was added to the flotilla primarily as anti-submarine training ship, but it was utilised for the sea training of recruits from HMIS *Akbar* when anti-submarine training became impossible during the monsoon. HMIS *Cornwallis* was decommissioned in July 1945, and HMIS *Lawrence* joined the flotilla in November of that year.

(ii) Boys (sailors)

The British had learned from experience that the best seamen ware those who have been trained in the profession from their early youth. This was especially the case in India, where the standard of literacy remained slow, and suitable material for the Navy was definitely limited in numbers. Much knowledge of technical subjects was essential for the naval seaman who would need as a basis a good standard of general education. This was fully appreciated in the RIN, and in 1937 a plan was made for a new and permanent Boys' training establishment to replace HMIS *Dalhousie*. In the following year building was begun at Manora, Karachi. The new establishment (HMIS *Bahadur*) was commissioned in May 1940 and was originally designed to accommodate 250 boys. To meet war requirements it was later expanded to accommodate 500 boys. *Bahadur* was a modern well-equipped school with adequate instructional apparatus and extensive playing fields.

During the war the recruitment of boys considerably increased. There was a shortage of boys of the requisite educational and physical standards, and it was decided to set up an establishment for junior boys between the ages of

14 and 15.5 years to prepare them for the entry into *Bahadur*. The construction began on Chinna Creek, Karachi, in September 1941, and the establishment was commissioned as HMIS *Dilawar* in February 1942. Boys were admitted on half-yearly basis, the capacity of the establishment being 240.

With the rapid expansion of the service, the need for more continuous service ratings grew. To meet the requirements as quickly as possible and to avoid further construction it was decided that entries into *Dilawar* should be of the same age as those for *Bahadur*, i.e., 15 to 17. Educationally entries into *Dilawar* were, therefore, one year higher. The annual output from these establishments was thus increased from 360 to 480. The hulk *Dalhousie* was moved to Karachi in 1944 where it was attached to *Bahadur* for training purposes. Early in 1946 she became unseaworthy and was sold (see Figure 4.1).

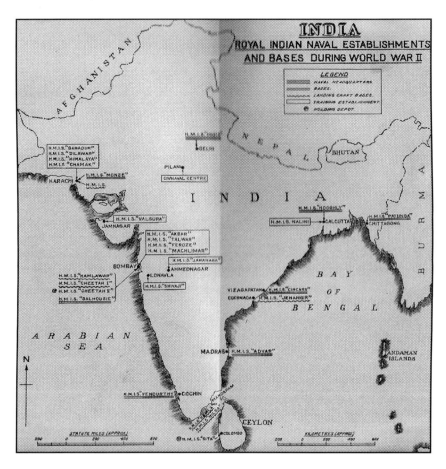

Figure 4.1 RIN establishments and bases during the war
Source: Naval History Division, Indian Navy, New Delhi

The Continuous Service Boys who entered *Bahadur* between the ages of 15 and 17 had to undergo two years of a pre-matriculation standard course. Fresh intake took place on quarterly basis. The course of 18 months covered general educational subjects and science (including electricity, wireless, engineering science and magnetism) and naval subjects, such as seamanship, divisional duties, service customs and regulations, naval history, and field training without arms. Advanced trainees received elementary instructions in navigation. On completion of this course, a boy had attained at least the matriculation standard of other Indian educational establishments, and in 1945 the passing out examination was accepted by the Madras Government as equivalent to the standard required for the service.

One of the main difficulties encountered during the period 1940–1943 was that of obtaining suitable schoolmasters. Men temperamentally and morally fitted for the instruction of boys and with the requisite high academic qualification were relatively few and not easily induced to join the RIN, where pay was comparatively poor. Later the pay and status of a schoolmaster was raised, and the situation eased. At the beginning of 1944 it was hoped to secure suitable graduates capable of giving specialised science and engineering training. "The products of Bahadur represent the Continuous Service Ratings of the Service for many years to come and so the importance of a high standard of educational and professional training cannot be overstressed."[21] The only other major development till VJ day was the provision of a sea training ship for boys, HMIS *Investigator*, in May 1945. Her copious accommodation made her especially suitable for that job. She made a number of training cruises, including two to East Africa.

Reserve Officers' training

At the outbreak of the war, Reserve Officers' training presented a large and difficult problem. Instructions were very short and the RIN had no officers' training school, whilst existing facilities were taxed to their utmost to cope with the training of ratings.

Towards the end of 1939 instruction began in the RIN barracks, all courses being of three weeks' duration except the anti-submarine course which was of one week. In 1941 training was transferred to Castle Barracks, and in May 1943 the duration of courses except anti-gas and divisional was increased to four weeks. Reserve Executive Officers received a month's Seamanship, a month's navigation, and divisional and anti-gas courses at Castle Barracks and signals, anti-submarine, torpedo and gunnery courses at the specialist schools.

There was no accommodation in the barracks for officers under training, some of whom were accommodated in the RIN Mess, and some of whom lived outside in private billets. The whole position was unsatisfactory; there was no mess life and officers dispersed to private life after working hours each day.[22]

In November 1943 the situation improved substantially with the commissioning of HMIS *Feroze*. This was a building on Malabar Hill, Bombay, and had formerly been the temporary location of HMIS *Himalaya*. It followed as far as possible the lines on which HMS *King Alfred* and HMS *Good Hope* in the United Kingdom were conducted. Officers undergoing training were accommodated on the premises and thus were subject to a more continuous service environment. All officers entering the RIN were required to undergo at least four weeks of a disciplinary course, and courses in Urdu, physical training and historical lectures at HMIS *Feroze*. Other courses were also carried out either at *Feroze* or at the specialist establishment concerned.

Courses were held for warrant officers, and also a boatswains seamanship course, a navigational course for gunners, gunners (T) and boatswains, and a course for lower deck personnel on promotion to commissioned rank. The total accommodation on VJ Day was for some 200 officers and 200 ratings.

The Mechanical Training Establishment

In the period prior to the opening of hostilities in 1939 progress had been made in modernising and expanding this establishment. This was based on the Nine Year Plan of the reorganisation of RIN. In 1938 Acting Leading Stockers courses were started, and the acute shortage of mechanicians led to the institution of an advanced Leading Stockers class from which ratings who qualified were promoted to Mechanician II Class. At the outbreak of war the ship's company comprised six officers and about 25 ratings and 150 trainees. Towards the end of 1940 an expanded school within the dockyard area was planned as a joint measure with a view to enlarging the training capacity to 500 ratings. The new school was completed towards the end of 1941. Training of various HO categories was then also undertaken, including motor engineers, boiler room chargemen, drivers, (steam i & ii), greasers, etc. Practical training was carried out afloat in HMIS *Lawrence* and other Local Naval Defence (LND) vessels. Prior to its expansion the Mechanical Training Establishment had little in the way of equipment, save the engineering appliances, steam and internal combustion engines, turbines, condensers, lathes and coppersmiths' hearths. A number of civilians were employed on the instructional staff, and courses covered both theory and practical work.

As a result of the expansion of the dockyard it became necessary to find another site for the establishment outside the dockyard areas, and in 1944 construction of a new school, HMIS *Shivaji*, was commenced at Lonavala in the Western Ghats, about 80 miles from Bombay. It was finally commissioned in June 1945, and was designed to train a maximum of 720 ratings of all categories with an instructional staff and ship's company of 50 officers and 329 ratings.

In September 1944 a Lt Commander (Engineer) was sent to the United Kingdom to study modern training methods in the Royal Navy, with particular reference to the training of engine room ratings and artificer apprentices. This was to ensure that training methods in HMIS *Shivaji* were kept up to date and provisions were made to depute officers to keep abreast of current methods in the future. Similar action was taken in respect to the engineering department of HMI Dockyard for the study of the latest developments and practice. Particular regard was paid to the large vessels with which the dockyard was then being called upon to deal.

In 1942 when difficulty was experienced in finding suitable men for Artificer Artisans Acting IV Class, a special pre-training scheme was evolved for the men of intermediate science standard. They were given six months' practical engineering instruction at the Civilian Training Centre, Pilani (Jaipur State) under the Labour Department. "This was made possible by Mr. GD Birla who generously supplied most of the training equipment free of charge." Later, it was felt that efficiency could be increased by conversion into a Civilian-Naval Centre under a RIN Engineer Officer. Subsequently, the change occurred in early 1944, and disciplinary training was added to the course with the naval staff consisting of 3 officers and 36 ratings.

Later in 1944, recruitment to the Centre, which till then had been poor, received considerable impetus. To cope with this and also to improve the internal administration, about which there had been some dissatisfaction, the Naval staff was increased to three Engineer officers (including a Lt Commander [Engineer]) in charge, three Executive officers and one Supply officer, in addition to the requisite regulating staff and ship's company.

Gunnery training

The pre-war gunnery requirements of the RIN were small, only one or two specialist officers and about four gunners mates being required for instructional purposes. However, it was realised that in the event of a war the existing training facilities that the Dockyard had inadequate, and the Nine Year Plan provided for a Gunnery School capable of training gunnery ratings for the new ships envisaged. This was recommended by the Chatfield Committee but was awaiting approval by Government at the outbreak of war.

In 1939 the first gunnery training expansion had taken place since the end of the First World War. Close to the existing battery in the Dockyard were installed an H/A Section, and R/F Director with FKC and FCB equipment. Then, in September 1939, the maximum possible expansion of the gunnery school took place in the space available, this being an extremely small maximum. Fire control, ammunition, land fighting, and direction sections were added in a building adjacent to the battery. In due course another temporary battery was added, giving a total of five guns (4" Mk IV QF; 4" Mk IX B/L; and 6" B/L – the last for training gun crews for AMC's fitting in Bombay) available for training. In the 1940 when the RIN Navy Office moved out, the main centre became available for theoretical and educational instruction. At the same time the increased flow of naval stores caused part of the already small parade ground to be absorbed for storage purposes.[23]

In the mid-1940s immediate provision for additional instructors became necessary, and a long course to fit RINVR officers for gunnery instruction was begun. Short three weeks course for Reserve Officers was increased, and with the opening of Fort and Castle Barracks the school had been split to deal with trainees living at these two widely separated points. All this threw a heavy burden on an already overstrained organisation.

At this point of time the British had decided to shift all training establishments out of the Bombay Dockyard. Various potential locations were considered, but to all of them there was an objection. It was after some considerable time that a suitable site at Manora Sandspit, Karachi, was finally found. Building construction was not seriously begun until early 1942. Meanwhile, the expansion of the school could not be delayed, and on 1 June 1942 it moved to II Palazzo on Malabar Hill, being commissioned as HMIS *Himalaya* in January 1943. Two blocks of flats and a bungalow were requisitioned for accommodation and by the end of 1942 there were some 500–600 ratings under training. This figure was still maintained in 1944 after the school had moved to Karachi in November 1943. Thereafter numbers remained more or less constant, showing a slight increase.

This new school had increased accommodation and was equipped in the most-up to date manner, being the most modern of its kind outside the United Kingdom. For the first time it was possible to give detailed practical instruction and to allow trainees to gain experience of the actual instruments concerned. A memorandum from HMIS *Himalaya* summed up the change by stating "the new Gunnery School in Karachi has proved in five months how vitally necessary an establishment of its kind was, and the results of the classes passing through during this period have been most gratifying."

The necessity for a fully equipped school was amply established by the fact that the results of the examination carried out at Karachi showed a vast improvement over the earlier examinations held in Bombay. The results of a few classes were as follows:

	In Karachi		In Bombay	
	Qualified	Failed	Qualified	Failed
Officers	14	3	15	5
Short courses	10	5	5	8
(4 classes)	15	3	5	11
	15	5	6	6
Total	54	16	31	30

	In Karachi		In Bombay	
	Qualified	Failed	Qualified	Failed
Anti aircraft	11	5		
Ratings II	9	2	5	8
Total	20	2	10	8
Anti aircraft	9	3	8	2
Ratings III	12	1	6	6
	7	5	4	6
	11	3	8	1
	12	4	7	5
Total	51	16	33	20

Regular RIN officers carried out their Sub-Lieutenant course in the United Kingdom and certain selected officers did the Gunnery Specialist course at HMS *Excellent*. All reserve executive officers were to undergo a four-week gunnery course at HMIS *Himalaya*; some were selected to do the long course as gunnery specialist officers. Ratings were trained in all gunnery non-substantive rates except QRI and AAI. Gunners mates were qualified up to Black Swan class with handworked mountings.

Apart from the earlier difficulties caused by cramped surroundings and lack of important equipment, the main problem to be faced was the provision of instructors. In the beginning of 1944, against a sanctioned establishment of 8 Chief Gunners mates, 16 Gunners Mates and 10 other Higher Gunnery Rate Instructors, Himalaya had only 3 Chief Gunners Mates, 5 Gunners Mates and 6 Higher Gunnery rate Instructors. This shortage was offset by a shortage of ratings under training. Himalaya had only one-third of its total capacity due to this manpower shortage. In mid-1944 if the full number of ratings had become available for training, the problem of providing instructors would have been serious.

In the final stages of the war there were no developments of note. In early 1944 HMIS *Lawrence* was allotted as a gunnery firing ship but was replaced in November by HMIS *Hindustan* when the latter was withdrawn from operational service. HMIS *Himalaya* was improved by 1944–1945 by the addition of new training equipment, and the firing point was extended to accommodate Defensive Equipment of Merchant Shipping (DEMS) and coastal force guns. An RIN Chief Ordnance Artificer was sent to the United Kingdom for training and was subsequently promoted as the first Indian Warrant Ordnance Artificer. Thirty-two RIN officers qualified in ordnance and two officers were therefore sent to the United Kingdom to undergo the necessary courses. They returned to India in January 1945 and were appointed to HMIS *Himalaya* and HMIS *Shivaji*.

Prior to 1941, Defensive Equipment of Merchant Shipping training was carried out in the Dockyard area, but in August of that year it was decided to establish a training centre at Colaba Point. Here all necessary instructional equipment was employed, the RIN providing officer instructors, whilst ratings instructors were found by the Royal Navy. Training was also carried out at Calcutta, Madras and Karachi and later certain training facilities were provided at Cochin and Vishakhapatam.

Anti-submarine training

The cardinal difficulties faced by the training establishments in the earlier years of war have already been discussed in earlier sections. The examples already given are typical and it is unnecessary to elaborate on the subject further. It suffices here to say that the Anti-Submarine School, when first opened in the Dockyard in July 1939, laboured under the same difficulties. The Anti-Submarine School was transferred to Castle Barracks in 1941 and it eventually carried out a further move to Varsora, 19 miles from Bombay, where a modern school had been built. Instruction was begun in April 1943, when the school was commissioned as HMIS *Machlimar*. The school was later extended to provide the training for Harbour Defence Operators, and instruction was given to Royal Navy, RIN and Ceylon RNVR ratings.

Since the submarine was the enemy's principal weapon at sea, efficient anti-submarine training was essential. The earlier schools were well equipped, whilst HMIS *Machlimar* had equipment enabling it to teach the highest anti-submarine courses for officers and ratings in all types of Asdic sets fitted in the RN, RIN and Dominion Navies. Instructions closely followed the syllabus of HMS *Osprey*, the anti-submarine school in Britain. The officers' long Asdic course lasted five months whilst all officers were required to undergo a three-week short course, and it was possible to train 220 officers and ratings at any given time.

It remained the policy for RIN officers to be sent to the United Kingdom for long courses, mainly to obtain up-to-date anti-submarine knowledge on problems under research and for liaison purposes with the RN. HMIS *Machlimar* was sanctioned as a joint measure with the RN. It was intended to train a certain number of RN ratings there. However, owing mainly to administrative problems within the Eastern Fleet, the RN School never worked at full strength. During the final stages of the war, no changes were made at HMIS *Machlimar*.

In 1945, HMIS *Gondwana* became the anti-submarine training ship, and Harbour Defence Motor Launch (HDML) 1084 was attached to HMIS *Machlimar* for similar duties. During the summer of 1945 some difficulty was experienced in carrying out anti-submarine training at sea as

EXPANSION OF THE ROYAL INDIAN NAVY

accommodation for the crew of an RN or Dutch submarine was not available at Bombay or on the Kathiawar coast during the monsoon. Facilities for anti-submarine training also existed at India's five major ports. At Bombay, an Anti-Submarine Tactical Training Unit was established on lines similar to the Western Approaches Tactical Unit at Liverpool. Officers of ships equipped with anti-submarine weapons were trained in the latest tactics of underwater warfare, and courses were kept constantly up to date.

Torpedo and electrical training

Torpedo Branch was the youngest service in the RIN. It was responsible for all torpedo, mining, paravane and depth charge gear in HMI ships and motor toepedo boats (MTBs) and also for the efficient working of all electrical apparatus, excluding W/T, radar and anti-submarine gear. The branch became essential when Bitten and Black Swan class sloops and other vessels with modern electrical equipment were required, the need being emphasised on the introduction of MTBs.

Originally certain engineer officers and electrical artificers (EAs) received courses in electrical maintenance and they were almost fully occupied at sea with their normal engineering duties. These men lacked the practical knowledge for maintenance of modern fire control gear. As a result, a number of wireless electricians were borrowed from the Admiralty and at the same time certain officers and EAs were sent for training to HMS *Vernon*, Torpedo and Electrical Training School in the United Kingdom. These officers and ratings were together with certain EAs who had received some electrical training at the MTE, Bombay. They formed the nucleus of the Torpedo Branch. A torpedo school was opened in the Dockyard in June 1942 and moved to a new location at Rozi Island, in Jamnagar, in December 1942. The school was commissioned as HMIS *Valsura* and was sanctioned as a joint measure with the Royal Navy and could be required to train Royal Navy ratings, from which Service came some of the instructors. In mid-1944 motor launch (ML) 420 was allotted to HMIS *Valsura* for torpedo firing duties.

Electrical mechanics

After the formation of the Landing Craft Wing, electrical maintenance was undertaken by three types of ratings, Wireman (HOs), Electrical Artificers from general service, and a newly created rate known as Electrical Artificers (LCW). Men employed on the same work were on varying conditions of service and had been trained in different ways. EAs (LCW) had received only a brief course in Bombay, and their performance was unsatisfactory.

The EA (LCW) Branch had worked independently of HMIS *Valsura* until December 1943, when an officer from the Torpedo School was deputed to take charge of the training of ratings for the Landing Craft Wing. The

EXPANSION OF THE ROYAL INDIAN NAVY

school was attached to HMIS *Khanjar* (later HMIS *Hamla*) and in February 1944 a new Electrical Mechanics Branch was formed. This was intended ultimately to be responsible for all electrical maintenance in Landing Craft Wing. Lack of equipment was a grave early problem which seriously dislocated the training programme as originally planned. This difficulty was overcome, but a shortage of instructors still remained a problem, and in early 1944 the school had only half the sanctioned number of instructors.

Candidates for entry into this branch were selected from Stockers and Seamen ratings undergoing their new entry courses at HMIS *Akbar*. The electrical course intended to fit them to take full responsibility for all electrical care and maintenance of 8 to 10 Landing Crafts. It was estimated that 60 electrical mechanics would be trained by the end of July 1944. As part of the reorganisation of the Landing Craft Wing, the training school for electrical mechanics, earlier located in HMIS *Hamla*, was transferred to HMIS *Valsura* in May 1945.

6. Specialised training

Signals training

Until 1941 the training of communication ratings was carried out at the Signal School in the dockyard area and up to 1939 the output of trained boys had been somewhat fewer than 100 annually. In 1940 the training of Communication boys was transferred to HMIS *Bahadur*, but the great increase in the number of Special Service Ratings necessitated the opening of a new school at Colaba in April 1941. The training of Special Service Ratings was then cut down to five and half months, including the new entry course. This was unavoidable but resulted in the drafting of insufficiently trained communication ratings to ships and shore stations. However, by 1944 the situation had eased, and the training period was increased to approximately eight and half months, including two months of sea training.

The Colaba School had accommodations for a maximum of 104 officers and 930 ratings. Some instructors were lent by the Admiralty but the majority of them were RINVR officers trained for this purpose. In the later part of 1943 the school was independently commissioned as HMIS *Talwar* and the Sloop *Cornwallis* was allotted to it for practical training. The school undertook Radar officers short courses, radio mechanics qualifying courses and RIN radar ratings preliminary and higher courses. The highest courses were V/S2, W/T2, P/O Coder and Convoy Yeoman.

Radar training

Until June 1943 the RIN had no qualified Radar Officers. Training was carried out at the Signal School with one type 286 set and an incomplete 285 set; the instructor was a W/Tel who had no expertise in this matter. Later, a qualified Radar Officer was obtained from the British Admiralty, and he carried out the instruction, but the general standard of those passing out was poor. Subsequently, two RIN officers who had qualified in South Africa joined the instructional staff. In 1944 it was decided to build a new Radar School at Manora. The site of the Signal School (HMIS *Talwar*) was found to be unsuitable for radar training. The new school (HMIS *Chamak*) was to be fitted with all radar sets in use in RIN vessels together with workshops both for overhaul and for the training of radio mechanics in radar upkeep and maintenance. The school would have the newest testing equipment, would teach fighter direction, and contain the Action Information Centre. The school was commissioned in June 1945 and all radar training was concentrated there. Further extension had been sanctioned at the end of the war to accommodate the latest radar and plotting equipment.

In early 1944 the long life of HMIS *Cornwallis* came to an end and in August 1944 HMIS *Madras* was allocated as a radar training ship and, after three months of conversion, she was made the first radar training cruise. At the end of the war she was in the process of being refitted with latest radar equipment found in sloops and with an Action Information Centre of the sloop type. HMIS *Karachi*, a Basset Trawler based in Karachi for local duties, was frequently employed on radar training and HDMLs 1261 and 1262 were also allotted for these duties. The main difficulties in radar training were the acute shortage of instructors and lack of equipment. In 1944 two petty officers (radar), RN, were lent to the RIN as instructors whilst two RINVR officers were in the United Kingdom undergoing a radar course. Considerable difficulty, however, continued to be experienced in the provision of instructors. The Admiralty was approached but it was also in a difficult position. Eventually 10 instructors were lent and arrangements were made for the secondment to the RIN of a small number of RINVR Radar officers to replace personnel lost by demobilisation.

Radio mechanics

The British considered that the training of radio mechanics probably provided more difficulties than any other branch of the service. Men with a satisfactory combination of theoretical, technical and, above all, practical training were most difficult to obtain. During 1943 some radio mechanics were sent to George Telegraph Institute Calcutta for a preliminary course, but results did not justify the scheme, and it was dropped. Radio mechanics were selected from the best of communications and radar personnel, and were trained at HMIS *Talwar*. Up to mid-1944, however, results of the training were not good.

After HMIS *Chamak* was commissioned in June 1945, in September the whole situation greatly improved. The headquarters, Bas Air Forces, South East Asia, made arrangements for a section of the number 2 School of Air

Force Technical Training, Ameerpet, to be placed at the disposal of the RIN, and for instructors and instructional equipment to be provided. Results from this school were excellent, and this high standard has been maintained since then.

After the Radio Mechanics Branch was reorganised,[24] training was as follows:

Radio Mech (W) – Shipborne Radar Basic Radio and naval W/T and W/T duties training at Ameerpet, and Radar training at Chamak

Radio Mech (S) – Shore station Basic Radio and naval W/T and Ship W/T training at Ameerpet, and duties only Shore station W/T at Mahul W/T Station.

Domestic training

New entry writers and stewards received their professional training at Castle Barracks under the supervision of an Accountant Training Officer. Cooks, after the six weeks' divisional course at the *Machalimar*, proceeded to a requisitioned house formerly part of HMIS *Khanjar* for an eight-week professional course. This was followed by four to eight weeks' practical experience of galley work. In 1944 the training of cooks, stewards and writers was transferred to HMIS *Akbar*.

Sick berth attendants

Until February 1944 the training of these ratings was carried out in Castle Barracks under the supervision of a medical officer. The most creditable work was done by the instructional staff. But training space was limited, and it was very difficult to give adequate practical training, an important feature of this course. The situation was radically improved by the opening of a new training establishment at Sewri, Bombay, attached to the RIN hospital. This ensured adequate practical work. The sick berth attendants had a highly responsible job in the service. Unlike the medical orderlies in the other services, they were frequently at sea for lengthy periods in ships out of call of a medical officer and carried the whole responsibility of treatment of sick personnel.[25]

Landing craft wing

The training of RIN Landing Craft began by the end of 1942, with HMIS *Hamla* being commissioned at Mandapam on 1 January 1943. The camp had an accommodation for 298 officers and 3,846 men with additional accommodation for another 800 men. There initial training was carried out;

EXPANSION OF THE ROYAL INDIAN NAVY

advance training was being done at HMIS *Salsette*. This latter was the RN establishment for the training of British ratings in combined operations. On completion of these courses, men were transferred to *El Hind*, *Barpeta* and *Llanstephan Castle* for flotilla training from ships and additional night wok.

In January 1944 HMIS *Khanjar* was taken over as a Landing Craft Centre and renamed HMIS *Hamla* (*Mandapam* became *Hamla II*). It replaced the training at HMIS *Salsette*. Men who passed out from HMIS *Hamla* went for combined training centres at Marvi (HMIS *Hamlawar*), and Cocanada (HMIS *Jehangir*). Base maintenance units for landing craft, motor engineers, and flotilla engineer officers were trained at the Landing Craft base at Sassoon Dock, Bombay.

Early in 1944 personnel comprising more than one assault brigade had been trained whilst a further brigade group had completed its initial training. Thereafter little training was possible as all the flotillas and units were engaged for extensive periods in the Arakan. Early in 1945, however, an officers' training flotilla and two ratings' training flotillas were formed in HMIS *Jahangir* to give ab initio training in Landing Craft with a view to making up for operational wastage. Before landing craft personnel moved to Bitter Lakes, to take over Landing Craft Training Squadron, some 100 officers were given short navigation courses at HMIS *Feroze* and about 100 ratings underwent a short A/A gunnery course at HMIS *Himalaya*.

Coastal Forces

Coastal Force training began in January 1943, after the commissioning of HMIS *Cheetah* at Trombay, the first Coastal Force Establishment. In 1944, a large new coastal force base was built at Vishakhapatnam, and was incorporated in HMIS *Circas*. This base was capable of accommodating some 100 officers and warrant officers and 1,000 ratings. During the non-operational season in 1944 and 1945, RIN Coastal Force Flotillas carried out intensive working-up programmes both at Vishakhapatam and Madras.

Firefighting and damage control

The Admiralty regarded it as essential that all naval personnel should be trained in firefighting, because many ships were lost during the war through fire. Early in 1944, a school was constructed at Bombay, and commenced to give short courses to officers and ratings. It continued in operation up to the end of the war. Damage control was first taught at HMIS *Valsura*, and at HMIS *Shivaji*, whilst a series of lectures was issued to ships and establishments. In 1944, a RIN officer was sent to the United Kingdom to undergo a course in damage control, and on his return he opened the Damage Control School in Bombay. It gave short courses to officers and ratings and continued to operate till the end of the war.

Education

Education cadre, as distinct from professional training, began in the service in 1928, and in 1935 the total strength of School Master cadre was nine. In 1938 the service of a Headmaster/Lieutenant (RN) was obtained on loan from the British Admiralty. At that time a Chief Petty Officer Schoolmaster was paid at the rate of Rs.70–5–100 per month. There were schoolmasters posted at Boys' Training Establishment, Signal School and Mechanical Training Establishment. At the initial years of the war the British decided to increase the cadre of school masters, raise their status and pay. In June 1941 all existing Petty Officer School Masters were renamed Chief Petty Officer School Masters at the same rates of pay as a Petty Officer. Later in 1941 the cadre was increased to 54 SchoolMasters, these comprising 10 Warrant School Masters and 44 Assistant Chief Petty Officer School Masters.

By February 1944 a great advance had been made and the sanction was for one Headmaster/Commander (RN) who was also Deputy Director of Education, one Headmaster/Lieutenant (RN) at Bahadur (who was under transfer to Shivaji) one Lieutenant (Sp) as Assistant Deputy Director Education, four Headmaster/Lieutenant (RINVR), 40 Commissioned Warrant School Masters and 180 Chief Petty Officer School Masters. Under the new rates of pay promulgated in November 1943, a Chief Petty Officer School Master started at Rs.150/-, rising to Rs.200/-, with many chances of promotion to warrant rank than before. New entry School Masters underwent an educational course at Castle Barracks, while promotion to warrant rank required the passing of a very stiff education examination.

Much difficultly was experienced in recruiting suitable men during the period 1941 to 1943, but the improvements in status and pay greatly eased the situation. All School Masters were required to be graduates in mathematics and although English and Urdu were the only official languages for instructional purposes, it was necessary to provide School Masters who could speak Bengali or other languages since recruits speaking only these frequently arrived. Subsequently School Masters were posted at Castle Barracks, Mechanical Training Establishment, *Talwar*, *Akbar*, *Hamla*, *Hamla II*, *Machalimar*, *Valsura*, *Bahadur* and *Dilawar* and others were attached to recruit reception camps at Jhelum, Meerut, Bangalore, etc., to the recruiting organisation itself. Simultaneously they were appointed onboard 10 ships, including all sloops.

With the strengthening of the branch, education within the service made strides, the RIN educational tests compared favourably with those of the Royal Navy, being higher in some respect, whilst the standard throughout the service had risen. In 1938, papers presented for the Higher Educational Test (HET) and for Educational Test I numbered only 12 or 14; in 1943 they were 953. An instructor branch was formed in August 1944. The service had never before had an officer equivalent of the School Master branch.

The Inter University Board (India) recommended to all universities in India that the Higher Educational Test of the RIN be recognised as the equivalent of matriculation. The recommendation of the Director of Training, that navigation and meteorology be introduced into Indian universities as a degree subject was accepted by the Inter Universities Board. The Government of Madras accepted the passing out examination of HMIS *Bahadur* as equivalent to the educational standard required for entry into the Madras Government Inferior Services.

7. Main problems

Sea training

Sea training and practical experience onboard ships were unavoidable in making a perfect naval man. Hence training ashore can never be more than a preparation for the essential training only to be acquired aboard a ship at sea. For preliminary training ashore the RIN was well equipped by 1944. But there was no modern training ship, and commenting on the training of officers the RIN Memorandum (OSD/F6) states that "All the theoretical instruction in the world will not make a man a practical seaman; it must always be a matter for contention whether it is possible to make a naval officer out of a civilian in a house at the top of Malabar Hill."[26]

The shortage of escort craft was a further handicap to practical training at sea. It meant that these craft could never be formed into escort or hunting groups for group or team training without which they could never become efficient escort units. For many duties aboard the ship this team training was of great importance. These deficiencies were eventually overcome with the formation of the Bombay Training Flotilla, consisting of five ships and three gunboats. As operational work in connection with minesweeping decreased ships of the Bangor and Bathurst class were released for flotilla training.

Every seaman had to go, in effect, for a double training. He had, first of all, to be made into a seaman, this being effected by a preliminary course ashore, plus the necessary experience afloat. Then followed his second training, when he was made into a technical rating competent to discharge one of the highly specialist duties requisite for the fighting efficiency of a ship. Torpedo men, gunners, telegraphists, radar operators, etc., were all essential, but they were seamen first and specialists afterwards. In normal times it was estimated that before a torpedo rating could be trusted to carry out his electrical maintenance duties, without constant supervision, he required five years' practical experience and in wartime this was impossible. This situation from the outbreak of the war onwards certainly could not have been peculiar to the RIN. "There was no time to train men to a high degree of efficiency through practical experience over a long period. Instead, and particularly in the earlier stages, to meet exigencies, officers had frequently to fill appointments before the completion of their courses, and for the same reason it was necessary to introduce new rates specially trained in only one small branch, e.g. the introduction of the QO Gunnery Ordnance Rate in August 1943." There was no time to turn out more highly qualified ratings. With the introduction of new training establishments and the progress of time these defects were gradually eliminated, but at first they were unavoidable.

Shortage of equipment

Particularly in the initial stages of the war one of the main difficulties was the very great shortage of training equipment. Indian industry was not then producing the hundreds of small items of naval stores it was to turn out later on, whilst the Far East was low on the priority list for items obtainable from the United Kingdom or elsewhere. Thus much training equipment had to be improvised, scrap material from the dockyard being converted into training models, etc.

In branches where such models were highly technical, improvisation was not easy. Radar equipment was very short of modern guns for the Gunnery Schools. In this case little had to be done by improvisation. That training was successfully maintained in spite of these handicaps reflects considerable credit on the staffs concerned. A point stressed by the RIN Memorandum was that much of the training equipment required was not of a type that Indian manufactures could properly be encouraged to produce. Apart from technical difficulties, the demand for a particular piece of apparatus was so limited in the Far Eastern area that no manufacturer was expected to incur the preliminary expenditure required before the item would be produced.

In the earlier periods of the war it occasionally happened that new equipment, notably new guns, was immediately installed in RIN vessels before similar equipment was available in training establishments. This seriously affected efficiency, and the lesson of first installing new equipment in training establishments was soon learnt.[27]

Instructors

Another pivotal limiting factor in training was a shortage of instructors, almost inevitable where large and rapid expansion occurs. It was aggravated by the introduction of new branches and new types of equipment, with consequent formation of new branches and new schools. Instances of this were radar, torpedo, and electrical training. The early difficult situation was overcome by hard work on the part of such instructors as existed, by the valuable assistance rendered by the RN instructors, and by utilising civilian instructors and facilities wherever possible.

Wastage

Training wastage as distinct from wastage owing to desertions, discharges on medical grounds, etc., varied considerably. In HMIS *Machlimar* at one period it touched 66.67%. At HMIS *Valsura* the figures for the first months of 1944 were:

Continuous Service Ratings	Practically nil
Special Service Ratings	About 10%
HO Ratings	About 50%

These figures were significant and emphasised the need to maintain the high educational standard for which the service had always striven. HO ratings filled an urgent requirement at the outbreak of war, but when these men were later required to undergo specialist courses aiming for a good standard of education fitting them for the handling of equipment and instruments of precision, many demonstrated their inability to do so. In the case of Landing Craft Wing training, "Wastage was abnormally high, undoubtedly due to the wholesale transfer of men from the Army units without any regard for educational qualifications."

The experience of the Royal Indian Navy throughout the war was fortunate in that battle casualty wastage was virtually non-existent. Wastage was increased at 'quite active' rate due to two causes, desertion and discharge. The desertion rate was extremely heavy, and the rate of discharge was only slightly less. The suitability of recruits for a naval life was not found altogether satisfactory, and weak ability even among men of the accepted educational standards was not all to be desired. Against an aggregate of 43,000 men recruited since the outbreak of war, the RIN lost, through either desertion or discharge (and an insignificant element of death and casualty) a total of more than 18,500. These figures do not include the boy and apprentice element of the Service nor do they provide for discharges consequent six years. See Table 4.2.

Table 4.2 Wastage of manpower during the war

Year (September to September)	Recruited	Wasted	Percentage wastage against intake
1939–1940	2,950	998	33.8%
1940–1941	3,359	1,169	34.8%
1941–1942	6,162	1,658	26.9%
1942–1943	13,017	3,981	30.6%
1943–1944	9507	5,880	62.0%
1944–1945	8,070	4,850	60.1%

Source: Monograph Approved by FOCRIN on the RIN Man-Power situation 1939–1945 (Secret) dated 10 October 1945, Page 7

The steep proportionate rise in wastage rate from 1942–1943 onwards can be attributed to (1) shortage of 'suitable' manpower and (2) inadequate and makeshift training facilities. With regard to the latter, for example, in 1942 HMIS *Dalhousie* was found insufficiently large to accommodate the number of recruits required to meet the target within the required operational period. Consequently an array of bungalows at Varsova, near Bombay, was taken over and converted into a training establishment for new entry seamen and stokers as an emergency measure. It was soon found that this establishment would be inadequate, but, in the meantime the ship was filled to overflowing in the early part of 1943. On the outbreak of the monsoon the inevitable happened: the congested condition under which recruits were having to live and work resulted in an alarming rise in the desertion rate. There is no doubt that the provision of liberal space, facilities and amenities in a training establishment amply would have repaid, not only as regards morale and discipline, but by reducing training wastage to the minimum. This wastage factor proved most uneconomical in the RIN during the war.

8. Conclusion

During the war the RIN had gone through a rapid development of the training establishments under the stress of war needs. In the early months of 1944 this growth was by no means at an end, but already the service had acquired a series of modern, highly equipped schools capable of imparting the specialised and technical training so essential for efficiency. This growth was all the more remarkable when compared with the modest establishments of 1939 and the limited personnel then available.

One of the results of the expansion and modernisation of these establishments has helped India to have a full-fledged Navy to protect her vast coastline in the post-independence era. In the post-war period, the New Construction Programme was due to be completed in stages, and ships were due to commission at intervals. This enabled a smoother intake, as it was obviously not of urgency at any one particular time to recruit certain categories of men when the ships for which they were required were not due to commission. Difficulties were encountered by the shipbuilding authorities in adhering to the planned assistance provided to the manpower situation, as continual postponement of commissioning dates gave more time to obtain and train recruits.

Notes

1 Composition and State of Training of the Royal Indian Navy, 30th September 1943, Naval Headquarters, New Delhi, p. 4.
2 Ibid.

3 Ibid., p. 5.
4 Ibid.
5 Ibid.
6 Ibid.
7 Ibid.
8 Ibid.
9 Ibid.
10 Ibid.
11 Ibid., p. 8.
12 Ibid.
13 Ibid.
14 Ibid.
15 Ibid.
16 Ibid.
17 Ibid.
18 Ibid.
19 Ibid.
20 RIN Memorandum, OSD/F6, Naval Headquarters, New Delhi.
21 Ibid.
22 Ibid.
23 Ibid.
24 Head 2, Final Review, Naval Headquarters, New Delhi, p. 5.
25 RIN Memorandum, OSD/F6, Naval Headquarters, New Delhi.
26 Ibid.
27 Ibid.

5

POST-WAR PLANS, DEMOBILISATION, DISCONTENT AND REVOLT

1. Post-war development plan

By the end of 1944, the hostilities were almost over and the British Government started to think about the future plan of the Armed Forces of India. The Directive for Reorganization Committee (India) of 1944 said that "It is considered that the time has now arrived to determine the size and composition of the defence forces which will be required in INDIA after the end of the war."[1] An appreciation of naval, land and air forces required to be maintained by India after the war was prepared by the Chiefs of Staff Committee[2] (COS) and it was accepted by the Commander-in-Chief and the Viceroy as the basis for planning. The Chiefs of Staff Committee prepared the report on the basis of the assumption that "Japan has been completely subdued; that the principal foreign powers with interest in East are Russia, America and China, that the relations to armed forces in India to the Crown remain as at present and that India will be responsible for maintaining sufficient forces to overcome a minor power and to hold out against a major power until imperial reinforcement can arrive."[3] The report emphasized on the share that had to be borne by the Commonwealth countries for the protection from any air- or sea-borne attack from an enemy country. The local defence was entrusted with the Commonwealth countries. The report said that "India, in common with other naval and air forces as are necessary to ensure the defence of her bases and the security of shipping within her coastal waters from submarine, mining and air attack to assist in the protection of trade in the ocean shipping routes."[4] Taking the matter of India's central position in the Indian Ocean in consideration, the report recommended the need for an increased naval force, especially for the larger warships for India after the war.

According to the recommendations of the COS Committee, the principal responsibility of the Indian Navy after the war was the safety of Indian and Empire shipping in the ports of India and their approaches; India had also to take her share in the protection of this shipping on the trade routes in the Indian Ocean.[5] The Royal Indian Navy was to provide facilities for combined operational training of the Army formations maintained in India and to provide a share of the escorts, assault shipping and craft required for landing.[6] This implied the maintenance in peace of a nucleus force of assault shipping and craft and the appropriate training organization, as well as personnel possessing expert knowledge in this subject. In addition, RIN in conjunction with the Air Force must be prepared to take its share in intercepting and attacking any foreign invading force which might attempt a landing on the shores of India.[7] The tasks assigned to the Army and the Air Force in India on the cessation of hostilities were the preservation of internal security in India and tranquillity among the tribes on North West Frontier, defence against possible Afghan aggression, and provision of garrisons for occupied countries. RIN units were assigned to proceed at short notice to ports in occupied countries in the case of disturbances and to patrol the river approaches to such ports.[8]

The British did not envisage any major power antagonistic to the security of India in the post-war period in the near future. But it knew that it would be unwise to assume that such a condition would remain for long and preparations would have to be made against any threat of this nature, should it develop later. It was impossible for the British Government to predict from which direction the next threat to India would arise, but foreign powers with both interest in East and large armed forces at their disposal would be Russia and the United States. The British expected that China might, with US assistance, develop into a naval power, but this would not be until a much later date.[9] It was foreseen that differences of opinion with Russia were possible and her influence in North Persia and her position in relation to India made her the most likely power to be a menace to India.[10] The Chiefs of Staff Committee report said that "Apart from a possible long term threat from China, Russia is the only major power from whom a major threat might be likely."[11] The British believed that, so long as India was connected with Britain, either by being a dominion or by a treaty guaranteeing assistance, hostilities between India and Russia could only be either the cause of or the result of the war between Britain and the USSR. And that would develop into another world conflict.[12]

For the industrial and economic prosperity of India, the security of her ports and overseas communications were most important. Therefore India would maintain adequate naval forces.[13] The coastal trade of India was not only an essential part of her peace and war economy but was also an important part of her transportation system. The requisitioning of the majority of India's coastal steamers at the beginning of the Second World War for naval purposes had greatly increased the congestion on the railways and might have been impossible had India been threatened from the outset. Therefore, the COS Committee recommended that "encouragement should be given to the coastal trade and the shipbuilding industry and the sufficient naval forces should be maintained to avoid being obliged to requisition mercantile shipping immediately on outbreak of war."[14] As in the case of a pre-war situation, the Report envisaged a joint responsibility in external security of India.[15] While India's contribution to a war of this nature would depend very largely on the defence policy of the British Empire as a whole, India must therefore be prepared at all times to defend her frontiers until Imperial reinforcements arrive.

During the war the British experienced shortages of suitable recruits for all three services and a low general standard of education, which were inadequate to contend with the technical recruitments of modern war. As a result of these setbacks, the COS Committee recommended the best use of the manpower resources of the country; new areas of recruiting that had been developed during the war would have to be maintained in peace as well as the improvement of the general standard of education and social services.[16]

The COS Report said that "In that event, her initial action might well be seizure of ports and air fields in Persian Gulf area and on Northern shores of the Arabian Sea on which to base her submarines and Air forces. The latter especially would constitute a severe menace to the sea communications to India."[17] To counter the air- and seaborne threat from Russia, RIN was to have close association with the Indian Air Force. The report recommended that:

> naval forces to counter these threats cannot be quickly improvised in time of war. The main task of Navy in peace, in common with other services, is to prepare for war but since the full strength of naval forces may be needed immediately on the outbreak of war and the long period is required both for the construction of the war ships and the training of the naval personnel, it follows that the naval forces and the air forces to co-operate with them must be maintained in peace at a high standard of preparedness.[18]

The Chief of Staff Committee Report envisaged a larger RIN in the post-war period by recommending that:

> we considered that a proportion of larger ships will also be necessary. The provision of such ships will produce a balanced naval force, form an added responsive to recruitment and increased pride in the service, besides assisting considerably in the training of the personnel which cannot be adequately carried out in small ships. In addition we attach great importance to the formation of an adequate air component for seaward reconnaissance and as a striking force and to the maintenance of modern coast defences and material for local seaward defences such as booms, mines, nets and indicator loops.[19]

The Chiefs of Staff Committee made the following main conclusion:

1. The future forces of India must be so organised that in addition to being able to carry out their immediate local roles, they are capable of operating outside the country as soon as war is imminent.
2. The forces to be maintained in peace must be of sufficient size to ensure rapid and adequate expansion in war, and they must be so composed and based to enable us to exploit the full manpower of the country at the outset.
3. Provisions must be made for the naval defence both as regards the development of the Royal Indian Navy and formation of an air component to work in co-operation with it.
4. Naval, Army and Air Forces organized and equipped on up-to-date lines must be maintained in India as the basis on which expansion can take place in the event of operations being required beyond the frontiers.
5. The Royal Indian Navy must be of sufficient size to undertake the local defence of shipping on the coastal shipping lanes and in Indian ports; to take its share in the protection of shipping on the trade routes within the Indian Ocean; to assist in the defence of India against the invasion from the sea; and maintain sufficient assault shipping and craft for training of the Army in India in peace. The aim should be to build up a balanced Naval Force to perform these tasks and which will form the nucleus on which the rapid expansion can take place in war.
6. In order to meet the manpower requirements of a major war new areas of recruitment which have been developed recently must be maintained and the general standard of education and social services must be improved.

Based on the above conclusions, the Chiefs of Staff prepared the estimates of the forces considered necessary for the post-war defence of India. Accordingly, the COS recommended the re-organisation of the RIN.[20] The COS had included the paper "The Future of Royal Indian Navy"[21] submitted by the Flag Officer Commanding, Royal Indian Navy, as an annexure to the COS Report. The British policy regarding the development of the Dominion and Indian Naval Forces was set forth in several papers of the Committee of Imperial Defence. This development can be summarized as comprising four successive stages:[22]

> **Phase I.** Local defence forces are provided and responsibility is assumed for the local defence. Preparations are made for Phase II by beginning the training of personnel for a seagoing force.
> **Phase II.** The first definite steps are taken in the creation of a force for work on the high seas as opposed to local defence. The necessary training, repair and fuelling facilities are built up in preparation of Phase III.
> **Phase III.** The local defence force and seagoing squadron under the orders of its own government takes over the control in peace of its own

home station. Interchange of ships with units of other stations is arranged and close co-operation is maintained with other squadrons.

Phase IV. Substantial contribution is made to the general scheme of Empire Naval defence by additional cruiser squadrons and capital ships.

The FOCRIN recommended to the Chiefs of Staff Committee that RIN would carry out local defence of harbours; protection of shipping on the coastal lines to take its share in the protection of shipping on the trade routes within the Indian Ocean; to assist in the defence of India against an invasion from the sea; and to maintain sufficient assault shipping and craft for the training of the Army in India in peace.[23] Towards the future plan of RIN, the COS Committee expressed the view that "the RIN has completed the second phase of development of small navies viz 'local defence plus the first step in creation of a sea-going force e.g. small escort vessel'."[24]

The Flag Officer Commanding Royal Indian Navy had brought out the future principal form of air and seaborne (submarine) attacks which the RIN has to counter and the proposals for the post-war RIN in his paper "The Future of Royal Indian Navy." The paper recommended the future RIN force which India should maintain: one cruiser squadron (three ships); one flotilla of destroyers (eight ships plus one leader); one flotilla of sloops (eight ships) employed mainly on miscellaneous duties; one flotilla of Bangor/Bathrust minesweepers (eight ships); one flotilla of motor minesweepers (eight ships); one flotilla of coastal craft (one each of eight MTBs, eight MLs and eight HDMLs); two surveying vessels, auxiliaries and trawlers; a nucleus of assault ships and craft and one repair ship.[25]

In considering a plan to develop the naval force in 1944 outlined in the said paragraph, the Chiefs of Staff had taken into consideration the difficulty of obtaining larger types of ships for the Royal Indian Navy until after the Japanese War.[26] The COS therefore suggested that development should be carried out in two stages.

Stage I Development from 1944 until the end of the Japanese War
Stage II Development after the end of the Japanese War

The COS recommended the immediate commencement of Stage I for the replacement of existing and inefficient ships, the acquisition of destroyers and in preparation for stage II in which this latter type of ship could be acquired.[27] The COS recommended that the total force was to be attained in two stages, each phase as below:[28]

Stage I Progressively for three years 1945, 1946 and 1947. This would include

1. Replacement of existing inefficient ships by frigates and modern sloops, and their disposal, 1945

2   Acquisition of eight destroyers, over two years, 1946–1947
3   Training of personnel for cruisers

Stage II Progressively for four years from the end of the war with Japan

1   Acquire in the first year one cruiser, one destroyer leader and assault ships and craft
2   Convert two frigates for survey duties and reintroduce the Hydrographic Dept.
3   Readjust the smaller types of ships
4   Institute a long-term program for replacement with up-to-date ships

Towards the development to Phase III, the COS Committee recommended that, until such time as the training had advanced sufficiently for the cruisers and destroyers to be manned and maintained entirely by RIN personnel, this should be done on the New Zealand model.[29] Thereby the ships would be lent (and replaced) by the British Government in the United Kingdom and partially manned by Royal Navy officers and ratings, the number of RIN officers and men being gradually increased.[30] The whole cost of maintenance would fall on India, and the ships would go to the United Kingdom for large refits and modernization every two or three years.[31] Further the Committee recommended the induction of some 1,500 regular officers and 15,000 ratings at the end of the war with Japan, continuation of HMI dockyard at Bombay and creation of base establishments and repair facilities on both the West and East coasts.[32]

2. Demobilisation

By mid-1945 the hostilities in Europe were almost over. The end of hostilities in Europe and the trend of the war against Japan had made post-war planning (for the post-war RIN), demobilisation and resettlement questions matters of urgent import.[33] Demobilisation was commenced immediately on officers' records, and two officers of the appointments directorate were wholly employed in allotting priority group numbers to all officers of the Royal Indian Navy. A signal was issued warning personnel not to be too optimistic regarding release from the service, as commitments would probably be heavier for the Navy than for the other two services.[34] A demobilisation and resettlement section was added to the department of the Chief of Personnel in early 1945 and it was responsible for the planning and operation of demobilisation and resettlement arrangements for officers and men.[35] Close liaison was to be maintained with the appropriate military and air force directorates and the department of labour.

Release Regulations of RIN had been drafted mutatis mutandis on the lines of Release Regulations of the Indian Army in 1945.[36] The Commander-in-Chief in India formed an Inter-Services Demobilisation Planning Staff (ISDPS)

to co-ordinate all demobilisation plans of the three services. The Flag Officer Commanding, Royal Indian Navy, was represented on this staff. A demobilisation progress report was submitted to the ISDPS on a monthly basis. Post-consultation with the departments of Naval Headquarters, it was decided that, the day for compiling priority roll for ratings would be 16 July 1945, and a general warning signal was issued, stating that all returns for RIN ratings were to be submitted by 10 August 1945.[37] The officers were permitted to volunteer to continue serving for one or two years after release of their group. On receipt of applications from officers, the rolls were amended accordingly, and officers notified of the priority group number allotted to them.[38]

In September 1945, HMIS *Hamla II* was paid off and re-commissioned as HMIS *Kakauri*, the demobilisation centre for ratings.[39] In October 1945, resettlement work was re-transferred to the welfare section and the demobilisation section started to deal only with demobilisation matters. Arrangements were made to extend some release benefits to Hostilities Only ratings and an RIN Instruction was issued to this effect.[40]

In accordance with the Commander-in-Chief India's directives dated 19 March 1945, the following upper and lower limits of demobilisation for the Royal Indian Navy were set out:

(a) *Upper limit (stage I)*
This represents the forces required immediately after the collapse of organised resistance by Japan and was governed by the Indian forces required by the British Government. The British Government required all ships of anti-aircraft assault (A.A) Sloop, modern Ocean Escort and Minesweeping Classes and Naval Assault Force units for employment in the East Indies and Pacific Stations as guard ships, mine clearance forces, port parties and to support small operations to clear up isolated areas.[41] The British Government wanted the RIN to have the following upper limit strength.

   (i) Seagoing: 7 Sloops, 9 Frigates, 3 Corvettes, 16 Minesweepers, 20 Bassat Trawlers and 10 Motor Minesweepers
   (ii) Coastal Forces: 6 Flotillas HDMLs (27 boats), 3 Flotillas MLs (27 boats) and 1 Coastal Force Depot Ship
   (iii) Seagoing Training Ship (to maintain flow into above seagoing forces): 6 No 1 Boys' Training, 2 Special Service Training, 1 Gunnery Firing Ship, 1 Radar Training Ship, 1 A/S Training Ship and 1 ML for Torpedo Running
   (iv) Landing Craft Wing: 2 Landing Ship Infantry (Large) (LSI (L)) with 40 Landing Craft Assault (LCA), i.e. 20 each, 1 Landing Ship Infantry (Large) (LSI (L)) with 10 LCA, 1 Landing Craft Tank (LCT) Squadron (36 LCT, 1 LCT (E) and 3 Landing Craft Administration (LCQ)). At CTC: 48 LCA, 30 Landing Craft Mechanised (LCM), 8 Landing Craft Personnel (LCP) and 6 LCA (HR). At Karachi: 4 LCA, 4 LCP and 4 Landing Craft Mechanised (LCM)

(v) Shore Establishments: Shore establishments sufficient to administer, supply, train and operate the above forces during the period
(vi) Strength: 2300 Officers & Warrant Officers and 23000 Ratings

(b) *Lower limit (stage III)*

The Lower Limit which represented the minimum force considered by the British Government for the military necessary for India's local defence and to enable her to hold out, in the event of a major war, until reinforcements could arrive from other parts of the Commonwealth.[42] The British Government envisaged cruisers for the RIN in the post-war period as part of the Lower Limit. There were strong reasons for the introduction of Cruisers into the post-war navy. Cruisers of the smaller classes were ideally suited to Indian requirements both for operational and training purposes. The main role of the RIN in the post-war era was envisaged as "the defence of India's coasts and sea borne trade."[43] It was expected that "cruisers form the corner stone of this edifice as they possess the armament and sea keeping qualities to protect long haul naval convoys whose main enemy in the early stages of any war will be enemy air forces."[44]

		In commission	In reserve
(i)	**Seagoing**		
	Cruisers	3	
	Modern Sloops	8	
	Frigates	4	4
	Minesweepers	8	8
	Surveying Vessels	2	
	Trawlers	5	6
	Gunnery Training ship	1	
	Hulks for Reserve Training	2	
	Motor Minesweepers	4	4
(ii)	**Coastal Forces**		
	HDML	8	
(iii)	**Landing Crafts**		
	1 Landing Ship Dock (LSD)		24 Landing Craft Assault (LCA)
	1 Landing Ship Tank (LST)		12 Landing Craft Vehicle Personnel (LCVP)
	3 Landing Craft Tank (LCT)		12 Landing Craft Mechanised (LCM)
	1 Landing Craft Headquarters (LCH)		3 Landing Craft Support (LCS)
	2 Landing Craft Infantry (Large) (LCI(L))		1 Landing Craft Navigation (LCN)
			1 Landing Craft Control (LCC)
	2 Landing Craft Administration (LCQ)		1 Landing Craft Emergency (LCE)
			9 Landing Craft Personnel (LCP)

(Continued)

DEMOBILISATION, DISCONTENT AND REVOLT

(*Continued*)

	In commission	*In reserve*
(iv)	**Shore Establishment** Naval Headquarters (India) and requisite administrative and training establishments to maintain the above said force level	
(v)	Strength: 1,000 officers and Warrant Officers and 10,000 ratings	

Intermediate demobilisation was considered as Stage III of the demobilisation. It was difficult for the British Admiralty to forecast the intermediate stage, because the RIN ships were under the operational control of the British Admiralty and were working in mixed forces with Royal Navy and Dominion ships.[45] Thus the demobilisation stages can be summarised as follows:[46]

	Officers & WO	*Ratings*
Stage I	2,300	23,000
Stage II	1,600	16,000
Stage III	1,000	10,000

Demobilisation planning commenced in April 1945 in three stages in common with the other two services. The three stages were as follows:[47]

Stage I – Demobilisation of men and material possible after the end of the war with Japan, i.e. reduction to the "upper limit."

Stage II – The intermediate stage, during which a proportion of the forces required after the cessation of hostilities with Japan could be released.

Stage III – When the sanctioned strength of the RIN, i.e., the "lower limit," would be reached.

Stage I was again sub-divided into two stages. This was necessary as the Admiralty had stated that the majority of the RIN seagoing fleet would be required on a wartime basis for approximately nine months after the end of hostilities with Japan.[48] A uniform release system was adopted on the basis of combination of age and length of service, with the special provision that men of 50 years of age and over would be treated as a priority class.[49] The general scheme of release by age and length of war service was known as Class A release. Class B releases were the men released for work of national importance, irrespective of age and service group. Class C release was on compassionate grounds.[50]

Release (demobilisation) of officers and ratings commenced on 1 September 1945, and continued according to the plan. By end of 1945, the plan was revised to attain the "lower limit" cadre shown in Table 5.1.

The programme of release of ratings accelerated considerably. In order to attain the lower limit cadre of approximately 11,000 ratings by June 1946,

Table 5.1 Demobilisation – officers

Branch	December	January	February	March
Executive	21–28	29–33	34–49	50–70
Special	20–29	30–38	39–46	47–65
Supply	10–20	21–25	26–27	28–29
Engineer (Steam)	11–15	16–20	21–24	25–27
Engineer (Motor)	11–15	16–25	26–34	35–65
Electrical	25–29	30–36	37–44	45–47

Source: Demobilisation and Resettlement Planning, Upper & Lower Limits of Royal Indian Navy, COS (45) 685 (Revised), (1945), History Division, Ministry of Division, New Delhi

the upper limit strength was cancelled by the end of 1945.[51] The plan of elimination was divided into four phases and the Phase A was completed in the second half of 1945, as follows:[52]

Ex-Army personnel in the landing craft wing	1,000
Hostilities Only ratings (expiration of agreement)	2,026
Pensioners, supernumeraries, reservists	152
Recruits under training in HMIS Akbar	1,090
Recruits under training in other establishments	308
Trained men (partially by groups)	1,250
Civilians	78
Total	**5,904**

Release by priority groups up till December 1945 includes those in phase A, listed in Table 5.2:

Table 5.2 Demobilisation – Phase 'A'

Branch	Groups
Artificers	1–20
Topasses	1–30
Seamen	1–33
Supply and Secretariat	1–35
Stokers	1–30
Stewards	1–30
Cooks (O) and (S)	1–25
Regulating	1–25
Communications	1–30
Sick Berth Attendants (S.B.As)	1–40

Source: Demobilisation and Resettlement Planning, Upper & Lower Limits of Royal Indian Navy, COS (45) 685 (Revised), (1945), History Division, Ministry of Division, New Delhi

Table 5.3 Planned strength of RIN warships

Class	Strength in Sept. 1945	Planned Strength	
		Max	Min
Cruisers	Nil	3	3
Sloops	8	8	6
Frigates	9	8	8
Corvettes	4	Nil	Nil

Source: File Minutes, Royal Indian Navy-Demobilisation Planning: Recommendations for regular and reserve forces and requirements in immediate post-war period Admiralty observation, Requirement of R.N officers for secondment to R.I.N, (1945), The National Archives, Kew Gardens, United Kingdom, ADM 1/18488

As part of demobilisation the target dates for closing down the naval stores organisation at Karachi was planned for the end of January 1946 and at Calcutta and Madras by the end of February 1946. The naval stores organisation at Cochin was taken over by the Royal Navy in 1945. By the end of 1945, out of 37 auxiliary vessels which had been requisitioned during the war, 15 were returned to their owners, 9 were taken over by other Services, 5 continued in commission and 8 were in the process of being paid off.[53]

The British Admiralty wanted all Dominion Navies to follow a policy similar to the Royal Navy by retaining a proportion of their Fleet in reserve in peacetime in order that the Dominion contribution on the outbreak of war might be as large as possible.[54] As far as the British Commonwealth defence policy was concerned, it is clear that an increasing share was to be borne by the Dominions. In 1945, the request of the Government of India for cruisers was under consideration of the British Admiralty and the numbers in Table 5.3 were proposed as the planned strength of the RIN:[55]

3. Resettlement

The problem of the post-war resettlement of its 'temporary personnel' was always a concern for the RIN. Before the end of hostilities, in July 1944 a personal letter was sent to every Reserve officer in the RIN, enquiring about his future plans and ambitions, and asking him whether he would require assistance after demobilisation in obtaining employment, or alternatively, further education or training to fit him for employment.[56] Ninety percent of the officers addressed replied to these enquiries with a promptitude which indicated the importance they attached to the problem of their futures. In August 1944, the second letter, in the form of a comprehensive questionnaire, was sent for obtaining all the necessary facts about each individual officer at Naval Headquarters.[57] The RIN Report of 1945 says that "steps were taken at a time when it was anticipated that the resettlement of demobilised personnel would become the responsibility of the individual Services concerned, and the RIN idea at that time was that a kind of Naval labour exchange would be set up, either at Naval Headquarters or in Bombay, as soon as the war was over."[58] The policy on resettlement was changed in 1945, and since the services were precluded from setting up independent machinery for the resettlement of their own personnel, resettlement became the joint responsibility of the Resettlement Directorate in Simla and the Labour Department in the Government of India.[59]

Towards the resettlement of naval personnel, pre-release training was arranged for all personnel awaiting demobilisation. This included classes designed to improve general education, further technical training for those already doing technical work, lectures in health and hygiene, instruction in civics, and, to a limited degree, participation in some of the training courses arranged for their own personnel by the Army.[60] The war information rooms of all shore establishments were converted into resettlement information rooms, and a very large volume of literature, posters, etc., was supplied for display there. Similar literature was sent to all ships afloat. The RIN had a close liaison with Resettlement Directorate and Labour Department. Details of vacancies for appointments in Government and other services were promptly notified to all ships and establishments, and a number of RIN applicants were successful in obtaining posts.[61] In the post-war period many Reserve officers got the opportunity to obtain Government jobs. Mrs. Ray states that "My dad, Lt Commander Ram Mohan Ray served the Royal Indian Navy between 1941 and 1946 and at the end of the war he was placed at the Ministry of Labour."[62]

The Government's Rehabilitation Scheme was made applicable to the RIN. Under this scheme all disabled personnel were retained in the Service while being prepared for civil life.[63] This preparation was carried out in three stages; hospital treatment, post-hospital rehabilitation and training for employment. Labour exchanges were opened, appointments were offered, and a rehabilitation scheme started with the objective to ensure that every disabled or diseased rating, provided that he was capable of cure or improvement, would be physically rehabilitated, and if necessary, taught a trade at which he could earn his living, before he was finally released from the Service.

However, most of the RIN personnel were unaware of the resettlement programmes. The RIN Report of 1945 says that "unfortunately there is still a strong tendency, amongst officers and ratings alike, to believe that a man has only to sit back and wait for Government to find him a job. Steps are being taken to inculcate into all ranks and ratings the correct outlook on resettlement, which is that every man is expected to do everything possible himself to resettle himself, and that the function of the government is to advise and to assist."[64]

In one type of resettlement the RIN had suffered a severe disappointment. It was hoped that many released ratings would be given official preference when seeking employment in India's Mercantile Marine. When the matter was mooted, however, the seamen's unions refused unconditionally to agree; the reason given was that the number of jobs available was not sufficient even for the non-service members of the unions.[65] As a general strike of all merchant seamen was threatened in the event of the project being pressed, it had to be abandoned.[66] The majority of the RIN ratings wanted to continue in the Navy because of the non-availability of highly paid jobs they were looking for. The RIN Enquiry Report says that "the resettlement arrangements which looked well on paper did not provide the kind of jobs which ratings had expected and considered to be their due."[67] This discontent of ratings later became one of the main causes of the RIN Revolt of 1946.

4. RIN Revolt

Mutiny or Revolt in armed forces is not a new phenomenon. In military legal terms, any grievance represented by more than one person is considered as a mutiny against the system; this resulted in calling many revolts/strikes in armed forces mutinies. This law was created and implemented by the imperial government in the colonies. Interestingly most of the armed forces around the world have been following the same rule. Because of the above stated colonial law, most of the protests, agitations, strikes, uprisings and revolts against the colonial rule were termed as mutinies. And this was always supported by the British historians. The 1857 Revolt, "the first war of independence" is the finest example of the so-called Sepoy mutiny.

The *Oxford Encyclopaedia of Maritime History* defines mutiny as follows: "Mutiny is insubordination of two or more persons against the lawful authority onboard: the captain or the master. It is collective action by the crew members to achieve their own goals against the will of those in command. Before the twentieth century authorities ashore considered mutiny, and even the preparations for an unexecuted or discovered mutiny, as a capital crime."[68] In 1969 Dutch sociologist D. J. Lammers characterised the mutinies as protest movements that, according to their aims, could be divided into three categories: (1) promotion of interests, (2) seizure of power and (3) secession.[69]

> In categories 2 and 3, the mutineers want to seize the ship's command to pursue their own goals. Mutinies of the first category strive for better labour conditions. In the twentieth century this sort of mutiny would be called a strike, but in the past this distinction was not made. The seizure of power and secession are usually prepared by a small group of conspirators, who seek wide support only after the start of their coup. They rely on surprise action by violence according to a carefully planned strategy. Within a relatively short time, either the goals of their actions are realized or the armed resistance of superiors and loyalists crushes the mutiny.[70]

DEMOBILISATION, DISCONTENT AND REVOLT

There were nine so-called mutinies in the Royal Indian Navy between March 1942 and April 1945.[71] According to the RIN Enquiry Commission Report, "the ostensible reasons of the mutinies were related to grievances regarding the pay scale, quantity of rations, bad cooking, inadequate arrangement of lodging, refusal of men to carry out certain duties like cleaning ship, cleaning the deck, sentry duties, messenger duties, etc." These 'mutinies' happened due to the discontent among the RIN ratings; however these so-called mutinies were not politically motivated.[72] Most of these mutinies were suppressed by the British officials, and the details were never revealed to the world. A Revolt took place in the Indian Army, almost at the same time as the RIN Revolt, in February 1946. Two of the Indian Pioneer units of the Eastern Army Command at Calcutta refused to obey orders, and the matter was resolved quickly and in secrecy. The 'mutiny' was suppressed by the British and Gurkha troops at night, and the mutineers were soon after sentenced without leaking the news to the political parties and press.[73] Naturally, the previous revolts had an impact on the RIN Revolt of 1946. The RIN enquiry said that, "Not only, in as much as they bequeathed a state of discontent and indiscipline contributed in no small degree to the present mutiny, but they also indicate that there was something seriously wrong with the condition in the service and that the warning to the Naval authorities, given in the form of successive mutinies, were not sufficiently heeded."[74] During this period, there were 'mutinies' in Royal Air Force and the Royal Indian Air Force. See Figure 5.1.

Figure 5.1 Ratings standing in the queue for food
Source: Naval History Division, Indian Navy, New Delhi

Investigations which followed some of the 'mutinies' have disclosed that there were faults in the administration.[75] The Naval Revolt of 1946 played a significant role in the freedom struggle of India, and the British Raj realized the fact that their men in armed forces were no more trustworthy to continue their colonial regime in India.[76] Pandit Nehru said that "The RIN strike has altogether opened a new chapter in the history of our armed forces."[77] This study seeks to analyse the RIN Revolt of 1946, which the British archival records dismiss as mutiny.

Events prior to the Revolt

At the end of Second World War, about 20,000 men of the RIN were located in the ships and establishments in Bombay. HMIS *Talwar* was the communication ratings training school, accommodating the communication branch ratings and 'draft reserves' many of whom were awaiting demobilisation.[78] These ratings had lost all interest in the service, and they were not concerned with the future of the RIN.[79] The RCO and CCO division consisted of 200 communication ratings with only one divisional officer. He was a warrant officer who was also in charge of the RCO. Besides this, there were about 700 other ratings in these establishments under training and there was considerable overcrowding. The number of divisional officers was far too small to look after the welfare and discipline of the ratings living there.[80]

On 30 November 1945 anti-British slogans, like 'Quit India', 'Kill the white dogs', etc. were written in places in HMIS *Talwar* in anticipation of the 'Navy Day' celebrations.[81] The RIN official made efforts to trace the personnel who were responsible for this act of indiscipline, but all went in vain. The report by the Deputy Director of Morale shows the interest of both Indian officers and ratings in politics.[82] R. K. Singh (Rank not known), who was inclined towards the Gandhian method of open defiance of the British Raj, sent his resignation letter. R. K. Singh was charge sheeted for sending his resignation. When he was summoned before the commanding officer, he threw the naval cap and kicked it, signifying his utter contempt for the Crown and the Service.[83] The news of the act of Singh spread like a fire in the barracks. Anti-British slogans again appeared in HMIS Talwar on the night of 1–2 February 1946, in anticipation of the visit of the FOCRIN.[84] On 2 February 1946, B. C. Dutt, a leading telegraphist (naval rating), was placed under close arrest for writing these slogans.[85] Even after the arrest of B. C. Dutt, the slogan writing continued. 'Quit India' was written on the car of Commander King, the Commanding Officer of HMIS *Talwar*, and his tyres were deflated on the 6 and 7 February 1946.[86]

RIN Revolt

On the morning of 6 February 1946, when Commander King entered one of the barracks where some of the communication ratings not on duty were either smoking or lying on cots and did not take any notice the arrival of the Commanding Officer. As soon as they noticed his arrival, they paid due attention to him.[87] Commander King as soon as he entered the barracks addressed these ratings as 'Sons of bitches', 'Junglies' and 'Coolies'.[88] As a protest against Cdr King's language, 14 ratings made their individual complaints to Lt Commander Shaw, who was the Executive Officer (Second-in-Command). Shaw forwarded the complaints to Cdr King and appraised him of the gravity of the situation. However Cdr King deferred the matter for CO's normal day for hearing requests, which was once in a week.[89] King heard the complaints on 16 February 1946 and told the ratings that they were making false complaints against the Commanding Officer. He gave them 24 hours to rethink. On the same day B. C. Dutt was brought before the CO, who informed him about the RIN authorities' decision to demote him and discharge him from the Naval Service.[90]

On 18 February 1946, the ratings found the breakfast served was not properly cooked and inadequate. B. C. Dutt says that "Suddenly a murmur went up. No one was sure as to who started it. Soon there was an uproar from all corners."[91] As a protest the ratings walked out of the mess hall. "Someone shouted the slogan in one of the mess halls: No Food, No Work."[92] The RIN Revolt began on 18 February 1946 in HMIS *Talwar* and it spread to almost all RIN ships and establishments. Only a few remained unaffected. The ratings formed a Naval Central Strike Committee (NCSC); MS Khan and Madan Singh were elected as the president and vice-president respectively. On 19 February 1946, the Flag Officer Bombay arrived at Talwar, and a meeting was held with the RIN officials and 14 representatives of the Naval Central Strike Committee. The Naval Central Strike Committee representatives put forwarded the following demands:[93]

1. No victimisation of strikers
2. Release of R. K. Singh, Telegraphist, from Arthur Road Prison immediately
3. Speedy immobilisation according to age and service group with reasonable peacetime employment
4. Immediate disciplinary action against Commander King for inhuman behaviour and vulgar language
5. Best class of Indian food
6. RN scales of pay, family allowance, travelling facilities and use of NAAFI stores
7. No kit to be taken back at the time of release
8. Immediate grant of more gratuity and treasury pay to men on release
9. Good behaviour of officers towards lower deck personnel
10. Quick regular promotion of lower deck personnel to officers. Officers from abroad to be stopped.
11. A new commanding officer of the signal school to be appointed

DEMOBILISATION, DISCONTENT AND REVOLT

Naval Central Strike Committee representatives asked that all demands be decided by the authorities concerned by 1700 hours of the same day through a national leader who would be nominated. They also demanded the following protests were also put forward to be registered with the Government of India:[94]

1. Immediate release of political leaders as well as INA including Captain Rashid
2. Immediate and impartial enquiry into the firing on the public all over India
3. Immediate withdrawal of Indian troops from Indonesia and Middle East

The immediate cause of the 'mutiny' in other ships and establishments were sympathy with *Talwar*, inflammatory articles in the press and incitement by ratings from other establishments. One common feature of the mutiny was that the Union Jack was hauled down and Congress and Muslim League flags were hoisted.[95] A meeting was held in Azad Maidan by the 'mutineers', and they marched in processions shouting slogans some of which were anti-British and included slogans like "Release INA and political prisoners," "Withdraw Indian army from Indonesia," etc.[96] The RIN Enquiry Commission Report says that "the ratings paraded the streets and did not wear their uniform caps. Some of them asked people to remove English caps which they were wearing; although their behaviour in general was rowdyish, the mutiny was still non-violent."[97] The news of the strike in Bombay was broadcast on the All India Radio and was also published in all the leading newspapers. This news reached places like Calcutta, Karachi, Vizagapatnam and Madras, where other units of the RIN were located. The report, on the incidents which took place and the Strike of the naval ratings in HMIS *Talwar*, in newspapers spread like fire and considerable sympathy was shown towards the demands of the ratings of the RIN.[98] In those units also, whispers of a sympathetic strike started on the 19th.[99] On that day in 1946, around 2,000 ratings from various establishments and ships came down on the breakwater about 0930 hours, inciting the ship's companies to carry out "a sit down strike."[100]

One common feature of the 'mutiny' was that the Union Jack was hauled down and the ratings hoisted the Congress and Muslim League flags tied together onboard ships. The flags signified the unity and demarginalisation of communal issues among the mutineers. A general strike in support of the revolt took place in Bombay on 22 February, and in Karachi on both 22 and 23 February 1946. The most significant factor of this revolt, with hindsight, came to be that Hindus and Muslims united to resist the British, even at a time that saw the peak of the movement for Pakistan.

DEMOBILISATION, DISCONTENT AND REVOLT

The revolt came to receive widespread support from the public even for the short period that it lasted, not only in Bombay, but also in Karachi, Calcutta, Ahmadabad, Madras, Trichinopoly, Madurai, Kanpur and several places in Assam. The happenings in the city of Bombay were condemned by Sardar Patel[101] as acts of indiscipline and defiance of the authority. However, on the 22 February 1946 after the riots and troubles in the city, Sardar Patel sent the following message to the mutineers: "The strikers should lay down all arms and should go through the formality of surrender, and the congress would do its level best to see that there is no victimisation and the legitimate demands of Naval ratings are met as soon as possible."[102] This advice was eventually accepted. The revolt was called off following a meeting between the President of the Naval Central Strike Committee, M. S. Khan and Sardar Patel of the Congress. Patel issued a statement calling on the strikers to end their action, which was later echoed by a statement issued in Calcutta by Mohammed Ali Jinnah on behalf of the Muslim League. The agitations, mass strikes, demonstrations and consequently support for the revolt continued several days even after the revolt had been called off.

It is notable that the revolt more or less disappeared from the nationalist narratives at the end of the empire. This is in contrast to the trials of the officers of the Indian National Army, which were under way at the same time. In fact, the INA trials have often been incorporated into the narrative of the final push for independence. The RIN revolt, by contrast, usually vanished from sight. Subrata Banerjee says that "The RIN Revolt as a spontaneous nationalist uprising that was one of the few episodes at the time that had the potential to prevent the partition of India, and one that was essentially betrayed by the leaders of the nationalist movement."[103] However, criticising the view that the revolt posed a fundamental threat to the British.

> In fact, the upsurges demonstrated that, despite considerable erosion of the morale of the bureaucracy and the steadfastness of the armed forces at the time, the British wherewithal to repress was intact.... It was one thing for the British Government to question its own stand of holding the INA trails when faced with opposition from the army and the people; it was quite another matter when they face challenges to their authority. Challenges to law and order and peace, the British were clear, had to be repressed.[104]

Causes of the Revolt

The key to understanding the morphology of the Naval Mutinies lies in the British Naval policy of expansion, consolidation and radical contraction followed by demobilization.[105] The general tendency of RIN post–World War II was towards consolidation and contraction. The end of hostilities in Europe and the trend of the war against Japan made post-war planning, demobilization and resettlement questions matters of urgent importance. In 1943, when the Demobilization Committee was set up, it appeared probable that the Japanese War would last for a long time after the German war came to an end. It was known that at the end of the German war it would be possible to release a moderate portion of the forces, but that the remainder would probably have to serve until the end of the Japanese War.[106] Large numbers of personnel were released in a phased manner and arrangements were made, as far as possible, for re-settlement of a number of young officers and men, who had come forward to serve during the war, in civil placements in government and elsewhere.[107]

The wartime strength of the ratings (sailors) reached the maximum figure of 27,651 towards the middle of 1945. The RIN had expanded about 20 times during the period of war. Owing to sudden end of the war against Japan in August 1945, the process of demobilization was therefore bound to start. It was at this stage that those who were about to be demobilized would expect fulfilment of the promise made at the time of recruitment and contained in the resettlement schemes and many advertisements of post-war jobs[108]. The booklets entitled "The Navy and Its Job"[109] and "Indian Navy"[110] created an expectation of having a post-retirement career option on completion of the war. The letters of ratings and posters pasted at many ships and establishments shows the discontent, dissatisfaction and resentment of ratings against the maltreatment and discrimination in the Navy.[111] The frustration and disillusionment caused by the failure of the resettlement schemes in practice was another potent cause of discontent which contributed towards the RIN Revolt.[112]

The immediate issue for the Revolt was service conditions and food, but there were more fundamental matters, such as racist behaviour by Royal Navy personnel towards Indian sailors and disciplinary measures being taken against anyone demonstrating pro-nationalist sympathies. There is considerable evidence to establish that the RIN ratings were often subjected to harsh and at times even inhuman treatment by European officers. Treatment of British sailors was indulgent. At times their acts of indiscipline were ignored while no indulgence was shown to the Indian ratings. Racial discrimination operated not only between British officers and Indian ratings but also between British officers and Indian officers in the Service.

At the end of the war the world was in a state of unrest both political and economic. The transition from a wartime to a peacetime economy was inevitably attended by strained and unsettled relations between the employers and the employees, owing to troubles over retrenchment, wages and costs and a sense of general disillusionment with the fruits of victory. The political situation was equally tense, particularly in India, where the effect of demand for freedom and the withdrawal of British control was reinforced by an insistent demand from all parties for withdrawal of

Indian troops from Indonesia and later by general sympathy with the INA and agitation for their release. Another cause for the revolt was the war brought to RIN ratings many opportunities for visiting foreign countries and their experience particularly in regard to pay and amenities available in the Royal Navy and the other navies of the Empire had an unsettling effect on their minds.

The RIN Enquiry Commission concluded the origins and causes of the RIN Revolt broke out on 18 February 1946 as a result of the discontent due to grievances, the low state of morale, bad management, the unsuitability of a number of the ratings and politics.[113] These causes were aggravated by the lower standard of morale and discipline and brought to a head by the 'Commander King incident', culminating with the food served on the evening of 17 February 1946 and the morning of 18 February 1946.[114] The foul language of Cdr King, the CO of HMIS *Talwar* on the morning of 6 February 1946 and the unresolved grievances of ratings on the same issue led to sudden fire on 18 February 1946. Cdr King stated before the RIN Enquiry Commission that what he said was "normal Naval Manners."[115] The use of foul language was nothing new to the ratings; they had been listening to foul language from the day they joined the RIN. B. C. Dutt says from his experience on the use of foul language in the RIN in his book. On the very first day in the RIN, an Indian Petty Officer shouted at the newly inducted ratings, "Shut up, you bastards. Navy does not need your bloody opinions; Navy damn well expect you to obey the bloody orders; I am here to knock some discipline into your sickly, uneducated heads. Let that son of a bitch who has any suggestion, speak up."[116] During training, the use of foul language was common. In another incident, the instructor addressed the fresh ratings at a parade ground in the following words, "You bunch of sickly monkeys, you bloody cross between pigs and goats, bloody Sissies, I will have the whole bloody lot raped and that will teach you how to fall in line; right turn; let your arse look towards the sea. Double march."[117] In another occasion the instructor shouted at Dutt: "you bastards, you miserable cross between a pig and a goat, you have been sleeping all these years with your mothers and sisters; I am going to make such men out of you"[118] Biswanath Bose, who was a member of the RIN Strike Committee, says that:

> the instructors, mostly Indians, hailing from Punjab, Sind and Chittagong as also a few Britishers from Royal Navy, were very rough and extremely harsh towards the trainees. They always reported against each trainee to their superior officers, responsible for each Division who turn reported the same to the Commanding Officer of the establishment. . . . The food offered to the trainees was not edible. Those who complained of bad food were not in good books of the instructors and officers.[119]

This clearly shows that the foul language used by Cdr King did not trigger the Revolt. All frustrations, which I have talked about above, led the ratings to protest against the existing system of governance. The main causes which led to the RIN Revolt are described in the succeeding paragraphs:

Racial discrimination. Racial discrimination is based on the theory of superiority and inferiority complexes between the conqueror and the conquered.[120] "The injustice and ill treatment in the RIN were believed by the ratings to be the outward manifestation of racial arrogance on the part of the European personnel in the services. The ratings and even many of the Indian officers genuinely felt that colour bar in all its grim nakedness was present and influenced the conduct of Europeans towards Indians."[121] The RIN Enquiry Report said that "He (RIN Rating) cannot be put up being discriminated against, in his own country by European officers who draw their salaries from the revenue derived mainly from the contributions of his own people."[122] It further says that "The racial discrimination operated not only between the British officers and the Indian ratings but between the British and Indian officers also. Sometimes the Indian officers also behaved with the Indian ratings on the same lines."[123] Discrimination was more prevalent in the Indian Army than the RIN.[124] The British personnel in the Army had preferential treatment, better accommodations and better amenities. The British Servicemen were not required to salute Viceroy's Commissioned Officers.[125] The discrimination was crude, and was calculated to make the Indians feel inferior to the British.[126] B. C. Dutt says that "The British sailors received better pay and enjoyed more amenities but that did not trouble us much as we seldom served together onboard the same ship or establishment. It was when we had to work with the Army personnel that we felt humiliated at every turn."[127] Maulana Abdul Kalam Azad said that "If they (RIN Ratings) suffered from racial discrimination, this was not an evil peculiar to them but one common to all sections of the Army and the Naval force. They were justified in protesting against the discrimination."[128]

Exposure to other countries and navies. The ratings had the opportunities to visit the foreign countries, especially the United Kingdom and Australia, and to meet the men of other navies. "While aboard they saw the standard of living which was far higher than that to which they were accustomed in their own country."[129] They saw the world outside India during the war.[130] The RIN Mutiny Enquiry Report says that "while employed at times on the same task as the Royal Navy and other navies of the empire they found that they were being paid less and some considered that their food, accommodation and amenities were inferior."[131] This new awareness led to them to feel that equal work deserved equal treatment. More than that they found that the canteen facilities in the

Royal Navy and other navies were far superior. At the end of hostilities they realised that most of them had reached the end of their career in the RIN. B. C. Dutt says that "Having travelled and also having learnt what the war was all about, most of them had become more sensitive to the condition of their own country."[132]

Expansion and misleading recruitment advertisements. On the outbreak of war, 31 auxiliary vessels were taken up and fitted out as minesweepers of patrol vessels. By 3 December 1939, the number of both officers and ratings had been almost exactly doubled.[133] During the recruitment rallies the recruitment officers gave a rosy picture about naval life and false post-war resettlement, a dissatisfaction which led to many desertions and also became one of the causes behind the RIN Revolt.[134] Several ratings complained that false hopes and assurances regarding pay, promotion, prospects of a career in the Navy and of post-war jobs besides good food, accommodation and treatment were held out to them by the recruiting authorities at the time of enrolment.[135] The high caste Hindu ratings or those recruited for skilled work complained that they were misled by not being informed that they would be required to perform certain disagreeable duties such as cleaning the ship and lavatories or acting as mess messengers.[136] Many recruits were told glowing tales of life in the Navy, and Service life was consequently a shock.[137] The posters, pamphlets and booklets circulated to attract the recruits were misleading and tended to represent to the recruits that the Navy offered a permanent career, a happy life, good and ample food and clothing, liberal pay plus many allowances, quick promotion and sympathetic and helpful officers.[138] The booklets entitled "The Navy and Its Job" and "Indian Navy" created the following misunderstanding by implication or direct statement:[139]

1. RIN is moulded on the lines of Royal Navy. The ratings therefore felt justified in their demand for pay and amenities approximating to that of Royal Navy.
2. Incorrect idea of the duties of various branches in that 'cleaning ship' was omitted from the list enumerating such duties.
3. Ambiguous wording of certain conditions of Service conveyed an impression that though enrolment was for 5 or 10 years, the recruit could stay on with good prospects of promotion and qualify for a pension.
4. Overstatement of prospects of advancement to higher rates and even promotion to Warrant Rank in the Communication Branch.
5. The posters and pictorial pamphlets painted an even more misleading picture. The net result was that the ratings become disappointed and aggrieved when the promised promotions did not come their way.

The RIN recruiting officers had stated before the RIN Enquiry Commission that if true conditions of service were known, no recruits would have joined the technical branches of Royal Indian Navy, as prospects of pay and promotion were much better in the Army and the Royal Indian Air Force.[140] Vice Admiral Godfrey, FOCRIN, in his report on the cause of the 'mutiny' said that "the average rating firmly believed that he was going to be found a post-war job by the service. Government and the Navy cannot be held blameless for this. Much of the recruiting advertising was literally on the lines of join the Navy and Secure yourself a post war job. Admittedly in the text of the advertisement no specific promise was made but the caption definitely implied that this would be the case. We stopped it later in the war but the damage was done."[141]

Rear Admiral Rattray, Flag Officer Bombay, in his report on the same subject said that "Too many ratings at the end of the war brought alluring prospects of return to civil life on a high scale of pay. This state of mind has been largely engendered by war time recruiting propaganda on the theme of 'Join the Navy and learn a job for after the war'."[142] Commander Gill, the Commanding Officer of HMIS *Cheetah*, in his report on the 'mutiny' submitted that

> The rating was strongly of the opinion that he had been let down by the Recruiting Officer who recruited him. He was assured at the time of recruitment that he would get rapid promotion in the RIN, that on release he would be guaranteed a job or failing that, adequate subsistence allowance, whereas he now saw from the experience of those released already, that no such facility is being provided by Government and that they are being just left in the streets.[143]

Commander Gill submitted the following before the RIN Enquiry Commission:

> The real reason of the RIN mutiny can be easily traced back to the policy adopted by the Recruiting Organisation earlier in the war. Masses of ratings were enrolled on promises of quick and substantial promotions while in the service and an equally satisfactory resettlement in civil life on the termination of hostilities. The experience of the great majority of ratings while in service tended to belie this exaggerated and rosy picture painted by the official recruiting agencies. With the close of the war the unplanned and large scale demobilisation that took place without any sensible programme of resettlement that has been rapidly overcoming the morale of the ratings.[144]

The morale reports of commanding officers of various ships and establishments talked about the complaints about false promises. The Morale Report of NHQ for the quarter ending 31 December 1945 said that

"Complaints by men who state that they had been recruited by false promises are still prevalent. They argue that they were taken into the Navy with all sorts of tempting promises and now they are being sent out of the service without any adequate provision for employment in civil life."[145]

Commodore Lawrence produced certain recruiting posters, pamphlets and booklets before the Enquiry Commission and stated that "they contained promises and tried to encourage people, but they were not quite as they should have been"[146] Further he stated about the complaints from the training school, Pilani, that

> the recruits were grossly misinformed at the time of original recruitment. The weight and diversity of evidence is too great to leave much doubt about this. I think the view of FOCRIN is explained in his letter wherein he admits that men were recruited with false promises. . . . [T]here is no doubt in my opinion that the average rating firmly believes that he has no post war job in the three services. Advertising to join Navy was done on the lines of ratings securing post war jobs. In a large number of cases he (the rating) is joining the service to secure himself a post war job. The recruiting staff was overstating the matter and that was discovered sometimes in 1942–43. From 1942–44 onwards they have been taking action to stop this kind of thing. An enquiry was made and it was found that the paid recruiter in the field was the delinquent. As he was not under any particular military authority, we could only ask him that he should not make these statements again. A premium was put on the number secured.[147]

He also stated that the recruiting slogans were apt to be misleading and he quoted recruiting posters which were in these terms:.[148] "Permanent careers in RIN. Learn while you earn. Promotion to Warrant Officers and Commissioned rank. Must have completed 2 years college course and the inter-class with mathematics and physics. Pay during training at Civil Naval Centre, Pilani – Rs. 70/- and all found. Pay during advance training – Rs. 100/- rising to Rs. 250/- and all found."[149] He said "I feel that the above is definitely misleading. As these are short service men, they cannot hope to rise even to Warrant Officers, leave alone commissioned ranks."[150]

Lieutenant Kohli said before the RIN Enquiry Committee that "In spite of the fact that many promises were made by the recruiting authorities about the post war settlement of ratings when they joined, the actual number of jobs which the ratings can be offered or will get was extremely few with the result that the rating is sadly disillusioned and bears malice and bitterness towards the service."[151]

The recruitment advertisement posters were misleading. A poster with the following words at the top "Boy proud of your son," below occur the following statements. "Let him join the RIN if he wishes to. Give him your blessing. The navy will give your son a healthy open air life with good fellowship, good pay and plenty of food and good clothes. He will meet the best of his countrymen and be a real man. The RIN has a great tradition and a glorious future. Let him join up."[152] It is pertinent to mention about a pamphlet of 1943 entitled "The Story of Kishore and Khalil" and its misleading statements. It contains at the top the pictures of Kishore, a rating in his naval uniform and Khalil, his friend in civilian dress. The story is related in the form of a dialogue and is on the following lines. Kishore, a lawyer's son, ran away from his home and joined the RIN as a communication rating with a salary of Rs 60/- per month. When he meets Khalil during his leave, he advises Khalil to join as an artificer and earn Rs 40/- more than he himself does. Khalil and Kishore are able to persuade Khalil's parents to agree and after telling them about the service in the RIN and its benefits. Khalil's father tells him that the war would not last indefinitely and as soon as the war is over, he will be asked to leave. Khalil replies to his father, "No, Sir, the contract is for ten years and it is believed that after the period is over a great majority would be retained in the permanent service. I have seen an article in a newspaper saying that India has a coastline of 4000 miles and it must have an adequate navy." In answer to his father's enquiry about scale of pay the son tells him, "I believe the pay goes up to Rs 460/- p.m."[153] The RIN Enquiry Commission's opinion about this pamphlet was that "this pamphlet is definitely misleading on the question of Special Service ratings who are taken on a 5 years contract as disclosed in the booklets and regulations. It is doubtful if the real position was ever brought home to these ratings. In any case they would have left their native homes and signed their enrolment on the strength of assurances such as those conveyed by this pamphlet."[154]

Demobilisation. By early 1945, the war almost came to an end in Europe and the British Government began the process of demobilisation. The majority of the RIN ratings wanted to continue in the Navy because of the non-availability of highly paid jobs. The RIN Enquiry Report says that "the resettlement arrangements which looked well on paper did not provide the kind of jobs which ratings had expected and considered to be their due."[155] Biswanath Bose says that "What the Indian sailors gained after serving the RIN . . . with full skill and acumen and spending the best part of life? This question was highlighted then. They have gained during such a long period of time would be a very little or no use to any entity. . . . They would be provided with any other job when they became civilians nor would they get any priority in securing an alternate job even if they were selected on merit. In some cases settlement of dues was also delayed. Therefore, everywhere there have been signs of discontentment in RIN."[156] "Large-scale demobilisation from 1945 spread fear and anxiety amongst Indian ratings facing uncertain future and broken promises of post-war employment."[157]

Failure of Divisional System and Discipline. The stoppage of recruitment between 1921 and 1928 led to the chronic shortage of experienced officers during the war. During the first three years of the war, till 1942, RIN was focussed only on the Local Naval Defence.[158] The new commitments given by the British Admiralty and the Government of India forced the RIN to go in for a massive expansion. The rapid expansion especially during 1942–1945 compromised on the training of officers and ratings and the appointment of less experienced officers, as Commanding Officers were also other factors of the RIN Revolt. Vice Admiral Godfrey, the Flag Officer Commanding the Royal Indian Navy, stated before the RIN Enquiry Commission that

> the British Admiralty, the Indian Government, Indian Army and SEAC were continuously asking the RIN to take on new commitments. . . . [I]t was bad for the service to take on so much and to inflate itself without acquiring the necessary officers, or administrative staff. . . . [W]e must accept the mutiny as a casualty arising out of the vigour with which India carried on with the war, and which might have been avoided if we had continued the go-slow policy between 1942 and 1945. We did 'go-slow' before 1942, except in fulfilling the Navy's first commitment of local naval defence.[159]

It is evident from the RIN Enquiry Report that the gap in the relation between the officers and men became wider, especially between the white officers and the black sailors. There was a lack of divisional system[160] and a command and control system due to inexperienced officers and less-trained ratings. In the post-war period, the RIN personnel had lost the loyalty towards the Service due to the demobilisation. Even though discrimination in pay, allowances and status existed even before and during the war, many of the ratings wanted to continue in the RIN. Demobilisation and the service conditions in the post-war period made the Indian ratings think that they were utilised by the colonial government for their imperialistic interests and now they were going to be thrown out. The ratings had written in the poster pasted on the walls of HMIS *Kakauri*: "Is this the REWARD of our loyalty and service during the war?"[161] Men had insufficient work and they were unlikely to be interested in their work when they expected to be out of service shortly and had no clear future before them.[162] This invoked feelings of hatred towards the Service, and the ratings started to respond to minor issues, which they had never done before. B. C. Dutt says that, "The 'Talwar' was completely managed training establishment during the war. But on my return I noticed a great deal of deterioration due to overcrowding, the standard of discipline had fallen. There was no training programme to keep the ratings occupied. The establishment was far less clean. Every week new batches of ratings poured in from different parts of the world to await demobilisation or new posting."[163]

There were several 'mutinies' in the RIN due to lack of discipline. Lt Cdr Soman stated before the RIN Enquiry Commission "that the higher authorities took no notice of the warning given as early as September 1942."[164] According to him the 'mutiny' which took place in HMIS *Orissa* in September 1942 was found on investigation to be due to bad discipline and to the fact that there was little contact and no sympathy between the officers and men.[165] Vice Admiral Fitz Herbert came to the conclusion about the previous 'mutiny', which took place in March 1942 in the Mechanical Training Establishment at Bombay, that "had the officers maintained proper contact with the apprentices and had the general discipline of the establishment been in a satisfactory state, the outbreak of indiscipline could not have occurred."[166] In January 1943 Admiral Fitz Herbert was alarmed at the state of indiscipline in the Navy. The RIN Enquiry Commission concluded by stating that "the several factors which in varying degrees contributed to the February Mutiny in the R.I.N (which includes Divisional Duties, Man-Management, and administration from Naval Headquarters downwards)."[167] Admiral R. D. Katari[168] says in his autobiography that, "The senior officers of the Service, who were all British, were particularly culpable in not sparing some thought to what was required to maintain the discipline and morale in the Navy."[169]

Question of nationalism

Most of the English educated youth did not return to their village homes; they either joined the government service or one of the learned professions. B. C. Dutt, who had written anti-British slogans on the walls of HMIS *Talwar*, admits that he really wanted to join the RIN.[170] Except six, all ratings who participated in the RIN Revolt were recruited between 1939 and 1944.[171] The ratings who had seen the peak of the nationalist movement and the Quit India Movement continued in or joined the RIN. Most of the men who joined the Indian Defence Forces belonged to lower-class families and were ready to serve under the colonial government in any circumstances for a better economic and social life. The distance between the officers and men of the defence forces existed even before the First World War. The Indian ratings revolted for parity in pay, perks, allowances and good treatment by officers. If this issue would been addressed by the divisional officers or by the commanding officers, the RIN ratings would not have protested. The protest started with a hunger strike, which led to a massive strike and finally went out of control of the RIN Strike Committee leaders. By that time, it was too late for the ratings to stop their protest, and they realised the consequences of the indiscipline they have shown. Then they wanted to give the colour of nationalism to their protest and get the support of the political leaders in order to avoid the military trails. That is why Gandhi advised the RIN boys to resign. (And, they wanted to get the support from the INA officers.) Even though Pt Nehru had agreed to give leadership to the RIN ratings on the request of Aruna Asif Ali, however, when he returned from Singapore he asked the RIN ratings to follow non-violence. Nationalism is a feeling and it has to come from the individual. Now the nationalism of the RIN ratings is questionable. The ratings have written in the poster at HMIS *Kakauri* that "Is this the REWARD of our loyalty and service during the war?"[172] If they had nationalism in their minds, why did they join the colonial force and fight the war for the colonial government? The answer is that they never had any feeling of nationalism towards the motherland. If the issues of the ratings would have been resolved, they would have been continued in the service. Many of the ratings wanted to rise to a commissioned rank, knowing the fact that there was discrimination between the British and Indian Officers, to get a better life and for financial benefits. Lt Cdr Shaw submitted before the RIN Enquiry Committee that "By all accounts recruiting officers and the service life has consequently been a great shock. This has led to there being men in the service who have been discontented from the day they joined. To my personal knowledge in 1945 several gentlemen applied for commissions who at the time of their application were drawing a salary of Rs 70/- per month. It is considered reasonable to assume that the pay for a sub-lieutenant of Rs 450/- proved an attraction."[173]

The most significant factor of this revolt, with hindsight, came to be that Hindus and Muslims united to resist the British, even at a time that saw the peak of the movement for Pakistan. "The communal unity evident in the RIN was limited, despite Congress, League and Red flags being jointly hoisted on the ships' masts."[174] Muslim ratings approached the Muslim League for advice on the future course of action, while the rest sought advice from the Congress and the Socialists.[175] The revolt was called off following a meeting between the President of the Naval Central Strike Committee, M. S. Khan, and Vallabhbhai Patel of the Congress. Patel issued a statement calling on the strikers to end their action. However, Mohammed Ali Jinnah's advice to surrender was addressed to Muslim ratings alone, who duly heeded it.[176] From these incidents one can conclude that their communal identities and feelings were greater than their 'nationalism'.

Question of political influence

The rating approached Aruna Asif Ali, a left-wing Congress leader, who was in Bombay at that time, with a strong expectation that she would lead the strike.[177] However Aruna Asif Ali advised the ratings to "remain calm" and she explained the loopholes in their demands.[178] Aruna told the ratings that, they were wrong in mixing up "political demands" with "Service grievances."[179] Therefore she asked the ratings "to separate the two and formulate their demands" to the Naval Authorities.[180] On realising that the ratings were not seeking her guidance to draw up their demands, but looking for a national leader to lead them, promptly she advised the ratings to approach Sardar Patel. Later Aruna told the press that, "what the ratings sought was the support of the national forces for their just cause."[181] Then the Strike Committee approached Sardar Patel, a member of the Congress working committee, on 21 February 1946, when the firing had been started by the military at Castle Barracks.[182] B. C. Dutt says that, "The men to whom we looked for leadership tried to ignore the uprising."[183] Sardar Patel, however, declined to interfere.[184] He was of the view that the ratings ought not to have taken up arms and he condemned their act of indiscipline in staging a mutiny.[185] He expressed the opinion that there ought to be discipline in the armed forces.[186] Before leaving Bombay, Aruna send a telegram requesting Nehru's intervention to avoid a tragedy. The telegram read, "Naval Strike tense. Situation serious. Climaxing to grim close. You alone can control and avoid tragedy. Request your immediate presence in Bombay."[187] B. C. Dutt says that "From later events it became clear that her (Aruna) telegram was a neat summing up of the attitude of the national leaders towards our endeavour and aspirations."[188] In the 1920s Gandhi pleaded with Indians not to cooperate by resigning from the Police and Army.[189] It clearly shows that the Indian National Congress was not in favour of Indians joining the Armed Forces. On hearing the news on the RIN strike, Mahatma Gandhi, who was in Poona at that time, said that if the ratings were unhappy, they could have resigned.[190] The Strike Committee members approached each and every leader for political intervention and leadership, but all of their efforts went in vain. According to the RIN Enquiry Commission "the ostensible reasons of the mutinies were related to grievances regarding the pay scale, quantity of rations, bad cooking, inadequate arrangement of lodging, refusal of men to carry out certain duties like cleaning ship, cleaning the deck, sentry duties, messenger duties, etc. These 'mutinies' happened due to the discontent among the RIN ratings, however these so-called mutinies were not politically motivated."[191]

Mutiny or revolt?

Mutiny is a criminal conspiracy among a group of individuals (typically members of the military or the crew of any ship, even if they are civilians) to openly oppose, change or overthrow a lawful authority to which they are subject.[192] According to the American Heritage Dictionary, *revolt* is rejection of and rebellion against a prevailing state of affairs or a controlling authority and *mutiny* is revolt against constituted authority, especially by sailors: The sailors, who had received low pay and poor rations, were finally in a state of mutiny. "A strike in the armed forces is a mutiny."[193]

DEMOBILISATION, DISCONTENT AND REVOLT

The young ratings who took part in the Revolt were under the impression that they were carrying out a 'strike', like the political parties used to do against the British Government. Perry S. Gourgey says, from his experience, in his book that "Stopping a Leading Seaman who was on my staff, I asked why he was not at his post and in a sullen manner he replied: Strike Sir!"[194] M. S. Khan (Punnu Khan), President of the Central Strike Committee, told to Sub Lieutenant Percy S Gourgey that:

> Some of our friends got in touch with members of the Congress and other nationalists amongst the civilians. . . . They suggested plans for a mass strike. The authorities may call it 'mutiny' but we understand mutiny to be the violent and bloody overthrow of the officers commanding us. On the other hand, our original intention was, and still is, to have a mass sit-down strike in all ships and establishments, until the authorities take sincere, concrete steps to settle our grievances. But we want this strike to be peaceful. If we can achieve on our aims peacefully, why should we want any harm to come to our superior officers?[195]

It clearly shows that the so-called mutiny began as a strike. Historians have different opinions about the character and nature of the RIN Revolt of 1946. The British Government called it a Mutiny. Field Marshal Sir Claude Auchinleck, the Commander-in-Chief in India, said in a broadcast on 24 February 1946 that:

> The word 'Strike' has been loosely used. The correct word is 'Mutiny' and this refers to any collective act of a few persons subject to Naval, Military or Air Force against the legal authorities of the service. . . . [I]t matters not, what form collective disobedience takes place, whether negative as refusal to work or refusal to eat, or positive such as demonstration or march or an act of violence. Such acts are all mutinous though obviously they can and do very in degree.[196]
>
> To the British Government, "if the two persons sign a letter together it is a mutiny. A letter of protest of any kind of joint letter . . . is considered a mutiny officially."[197]

According to Bhagwatkar, "The British administration considered their political domination over India as legal authority and any action against that power was regarded as 'mutiny'. It clearly means that, from their point of view, the British imperialism and imperialism in general was legal and constitutional and the people's struggle for the liberation of their country was a 'mutiny'. In this sense, the national struggle becomes a 'mutiny'."[198]

The RIN Enquiry Commission brought out in its report that the so-called mutiny was non-violent except few minor incidents. The Commission had the opinion that, "The mutiny in all other places was non-violent. The technique of the mutineers was hunger-strike, or refusal to work. With rare exceptions, their behaviour towards officers was respectful and they paid the usual marks of respect."[199] In almost all of the ships/establishments, the strike began as sympathy with the ratings of *Talwar*.

5. Conclusion

The post-war actions of the British regarding the RIN were well prepared. When the hostilities were almost over by end of 1944, the British had started to prepare the post-war plans including demobilisation. During the war the British had to utilise the manpower of India to meet their defence requirements. To achieve this goal, they had to compromise in their 'martial race' recruitment by accepting the low educational, physical and medical standard of Indian youth. In the post-war period the British wanted remove the 'non-martial races' from the Royal Indian Navy and planned to begin the recruitment of 'suitable' candidates for officers and rating cadres. Consequently, the wartime-recruited ratings were demobilised on a massive scale without keeping the wartime recruitment promises. This led to a major discontent among the ratings and became one of the cardinal causes of the RIN revolt of 1946.

After the surrender of Japan, the British believed that the major powers in the East would be from among the United States, China and Russia. The British envisaged a local naval defence role to the RIN against only the 'minor dangers', and the Royal Navy was entrusted with the role against the 'major dangers', as in the pre-war situation. The British did not expect any attack on India by a major power in the near future of the post-war period. Therefore the British planned a slow pace of development of the RIN in the post-war period, not only to restrict local naval defence but also equip and train it to operate outside the country in a future war. Accordingly the British planned a Cruiser squadron comprising three ships to train 'suitable' Indian men so to make them fit for deployment in international waters in a future colonial requirement.

There were many 'mutinies' in the Armed Forces during the Second World War and most of these mutinies were suppressed by the British officials, who never revealed the details to the world. A revolt took place in the Indian Army at almost the same time of the RIN Revolt, in February 1946. There were nine so-called mutinies in the Royal Indian Navy between March 1942 and April 1945. Most of these mutinies were the result of discontent of the ratings regarding service conditions, pay, promotion and discrimination; however these so-called mutinies were not politically motivated. The wartime recruitment advertisements gave hope to the Indian youth in the post-war period for a better life in the RIN. The advertisement pamphlets were never given the real picture of the naval service and its career prospects. These recruitment advertisements, including posters, booklets and pamphlets, were made with the sole aim to attract Indian youths for the wartime requirements and made these advertisements in such a way that they gave a positive picture of the RIN.

The RIN Revolt took place as a result of the socio-economic-political and service conditions. The existing service conditions and the impact of the previous so-called mutinies in the RIN influenced the RIN ratings to respond to the immediate cause of the Revolt: the misbehaviour of Cdr King, the Commanding Officer, HMIS *Talwar*. The RIN ratings were discriminated and that led to a strike in the beginning as a protest against the service conditions and racial discrimination. "Training had been curbed by wartime expansion, while structural deficiencies had been exacerbated by a poor quality, predominantly white officer class, uninterested in the indigenous languages and customs. Some officers had no seagoing experience, others were tea or rubber planters who viewed Indians as servants, and some came from regions of strong colour prejudice like South Africa."[200] But in the later stages the Strike Committee had lost the control over the ratings of the other units, and it culminated as a revolt. The ratings were influenced by the national movement and the trial of the INA personnel. Indeed, the ratings expected that the political leaders would come forward to take the leadership of their fight for their rights. The ratings wanted representatives from outside and some political leaders who could negotiate for their demands with the top ranks in the RIN, because they had a feeling that if their representatives would be from themselves there were chances for compromises in the demands tabled before the higher authorities of RIN and victimization of the representatives in the name of mutiny. That is the reason; the ratings refused to listen to the appeal of Flag Officer Bombay and demanded the intervention of a national leader. The ratings said, "We want a national leader either from the Congress or the Muslim League or the Communist Party of India to negotiate between us."[201]

Even though the ratings had sympathy towards the INA people and the ongoing freedom struggle, they had no 'nationalist feeling' as they never wanted to move out from the RIN and to join the nationalist movement running parallel during that period. Secondly, in their initial charter of demands they did not put forward the case of B. C. Dutt (the rating who was imprisoned for writing anti-British slogans like 'Quit India' on the walls of HMIS *Talwar*). The question as to whether these ratings had had nationalist feeling if then their immediate demands would have been to release their fellow sailor who was imprisoned by the British Government. In their initial charter of demands, none of the demands mentioned or showed the nationalist sentiment. Their demands instead clearly showed that they wanted amelioration of the service conditions and treatment on a par with their British counterparts. Several government servants who had nationalist feeling resigned from the British Government organizations to join the nationalist movement; however none of the ratings did the same. Hence, here one can say that the prevailing socio-politico-economic situation and the nationalist sentiment of the masses as a whole overwhelmed the RIN Revolt, and the same was projected as part of the freedom movement by the participants and leftist historians. Later, these ratings added more demands like release of all political prisoners, INA soldiers etc. as they wanted to grab the attention of the national leaders. Also at the same time they wanted to take advantage of the prevailing political instability so to make their demands stronger and to get them incorporated into the nationalist demands as well.

But it indirectly helped the national movement for freedom. As a result of the RIN Revolt, the British Government in India had lost the faith in the Armed Forces, which was very much required for the existence of a colonial power in a foreign land. Even though the RIN revolt did not last for more than a week, it had a dramatic impact on popular consciousness and had a liberating effect on the minds of people.[202] In the aftereffect of the revolt, a weekly intelligence summary issued on 25 March 1946, admitted that the British Indian Armed forces were no longer trustworthy, and, for the army, "only day to day estimates of steadiness could be made."[203] However, Sucheta Mahajan differs from this view; she says that "The soldier-Viceroy, Wavell, gave a clean chit to the army a few days after the naval strikes." "Those who believed that the British would succumb to popular pressure, if only it was exerted forcefully, were proved wrong."[204] The 'mutiny' profoundly disturbed the delicate officer/man relationship in the service, which needed years of patient labour to repair and rehabilitate.[205] It came to the situation where if wide-scale public unrest took shape, the armed forces could not be relied upon to support counter-insurgency operations as they had been during the "Quit India" movement of 1942. This had become a movement characterized by a significant amount of inter-communal cooperation. The British government had made a commitment[206] in 1942 to grant dominion status to India after the war; but the INA, RIN Revolt, and public resentment it germinated, were important factors in the withdrawal of the Raj from India. India's internal politics would have been changed had the mutiny continued. However, the RIN Revolt is almost missing in the Indian history, as a forgotten episode. According to Bhagwatkar, "It has been stated that this uprising of the ratings was organized only to press their day to day demands like food, clothing and service conditions etc. while its great political significance in the freedom struggle has been grossly overlooked."[207] In June 1973, the Government of India recognised the contribution of RIN Mutineers in the freedom struggle and a total of 476 ratings, who had taken part in the 'Mutiny', were granted freedom fighter pensions.[208] Subsequently the RIN Mutiny was renamed as the Naval Uprising, and the mutineers were honoured for the part they played in India's

Freedom struggle. The impact of RIN Revolt is aptly reflected on the RIN Uprising memorial in Mumbai; "To Honour personnel of the then Royal Indian Navy for the sacrifice and courage to 'steer away from the course charted from them'; because of the discriminatory treatment meted out to Indians. Their contribution in February 1946 proved to be a turning point that hastened the India's Independence." See Figure 5.2.

Figure 5.2 The RIN Uprising Memorial erected by the Indian Navy at Colaba, Mumbai

Source: Capt Navtej Singh, Director Personnel Services, Indian Navy

"The INA trials, the post-war RIN Mutiny and RIAF 'Strikes' were all forceful indicators to the British that the writing was on the wall and that the time was ripe to begin their retreat from empire. Apart from its impact on the Indian freedom struggle, in purely military terms the war contributed immensely to hastening the process of Indianisation of the officer corps, the rapid expansion of the RIAF and the RIN, and the overall establishment of technical arms in the Indian military as well as laying the foundations of defence production in the country."[209] Since the Quit India movement of 1942, the British had repeatedly acknowledged that they could not rely on Indian officials in the event of large-scale popular unrest.[210] "The air force and naval mutinies in January and February 1946 respectively revealed the split in the military base of the empire. The mutinies came without any warning to the British. Though both mutinies were eventually put down, racial sentiment was now very strong, and the loyalty of the armed forces was clearly in doubt."[211]

Notes

1 Directive for Reorganization Committee (India), Naval Headquarters, New Delhi, 1944, p. 1.
2 Chiefs of Staff Committee Report on Composition and Size of Post-War Forces in India, COS (44) 636, Naval Headquarters, New Delhi, 1944, p. 1.
3 Ibid.
4 Ibid., p. 2.
5 Ibid., p. 3.
6 Ibid.
7 Ibid.
8 Ibid., p. 4.
9 Ibid., p. 7.
10 Ibid.
11 Ibid.
12 Ibid.
13 Ibid., p. 8.
14 Ibid.
15 Ibid., p. 9.
16 Ibid.
17 Ibid.
18 Ibid.
19 Ibid.
20 Ibid., p. 11.
21 Ibid.
22 Royal Indian Navy, Summary of Main Proposals in Paper 'The Future Royal Indian Navy', Annexure to Chiefs of Staff Committee Report on the Size and Composition of the Post-War Forces in India, COS (44) 636, Naval Headquarters, New Delhi, 1944, p. 1.
23 The Future Royal Indian Navy, COS (44) 637, Naval Headquarters, New Delhi, 1944, p. 1 and Chiefs of Staff Committee (India) COS (44) 642, 'Size and Composition of the Post-War Forces in India', Summary of Recommendations, Naval Headquarters, New Delhi, 1944, p. 3.

24 Chiefs of Staff Committee (India) COS (44) 642, 'Size and Composition of the Post-War Forces in India', Summary of Recommendations, Naval Headquarters, New Delhi, 1944, p. 3.
25 Royal Indian Navy, Summary of Main Proposals in Paper, 'The Future Royal Indian Navy', Annexure to Chiefs of Staff Committee Report on the Size and Composition of the Post-War Forces in India, COS (44) 636 Naval Headquarters, New Delhi, 1944, p. 2 and Chiefs of Staff Committee (India) COS (44) 642, 'Size and Composition of the Post-War Forces in India', Summary of Recommendations, Naval Headquarters, New Delhi, 1944, p. 3.
26 Royal Indian Navy, Summary of Main Proposals in Paper, 'The Future Royal Indian Navy', Annexure to Chiefs of Staff Committee Report on the Size and Composition of the Post-War Forces in India, COS (44) 636, 1944, p. 3.
27 Ibid.
28 Chiefs of Staff Committee (India) COS (44) 642, 'Size and Composition of the Post-War Forces in India', Summary of Recommendations, Naval Headquarters, New Delhi, 1944, p. 4.
29 The Future Royal Indian Navy, COS (44) 637, Naval Headquarters, New Delhi, 1944, p. 4 and Chiefs of Staff Committee (India) COS (44) 642, 'Size and Composition of the Post-War Forces in India', Summary of Recommendations, Naval Headquarters, New Delhi, 1944, p. 4.
30 Ibid.
31 Ibid.
32 Ibid.
33 Report on the Royal Indian Navy, January–June 1945, Naval Headquarters, New Delhi, 1946, p. 2, Naval Historical Branch of the Royal Navy, Portsmouth, UK.
34 Report on the Royal Indian Navy, July–December 1945, Naval Headquarters, New Delhi, 1946, p. 20, ADM 1/19413, The National Archives, Kew, UK.
35 Report on the Royal Indian Navy, January–June 1945, Naval Headquarters, New Delhi, 1946, p. 2.
36 Report on the Royal Indian Navy, July–December 1945, Naval Headquarters, New Delhi, 1946, p. 20.
37 Ibid.
38 Ibid.
39 Ibid.
40 Ibid.
41 Demobilisation and Resettlement Planning, Upper & Lower Limits of Royal Indian Navy, Together with an Intermediate Demobilisation Stage as Required by Demobilisation Policy Committee, COS (45) 685 (Revised), 1945, History Division, Ministry of Division, New Delhi, File No. 601/10605/H.
42 Commander in Chief in India Directives to the Chiefs of Staff (India) Committee: Demobilisation, 1945, Demobilisation and Resettlement Planning, History Division, Ministry of Defence, New Delhi, File No. 601/10605/H.
43 Ibid.
44 Ibid. A cruiser is bigger than a sloop or a destroyer and its larger size enables both additional officers and men to be trained.
45 Ibid.
46 Ibid.
47 Report on the Royal Indian Navy, July–December 1945, Naval Headquarters, New Delhi, 1946, p. 20.
48 Ibid.
49 Ibid.

DEMOBILISATION, DISCONTENT AND REVOLT

50 Ibid.
51 Ibid., p. 21.
52 Ibid.
53 Ibid.
54 File Minutes, Royal Indian Navy-Demobilisation Planning: Recommendations for Regular and Reserve Forces and Requirements in Immediate Post-War Period Admiralty Observation, Requirement of R.N Officers for Secondment to R.I.N, 1945, The National Archives, Kew Gardens, UK, ADM 1/18488.
55 Ibid.
56 Report on the Royal Indian Navy, July–December 1945, Naval Headquarters, New Delhi, 1946, p. 27.
57 Ibid.
58 Ibid.
59 Ibid.
60 Ibid.
61 Ibid.
62 Interview with Mrs. Ray, daughter of (Late) Lt Commander Ram Mohan Ray, RINVR, in October 2014 at New Delhi.
63 Report on the Royal Indian Navy, July–December 1945, Naval Headquarters, New Delhi, 1946, p. 27.
64 Ibid.
65 Ibid.
66 Ibid.
67 RIN Enquiry Committee Report, Naval Headquarters, New Delhi, 1946, National Archives of India, New Delhi, 1946, p. 17.
68 John B. Hattendorf (Ed), *The Oxford Encyclopaedia of Maritime History*, Oxford University Press, New York, 2007, pp. 604–606.
69 www.academia.edu
70 Ibid.
71 RIN Enquiry Committee Report, Naval Headquarters, New Delhi, 1946, National Archives of India, New Delhi, 1946, pp. 20–27.
72 V. M. Bhagwatkar, unpublished PhD thesis titled, *The Role of the R.I.N Mutiny of Feb. 1946 (Royal Indian Uprising) in the Indian Freedom Struggle*, p. 4.
73 Ibid., p. 5.
74 RIN Enquiry Commission Report, 1946, Naval Headquarters, National Archives of India, New Delhi, Para 40.
75 Summary of the Report of the Commission of Enquiry in to the RIN Mutiny, February 1946, War Department, GOI, New Delhi, National Archives of India, New Delhi, p. 3.
76 Kalesh Mohanan, 'War, Revolt and End of the Raj', *Journal of Indian Ocean Studies*, Vol. 21, No. 1, April 2013, p. 92.
77 Quoted by V. M. Bhagwatkar, unpublished PhD thesis titled, *The Role of the R.I.N Mutiny of Feb. 1946 (Royal Indian Uprising) in the Indian Freedom Struggle*, p. iii.
78 RIN Enquiry Commission Report, 1946, Naval Headquarters, National Archives of India, New Delhi, p. 49.
79 Ibid.
80 Ibid., p. 50.
81 Ibid. and B. C. Dutt, *Mutiny of the Innocents*, Sindhu Publications, Bombay, 1971, p. 80.
82 RIN Enquiry Commission Report, 1946, Naval Headquarters, National Archives of India, New Delhi, p. 50.

83 B. C. Dutt, *Mutiny of the Innocents*, Sindhu Publications, Bombay, 1971, p. 84.
84 Ibid., pp. 86–87 and RIN Enquiry Commission Report, 1946, Naval Headquarters, New Delhi, p. 50.
85 RIN Enquiry Commission Report, 1946, Naval Headquarters, New Delhi, p. 50.
86 Ibid., Subratho Banerjee, Deepak Das and Rear Admiral Satyindra Singh.
87 RIN Enquiry Commission Report, 1946, Naval Headquarters, National Archives of India, New Delhi, p. 51.
88 Ibid. and B. C. Dutt, *Mutiny of the Innocents*, Sindhu Publications, Bombay, 1971, p. 101. Cdr King, later, admitted before the RIN Enquiry Commission that what he said was "normal naval manners."
89 B. C. Dutt, *Mutiny of the Innocents*, Sindhu Publications, Bombay, 1971, p. 102.
90 Ibid., p. 106.
91 Ibid., p. 110.
92 Ibid.
93 RIN Enquiry Commission Report, 1946, Naval Headquarters, National Archives of India, New Delhi, pp. 52–53.
94 Ibid., p. 53.
95 Ibid., p. 54 and B. C. Dutt, *Mutiny of the Innocents*, Sindhu Publications, Bombay, 1971, p. 125.
96 Ibid., p. 54.
97 Ibid.
98 Ibid.
99 Ibid.
100 Ibid.
101 Sardar Vallabhbhai Patel was an Indian National Congress leader and the first Deputy Prime Minister of Independent India
102 Ibid. and B. C. Dutt, *Mutiny of the Innocents*, Sindhu Publications, Bombay, 1971, pp. 177–178.
103 Subrata Banerjee, *The RIN Strike*, People's Publishing House, New Delhi, 1954, The RIN uprising would have developed in a different direction; had it not been for the policy pursued by them in relation to every struggle that broke out in that period, we would have seen something different from the 1947 transfer of power, according to which the iron grip of British rule was allowed to continue. p. xvii, Introduction by E. M. S. Namboodiripad.
104 Sucheta Mahajan, *Independence and Partition: The Erosion of Colonial Power in India*, Sage Publications, New Delhi, 2000, p. 100.
105 Kalesh Mohanan, 'War, Revolt and End of the Raj', *Journal of Indian Ocean Studies*, New Delhi, Vol. 21, No. 1, April 2013, p. 87.
106 Royal Indian Navy Club Report, London, Naval Headquarters, New Delhi, p. 2.
107 Royal Indian Navy Club Report, London, 1950, New Delhi, p. 314.
108 RIN Revolt, Inquiry Commission Report, Part III, GF62/86 PR II, National Archives of India, New Delhi, p. 394.
109 Royal Indian Navy Recruitment Publicity Booklets, Caird Library, National Maritime Museum, Greenwich.
110 Ibid.
111 RIN Mutiny Enquiry Report Part III, GF62/86-PRII, National Archives of India, New Delhi, p. 397.
112 Admiral Godfrey, then FOCRIN, agreed before the RIN Inquiry Commission that "employment after release was probably the most potent cause of unrest

DEMOBILISATION, DISCONTENT AND REVOLT

in the service." RIN Revolt, Inquiry Commission Report, Part III, GF62/86 PR II, National Archives of India, New Delhi, p. 426.
113 RIN Enquiry Report Part III, GF62/86-PRII, National Archives of India, New Delhi, p. 118.
114 Ibid.
115 Ibid. and B. C. Dutt, *Mutiny of the Innocents*, Sindhu Publications, Bombay, 1971, p. 101.
116 B. C. Dutt, *Mutiny of the Innocents*, Sindhu Publications, Bombay, 1971, p. 42.
117 Ibid., p. 52.
118 Ibid., pp. 54–55.
119 Biswanath Bose, *Rin Mutiny 1946*, Northern Book Centre, New Delhi, 1988, p. 6.
120 V. M. Bhagwatkar, unpublished PhD thesis titled, *The Role of the R.I.N Mutiny of Feb. 1946 (Royal Indian Uprising) in the Indian Freedom Struggle*, p. 16.
121 RIN Enquiry Committee Report, Naval Headquarters, New Delhi, 1946, National Archives of India, New Delhi, 1946, Para 454.
122 Ibid.
123 Ibid.
124 B. C. Dutt, *Mutiny of the Innocents*, Sindhu Publications, Bombay, 1971, pp. 62–63.
125 Ibid., p. 63.
126 Ibid.
127 Ibid.
128 Abdul Kalam Azad, *India Wins Freedom*, Orient Longmans, Bombay, 1959, p. 131.
129 RIN Enquiry Committee Report, Naval Headquarters, New Delhi, 1946, National Archives of India, New Delhi, 1946, p. 16.
130 B. C. Dutt, *Mutiny of the Innocents*, Sindhu Publications, Bombay, 1971, p. 60.
131 RIN Enquiry Committee Report, Naval Headquarters, New Delhi, 1946, National Archives of India, New Delhi, 1946, p. 16.
132 B. C. Dutt, *Mutiny of the Innocents*, Sindhu Publications, Bombay, 1971, p. 60.
133 RIN Enquiry Committee Report, Naval Headquarters, New Delhi, 1946, National Archives of India, New Delhi, 1946, p. 1.
134 Ibid., p. 3.
135 Summary of the Report of the Commission of Enquiry into the R.I.N Mutiny, February 1946, GOI, New Delhi, 1946, p. 10.
136 Ibid.
137 Ibid.
138 Ibid.
139 Ibid. and the booklets entitled 'The Navy and Its Job' and 'Indian Navy'.
140 Summary of the Report of the Commission of Enquiry into the R.I.N Mutiny, February 1946, GOI, National Archives of India, New Delhi, 1946, p. 11.
141 RIN Enquiry Report Part III, GF62/86-PRII, National Archives of India, New Delhi, pp. 121–122.
142 Ibid., p. 122.
143 Ibid.
144 Ibid.
145 Ibid., p. 123.
146 Ibid., Commodore Lawrence, Was the Staff Officer, Operations, NHQ, from 1939 to End of 1941. He was the first witness examined at Delhi by the RIN Enquiry Commission.
147 Ibid., p. 124.

148 Ibid., p. 125.
149 Ibid.
150 Ibid.
151 Ibid., p. 126.
152 Ibid., p. 128.
153 Ibid., p. 129.
154 Ibid., p. 130.
155 RIN Enquiry Committee Report, Naval Headquarters, New Delhi, 1946, National Archives of India, New Delhi, 1946, p. 17.
156 Biswanath Bose, *Rin Mutiny 1946*, Northern Book Centre, New Delhi, 1988, pp. 13–14.
157 Daniel Owen Spence, 'Imperial Transition, Indianisation and Race: Developing National Navies in the Subcontinent, 1947–64', *Journal of South Asian Studies*, Vol. 37, No. 2, 2014, p. 324.
158 RIN Enquiry Committee Report, Naval Headquarters, New Delhi, 1946, National Archives of India, New Delhi, 1946, p. 18.
159 Ibid.
160 As per the Divisional system, a Divisional Officer, who is in charge of the ratings, is supposed to interact with ratings and resolve their service and personal issues.
161 RIN Enquiry Commission Report, 1946, Naval Headquarters, National Archives of India, New Delhi, p. 598.
162 Ibid., p. 18.
163 B. C. Dutt, *Mutiny of the Innocents*, Sindhu Publishers, Bombay, 1971, p. 74.
164 RIN Enquiry Committee Report, Naval Headquarters, New Delhi, 1946, National Archives of India, New Delhi, 1946, p. 27.
165 Ibid., pp. 27–28.
166 Ibid., p. 28.
167 Ibid., p. 242.
168 Admiral RD Katari Was an RIN Officer during the RIN Revolt and Later became the First Indian Chief of Naval Staff.
169 Admiral R. D. Katari, *A Sailor Remembers*, Prabhat Prakashan, New Delhi, 2012, p. 50.
170 B. C. Dutt, *Mutiny of the Innocents*, Sindhu Publications, Bombay, 1971, p. 31.
171 List of RIN Mutiny Pensioners.
172 RIN Enquiry Commission Report, 1946, Naval Headquarters, National Archives of India, New Delhi, p. 598.
173 Ibid., p. 125.
174 Sucheta Mahajan, *Independence and Partition: The Erosion of Colonial Power in India*, Sage Publications, New Delhi, 2000, p. 99.
175 Ibid.
176 Ibid.
177 B. C. Dutt, *Mutiny of the Innocents*, Sindhu Publications, Bombay, 1971, pp. 132–133.
178 Ibid.
179 Ibid.
180 Ibid.
181 Ibid., p. 134.
182 RIN Enquiry Commission Report, 1946, Naval Headquarters, National Archives of India, New Delhi, p. 58.
183 B. C. Dutt, *Mutiny of the Innocents*, Sindhu Publications, Bombay, 1971, p. 134.

184 RIN Enquiry Commission Report, 1946, Naval Headquarters, National Archives of India, New Delhi, p. 58.
185 Ibid.
186 Ibid.
187 B. C. Dutt, *Mutiny of the Innocents*, Sindhu Publications, Bombay, 1971, p. 134.
188 Ibid.
189 David Arnold, 'The Armed Police and Colonial Rule in South India, 1914–1947', *Modern Asian Studies*, Vol. 11, No. 1, 1977, p. 108.
190 B. C. Dutt, *Mutiny of the Innocents*, Sindhu Publications, Bombay, 1971, p. 138.
191 RIN Enquiry Commission Report, 1946, Naval Headquarters, National Archives of India, New Delhi.
192 http://en.wikipedia.org/wiki/Mutiny, accessed on 04 November 2014.
193 Percy S. Gourgey, *The Indian Naval Revolt of 1946*, Orient Longman, Chennai, 1996, p. 11.
194 Ibid., The author was a Sub Lt (RINVR officer) posted at HMIS Talwar during the revolt and witnessed the events.
195 Percy S. Gourgey, *The Indian Naval Revolt of 1946*, Orient Longman, Chennai, 1996, p. 23. Mistakenly the author calls him as Punnu Khan.
196 Bombay Chronicle, Bombay, 25 February 1946.
197 Quoted Pandit Nehru by Dorothy Norman, *Nehru-The First Sixty Years: Vol. II*, Asia Publishing House, Bombay, 1965, p. 202.
198 V. M. Bhagwatkar, unpublished PhD thesis titled, *The Role of the R.I.N Mutiny of Feb. 1946 (Royal Indian Uprising) in the Indian Freedom Struggle*, p. ii.
199 RIN Enquiry Report Part III, GF62/86-PRII, National Archives of India, New Delhi, p. 47.
200 Ronald Spector, 'The Royal Indian Navy Strike of 1946: A Study of Cohesion and Disintegration in Colonial Armed Forces', *Armed Forces and Society*, Vol. 7, No. 2, 1981, p. 278. Quoted in Daniel Owen Spence, 'Imperial Transition, Indianisation and Race: Developing National Navies in the Subcontinent, 1947–64', *Journal of South Asian Studies*, Vol. 37, No. 2, 2014, p. 324.
201 Subratho Banerjee, *The RIN Strike*, People's Publishing House, New Delhi, 1981, p. 10.
202 Sucheta Mahajan, *Independence and Partition: The Erosion of Colonial Power in India*, Sage Publications, New Delhi, 2000, p. 97.
203 James L. Raj, *Making and Unmaking of British India*, Abacus, 1997, Unpublished, Public Relations Office, London. War Office. 208/819A 25C, pp. 571–598.
204 Sucheta Mahajan, *Independence and Partition: The Erosion of Colonial Power in India*, Sage Publications, New Delhi, 2000, p. 100.
205 Admiral R. D. Katari, *A Sailor Remembers*, Prabhat Prakashan, New Delhi, 2012.
206 Judith Brown, *Modern India: The making of an Asian Democracy*, 2nd ed., Oxford University Press, Oxford, 1999, pp. 328–330.
207 V. M. Bhagwatkar, unpublished PhD thesis titled, *The Role of the R.I.N Mutiny of Feb. 1946 (Royal Indian Uprising) in the Indian Freedom Struggle*, p. i.
208 Rear Admiral Satyindra Singh, *Under Two Ensigns: Indian Navy 1945–1950*, Oxford & IBH Publishing Co., New Delhi, 1986, p. 90.
209 Rana T. S. Chhina, *Reclaiming Our Legacy*, Contribution of the Indian Armed Forces to the Second World War, IDSA Special Feature, January 2013, p. 37.
210 Some Reflections on Official Propaganda by H. V. Hodson, Reforms Commissioner, 26 August 1942, N.A.I. Reforms Office File No. 143/42-R. See also note

by Conran-Smith, 19 October 1942, and Maxwell to Laithwaite, 24 October 1942, *TOP*, Vol. 3, 1 60–61, 156–158. Quoted by Anita Inder Singh in her article 'Decolonization in India: The Statement of 20 February 1947', *The International History Review*, Vol. 6, No. 2, May, 1984, p. 195.
211 Anita Inder Singh, 'Decolonization in India: The Statement of 20 February 1947', *The International History Review*, Vol. 6, No. 2, May, 1984, p. 198.

6

INDIGENISATION, PARTITION, RECONSTITUTION AND BIRTH OF A NEW NAVY

1. Indigenisation of armed forces of India

On 24 September 1944 Gandhi himself offered Jinnah his plan for 'two sovereign independent States' with a treaty of separation on defence, foreign affairs, etc. Thus, from 1940 onwards, the trend was unmistakably against India's unity. Both Gandhi and the Congress had accepted the principle of Partition, based on consent of the areas concerned. Time was fast running out on India's unity[1]

In accordance with the Cabinet Mission Plan an interim government was formed on 2 September 1946. Jawaharlal Nehru, the Vice President of the Executive Council wrote to the Commander-in-Chief, that "one of our first tasks, as a national Government based on popular approval, is to attempt to transform the whole background of the Indian Army and make it feel that it is a national army of India. It was impossible for this to be done in the past because the whole conception of the Indian Army was different and the average soldier fought for more in terms of an external allegiance than for allegiance to his own country . . . it is equally necessary to make the Indian public feel that the army is theirs and is not some kind of hostile force imposed on them. They should be proud of their army."[2] In November 1946, Auchinleck informed the army commanders in his correspondence that "It has been decided, and in my opinion inevitably decreed, that we – the British officers – are to go."[3] The indigenisation of the Armed Forces could no longer be disputed. On 6 November 1945, the Admiralty requested RIN to inform them of the probable requirements of Royal Navy Officers for secondment to the RIN during its transition stage to full Indianisation.[4]

The Armed Forces Nationalisation Committee (AFNC) was set up under the Chairmanship of Gopalaswamy Ayyangar, on 30 November 1946, to nationalise the armed forces of India, within the shortest possible time, with due regard to Indian national interests and reasonable efficiency.[5] The Committee consisted of Pandit Hriday Nath Kunzru, Muhammad Ismail Khan, Sardar Sampuran Singh, Major General D. A. L. Wade, Brigadier K. S. Thimayya, Wing Commander Mehr Singh and Commander H. M. S. Choudri as members. Lt Colonel B. M. Kaul was the Secretary. The Committee aimed to nationalise the Armed Forces of India, and all Ancillary Services, both officers and men, within the shortest possible time, with due regard to Indian national interests and reasonable efficiency, and to enquire and report on:[6]

1. the ways and means, within the minimum possible period, of replacement of non-Indians in each Branch or Service;
2. the target date or dates of complete nationalisation for all or each category in different services, if possible;
3. the ways and means of retaining, if necessary, non-Indian personnel as advisers or experts in nationalised categories;
4. the enumeration of those departments, categories or personnel where non-Indian personnel could be replaced by Indians immediately.

A time limit of six months (from January 1947) was fixed for the Committee to submit its report. Accordingly the Committee circulated a questionnaire on 9 January 1947 to obtain the views of certain officers of the Indian Armed Forces.[7] Meanwhile initiatives were taken to expedite the indigenisation process of the officer cadre. Field Marshal Auchinleck, the Commander-in-Chief, informed in a meeting, called by S. Baldev Singh, Defence Member, that of the 22,000 officers of the Indian Army, 13,500 were British and the remaining 8,500 were Indians.[8] However there were not sufficient Indian officers of the right calibre to fill the officer cadre of a completely nationalised Army.[9] In a reply to the AFNC letter No.NC/14 dated 17 January 1947, Naval Headquarters had intimated that "No British Officers are now being commissioned and none are being transferred from British Services."[10]

The Committee envisaged a two-stage programme of Indianisation – the first ending in January 1947 and the second in January 1951. It did not provide for a comprehensive Indianisation, and even in 1951 almost 19% of officers would have been British. The Committee brought out the serious shortage of qualified Indian officers, other ranks and civilians in the technical areas and services of the Indian Army and the RIN, including Europeans domiciled in India who were in law Indian nationals.[11] The shortages were especially in the stores, engineering and the electrical branches. The shortage was aggravated by the following factors:[12]

1. The release programme
2. The delay in granting regular commissions to Indian Emergency Commission Officers (I.E.C.Os)
3. The age bar under the regulations for granting regular commissions to I.E.C.Os
4. The short service commission's lack of appeal to men with technical qualifications, for whom there were in most cases attractive openings in the civil market

INDIGENISATION, PARTITION, AND A NEW NAVY

5   Delay in publishing the new conditions of pay and service for the Armed Forces
6   Competition in the civil market for trained technical personnel

The service headquarters obtained the willingness of British officers through circulating questionnaires. A total of 75 officers (under 20 years' service) opted to transfer to the Royal Navy, 44 officers (under 20 years' service) opted for secondment to the RIN after transferring to the RN, 16 officers opted for retirement, 20 of them opted to serve in the RIN under an independent Government of India (self-governing Dominion within the British Commonwealth) and 11 (five opted for the previous situation as well) opted to serve under the new Government which did not elect to remain in the British Commonwealth.[13] In paragraph 3 of Chiefs of Staff Committee Report of 1946 (792 Revised (JAPC [46]3)) the total requirements in the RIN and IA were projected as 665 and 9,283 officers, respectively.[14]

Auchinleck's demand for the retention of British officers was also influenced by other considerations. According to Sharmila Singh, as late as March 1947 Auchinleck and most senior British officers were working under the assumption that division of the country would not entail bifurcation of the Armed Forces.[15] As such, retention of a substantial number of British officers in undivided Armed Forces would have ensured Britain's control over the defence and foreign policy of the successor states.[16]

In April 1947, Rajagopalachari discussed with Mountbatten regarding the question of complete indigenisation of Indian armed forces by July 1947 and the effect on their efficiency. Rajagopalachari had the opinion that Indianisation could not be completed in so short time without the gravest effect on efficiency, and five to ten years must elapse before it would be sound to withdraw British officers.[17] Most of the senior Indian officers of the armed forces had the opinion that complete indigenisation would take five to ten years. Brigadier Cariappa, the most senior Indian officer of the Indian Army, told the Indian press in London that it would take five years before they could do without British officers.[18] Commander Choudhury, the most senior Indian officer of RIN, considered it would take at least 10 years in the case of RIN.[19] Group Captain Subrato Mukherjee, in charge of training, Air Headquarters, India, met political leaders and tried to convince them of the need for a big Air Force in India and that the Royal Indian Air Force would not stand on its own legs.[20] According to him the RIAF would require at least five to seven years' close connection with the Royal Air Force and many more years would be required for an independent Air Force in India.[21]

Rajagopalachari told Mountbatten that the politicians were under the impression that the Indian officers wanted the British officers to be pushed out sooner for rapid promotion. When he raised the question of retaining British officers in India post-partition, Mountbatten informed him that those British officers who wished to continue in India had to resign their commission in order to serve a foreign power.[22] Mountbatten was not in favour of an immediate nationalisation of Indian armed forces. He said that "if nationalisation was to take place by June 1948, the Indian Army would not be worth much for several years to come, and if it had to be split on top of that, both parts would be virtually valueless. . . . Navy and Air Force would in any case be of very little value if they were nationalised in under ten years"[23]

In April 1947, Liaquat Ali Khan wrote to Mountbatten and informed him of the inadequate representation of Muslims in the Armed Forces.[24] Further he stated that,

> reorganisation and nationalisation are proceeding on the basis of a United India, having a single Army, Navy and Air Force. The fundamental constitutional issue of a United or Divided India is thus being prejudiced on a most vital point to the grave detriment of the Muslims. Because of the overwhelming preponderance of Hindus in the officer cadre and particularly in the senior ranks, the Indian Armed Forces organised as a single force for the whole of India will necessarily fall under the complete control of non-Muslims. The proportion of Muslims in the Other Ranks of the Army is being brought down from the pre-war ratio of 40% to less than 30% and steps are being taken to see that they are represented in each arm and service. Their representation in the Air Force (officers and men), and in the Navy (officers) is in the neighbourhood of 15% and in the technical services of the Army is much lower. Such strength as they have is dispersed all over and not organised into Muslim units. Indeed there are no wholly Muslim units even in Infantry, although there are a number of wholly Hindu units.[25]

Later Mountbatten turned down the League's plea to suspend nationalization of the army on the basis of a united India, and to reorganize it so that it could be divided easily when the time came. He told Liaquat Ali Khan that the British would not split up the army while they remained in India: it would have to be done by the Indians themselves after the British had left.[26]

2. RIN and indigenisation

The Flag Officer Commanding Royal Indian Navy submitted, 'The General Views on Nationalisation of the Armed Forces' before the AFNC on 3 February 1947, with an assumption that India would remain in the British Commonwealth.[27] FOCRIN had the opinion that:

> I am in entire agreement with the policy that the Armed Forces of India should be nationalized and in my opinion it should be carried out gradually but boldly if efficiency is to be maintained.

INDIGENISATION, PARTITION, AND A NEW NAVY

> It must always be remembered that in war one takes risks which are not permissible in peacetime. For instance, some young officers may find themselves in command before they really have sufficient knowledge or experience of commanding their men or the administrative ability to take charge of the accounts, returns, paper-work etc., quite apart from their technical knowledge. They may be lucky in not having to fight an action or run their ship ashore in the early period of their command before they have gained experience these risks can be accepted in war, but, I suggest, cannot be taken in peacetime. I am certain, however, that it is asking for trouble in peacetime to have young officers in command who have not had the experience or time to prove their ability in the handling of men. This was one of the out-standing lessons of the Mutiny in February, 1946.[28]

The FOCRIN considered the promotion of Indians to fill the higher ranks and the recruitments of the right type of Indian youth to fill the lower officer ranks as the two main problems of nationalisation. The British Admiralty and the RIN believed that "senior officers are not made in a day, it is experience that counts."[29] The RIN was not in favour of an immediate indigenisation and quick promotions to the Indian officers because they did not have adequate naval service and experiences for higher ranks. FOCRIN pointed out the length of time that it had taken the Australian Cadets Training College in Jervis Bay, which was started in 1910. The first Australian Officer who started his career at Jervis Bay was promoted to Rear Admiral on 8 January 1946, after completion of about 35 years of naval service. The Senior Indian Officer in the Royal Indian Navy was a cadet in 1931 and on the analogy of the Australian navy, he would be a Rear Admiral in 1966.[30] FOCRIN recommended the complete nationalisation of RIN by 1956 by stating that "as the RIN is a smaller and less complicated navy, it should be possible to complete nationalisation without undue loss of efficiency sooner than this and, I would suggest, it could be done in about another ten years. It follows, therefore, that senior British officers must either be retained in the Service or seconded from the Royal Navy until normal flow of promotion is to be retained."[31] With respect to the indigenisation of the Indian Army, Padeep P. Barua says that:

> Contrary to the popular belief, Indianisation was never meant to be a half hearted attempt to mollify Indian nationalist politicians. The evidence suggests that Indianisation was not a matter of political expediency to be achieved at any cost. Military efficiency remained a priority in this reform, and, had it become obvious over a period of time that the Indian officers were not up to the task, it is quite likely that the entire reform process would have failed.[32]

INDIGENISATION, PARTITION, AND A NEW NAVY

The RIN believed that when Britain Officers below the rank of Commander transferred back to the Royal Navy, the efficiency of the RIN would drop because trained officers would be leaving and their place could only be taken by Indian officers lacking in full naval training and experience. In order to avoid the loss of 'Specialist' officers, FOCRIN recommended the retention of some junior British officers in the RIN seconded from the RN until they could be entirely replaced by Indians.[33] For a fast indigenisation, induction of officers from the Indian Mercantile Marine, who were having enough sea experience, was another option. However they were not of the 'right type' because they were not qualified or experienced in handling men, nor had they the naval customs and traditions behind them; they would not be able to assume the role of naval officers without further training and experience in the Navy. He emphasized that "the transfer of British Officers to the RN in the near future will reduce the number of trained and experienced officers to a dangerous degree."[34]

By 1946 the recruitment of British Officers in RIN had ceased and the numbers and standard of Indian boys coming up for naval cadetships was not high and the numbers actually accepted fell far short of requirements.[35] In this aspect, the FOCRIN urged the Government to take this up as a priority matter and give all possible encouragement to bring the right type of boys forward to achieve the nationalisation of RIN. In the main, the lower deck (ratings) of the RIN was already nationalised, but there was a shortage of senior ratings in the artificer, electrical and radar branches. It was proposed to be filled by secondment of British ratings from the RN and it was hoped that the shortage in the electrical and radar branches would be overcome by 1950. But the shortage in the engine room branch was expected to take a longer time. FOCRIN recommended the drawing of engineers from civilian sources to fill the gap temporarily. See Table 6.1.

Table 6.1 RN officers on secondment to RIN in February 1947

Rank	Number	Appointment
Executive		
Vice Admiral	1	FOCRIN
Captain, RNR	1	INS Bahadur
Acting Captains	2	Directorate of Training, NHQ and Naval Officer-in-Charge Karachi
Commander	1	Staff Officer (I&S)
Acting Commanders	2	Deputy Director Personnel Service, NHQ and Dockyard
Lt Commander, RNVR	1	ISCo.Op, NHQ

(*Continued*)

Table 6.1 (Continued)

Rank	Number	Appointment
Electrical		
Commander (L)	1	NHQ
Supply and Secretariat		
Acting Captain	1	D (S) B, NHQ
Acting Commander	1	Secretary to FOCRIN
Instructional		
Commander	1	Deputy Director of Education, NHQ
Instructor Lieutenant	1	INS Shivaji
Shipwright		
Acting Lieutenant	1	Dockyard
Special		
Lieutenant	1	Radar School

Source: Report submitted by the FOCRIN on Armed Forces Nationalisation Committee's Questionnaire No.NC/32 of 9 January 1947, Appendix-B, dated 8 February 1947, Naval Headquarters, New Delhi.

To attain the goal of nationalisation, the RIN had to take necessary and immediate steps. To achieve the full nationalisation the time scale for promotion and pensionable age had to be reduced and preference was to be given to the Indian officers over the British officers, irrespective of their experience and potential, to promote the Indian officers to reach the higher ranks at the earliest time.[36] In order to reduce the number of senior British officers in the RIN, the retirement age of Commander and Captain was reduced to 48 from 50 and 52, respectively.[37] The time scale for promotion proposed by the FOCRIN follows in Table 6.2.:[38]

Table 6.2 Time scale for promotion

Rank	Till 1947	Proposed
Lieutenant to Lieutenant Commander	8 Years	6 Years
Lieutenant Commander to Commander	4 Years	3 Years
Commander to Captain	2 Years	3 Years
Captain to Rear Admiral	4 Years	4 Years

Source: Report submitted by the FOCRIN on Armed Forces Nationalisation Committee's Questionnaire No.NC/32 of 9 January 1947, Appendix-B, dated 8 February 1947, Naval Headquarters, New Delhi.

The Armed Forces Nationalisation Committee recommended the deferment of release of all Indian technical personnel and Indian Naval Reserve Officers who were considered suitable for the grant of short-term commissions and their retention in the service and the offer of sufficiently attractive terms to such individuals as had already been released to persuade them to rejoin. The Committee further recommended the following:[39]

1. Deferring final decision for obtaining officers from the Royal Navy for secondment to RIN
2. Offer of regular commissions to Indian Emergency Commissioned Officers (IECOs) who are still serving or who have been released and are at present debarred by the age limit
3. Grant of more short service commissions to IECOs.
4. Offer of short service commissions to suitably qualified civilians.
5. Grant of short service or regular commissions to VCOs and WOs and other ranks with technical qualification.

The Committee recommended the increase in the number of British officers and others ranks to be released to deal with the additional financial commitment involved in the retention (for the time being) of all Indian technical personnel as recommended by the committee. By early 1947 the British Government realised the fact that the partition of India was unavoidable. 'Preparation of Plan for the Partition of the Indian Armed Forces' says that "After H.M.G.'s statement of 20th February 1947, a United India with single Army, Navy and Air Force can no longer be taken for granted. In spite of this, the reorganisation and nationalisation of the Armed Forces are proceeding on the assumption that they are to continue as a single entity."[40] The Nationalisation Committee submitted its report on 12 May 1947. Its report was not made public in view of the changed political situation. In April 1947 the Government had in principle accepted that the partition of the country would also involve the division of the Armed Forces. Thereafter the issue of nationalisation of the Armed Forces was to be freshly taken up by each Dominion individually.

3. Armed forces and commonwealth

Mountbatten had a very strong emotional feeling for Commonwealth, and he took deep interest in keeping India in the Commonwealth. During the Viceroy's Staff Meeting, Mountbatten expressed his interest in keeping India in the Commonwealth and granting "some sort of" Dominion status to India towards the achievement of this.[41] The Viceroy made it clear in his discussions with the Indian leaders that there would be no question of the British remaining in India after June 1948, unless they were specifically asked to do so by a united request from all Indian parties.⁴² During the Viceroy's Staff Meeting held on 25 April 1947, Mountbatten expressed his views that "all possible assistance must obviously be given to India on request if she remained within the Commonwealth by the provision of officers to assist her armed forces, the task facing a British Governor General, as a high level umpire, with small team of advisers, would be fraught with frightful difficulties."⁴³ He further felt that there was a distinct possibility that, if a united request was made, His Majesty's Government might decide to accede it and leave a British Governor General (possibly himself), in India after June 1948.⁴⁴

The British knew that (according to Mountbatten) it would be disastrous to allow only either one of the parts of India (either India or Pakistan) to remain in the Commonwealth and thus back up one part of India against the other, which might involve the United Kingdom in war.⁴⁵

During Viceroy's Staff meeting Mountbatten said that Indian leaders should ask that India remain within the Commonwealth.⁴⁶ Regarding the retention of British officers in India, Mountbatten informed Rajagopalachari that it would depend upon India's membership in the Commonwealth.⁴⁷ Mountbatten tried to persuade the Indian leaders to retain India in the Commonwealth by informing them of the future military consequences in the situation that Pakistan opted for the Commonwealth and India did not. Mountbatten was of the opinion that the last thing he wanted to see, and it would indeed be most disastrous, would be that Hindustan left the Empire irretrievably and Pakistan remained within.⁴⁸ Mountbatten was personally in favour of British India as a whole being permitted to remain in the Commonwealth, and was using the Pakistan threat to remain in as a lever to help Congress to 'take the plunge'.⁴⁹ Mountbatten stated that:

> Pakistan will ask to be allowed to remain within the British Commonwealth. Whatever the views of the Viceroy or H.M.G. may be, a public appeal from the people of Pakistan to the people of the British Commonwealth not to desert them in their hour of need and not to throw them out of the Empire to which they have belonged for so long, may well produce a popular reaction to accept them into the fold and hold out a help in hand. Thus Pakistan would remain on the secret list of equipment and technique and, with our material and personnel, could rapidly forge ahead with their armed forces, thus constituting a very grave threat to Hindustan. Unless Hindustan chose to link up its fate with Russia (and accept the inevitability of coming under the consequent Communist influence), they would either have to remain out in the cold, with an entirely negligible Navy and Air Force and an out-of-date relatively inefficient Army, or throw in their lot with the British Commonwealth. By doing the latter they would prevent Pakistan from stealing a march on them, they would improve their position in the world, and they

would have a closer link with Pakistan than could be provided by any other means; since they would both be members of the British Commonwealth of Nations and could even call in representatives from the other nations of the Commonwealth to take part in their discussions it they so wished rather than advertise their differences by having to go to U.N.O.[50]

Mountbatten was not in favour of keeping Pakistan in the Commonwealth; he opined that "Although I shall keep my own position clear by saying that I shall not personally recommend the retention of Pakistan within the Commonwealth, I shall also point out that Jinnah is of the opinion that he will be able to appeal to the people of the Commonwealth over my head."[51] Ismay asked Mountbatten to request the Chiefs of Staff to examine the possible retention of parts only of India in the Commonwealth from a purely military point of view.[52] At the same time some British officials believed that keeping India in the Commonwealth would be an additional burden to post-war Britain in terms of defence matters. Lt General A. Nye pointed out to Mountbatten in his letter that "Surely it follows that if we take India into the British Commonwealth of Nations, we are taking, at least from the defence point of view, an ailing child who has literally nothing whatever to offer but who, on the other hand, constitutes a grave liability. We have seen two major wars in our lifetime. The one thing that our Empire needs is the means to recuperate from these awful losses – peace. How can we contemplate the risk of being involved in another war, by taking on this grave liability for the defence of India?"[53] Mountbatten pointed out to O. P. Ramaswami Reddiar that "for defence purposes India would not be even a third class power, and that it would be more of a liability than of a material advantage to have them in the Commonwealth."[54]

The British wanted India, at least the coastal states, in the Commonwealth in order to have a military base in the Indian Ocean. It is evident from the British Prime Minister's letter, which stated that "I should like the Chiefs of Staff in their discussion with General Ismay to consider the position in the event of (a) Western India, (b) Bengal or (c) one of the States with a sea board such as Travancore desiring to remain in the Commonwealth when the rest of India decides to go out. I should like to have their appreciation from the military point of view."[55]

At the same time some British officials considered the Commonwealth as a way of continuing to control the fate of Indians. Nicholls wrote to British Prime Minister:

> The actual partition and separation of Indian assets, services and responsibilities will be a task of immense difficulty, but it will be one of India's own making and one which she could only carry out with the active assistance of British experience and statesmanship.

Britain will thus remain as the arbiter of India's destiny and the moderating influence in her racial troubles and problems. It will continue to render India great service and remain indispensable in her affairs and a vital force in India's internal peace and welfare.[56]

The British Government expected to influence the successor states of India and Pakistan during the process of forging a new Commonwealth. The Labour Government under Attlee wanted to maintain a close relationship with India and Pakistan after 1947, but this was more difficult in the case of Pakistan because of the circumstances of the partition of the sub-continent.[57] Jinnah viewed the British critically, and they reciprocated fully.[58] The British Government was not sure about India in the Commonwealth for a longer duration. The British Government strongly believed that India would only remain in Commonwealth until the new constitution was framed.[59] They assumed the possibility of India being in the hands of a Socialist or Communist Government after the general elections and that India would go out of the Commonwealth.[60] During the Viceroy's 29th meeting, Mountbatten expressed his view that the British had many solid advantages in the immediate transfer of power.[61] He opined that an early transfer of power would gain her tremendous credit and the early transfer would involve the termination of present responsibilities.[62] A request by India to remain in the Commonwealth would enhance British prestige enormously in the eyes of the world.[63] From the point of view of Empire defence, an India within the Commonwealth filled in the whole framework of world strategy; a neutral India would leave a gap which would complicate the problem enormously; a hostile India would mean that Australia and New Zealand were virtually cut off.[64]

"The British deliberately avoided any mention of their defence interests to Indian leaders during the negotiations."[65] The British kept the discussions on Commonwealth as a 'top secret' matter, and it was strictly restricted to the high level officials like the Cabinet, the Viceroy, the British Chiefs of Staff, and the Commander-in-Chief India, and India Office officials at the highest levels.[66] Anita Inder Singh says that "Except for those who worked behind the scenes during the negotiations, such as Sir B.N. Rau and V.P. Menon, Indians were probably ignorant of the British keenness to retain India in the imperial security system."[67]

"India was the backbone of British military power east of Suez."[68] During the two world wars Britain exploited the Indian manpower for their victory. "Lord Wavell thought them an indispensable factor in Britain's victory over the Axis. India's manpower contribution in the Second World War roughly equalled that of South Africa, Canada, New Zealand, and other Commonwealth territories put together, and was surpassed only by that of Britain, which raised five million men."[69] Anita Inder Singh says that "The loss of India would weaken the British position in the Middle East and the Indian Ocean"[70] It would be in the British interest to have a stable and united India as a partner in the Commonwealth. A weak and divided India "would be a menace to our peace and a strong India within the empire would be the mainstay of our system of co-operative defence."[71]

The British wanted to have a large industrializing India as a partner in Commonwealth defence to maintain a defensive and highly mechanized force.[72] Ernest Bevin, one of the Labour members of the coalition cabinet, submitted his secret paper before the War Cabinet in June 1943 regarding the future role of the Indian subcontinent. He recommended to develop India including Burma up to the Persian Gulf as an organic defence area in partnership with the British Commonwealth.[73]

According to Anita Inder Singh, Britain's withdrawal from the Indian subcontinent was more spontaneous. Britain granted India independence because it could neither afford to hold the subcontinent with its own troops nor rely on Indian officials in the face of the Indian National Congress's overwhelming popularity. This reason for the rapid end of the Raj explains why, immediately after independence, Britain had to try harder than it had expected to preserve its diplomatic influence over India and Pakistan.[74]

In early 1947, due to unexpected partition, indigenisation of armed forces was dropped and the Indian leaders were requesting the British Government for the retention of British officers in India in the post-independence period. British knew that indigenisation of the officer cadre would take a minimum of five to 10 years and for that period British officers would be the top brass of the armed forces of India. Their dual allegiance to the Indian and British governments would not cause much difficulty as India and Britain would be co-ordinating military policy.[75] Military and foreign policy implications of Indian affiliation to the Commonwealth received top priority in official memos and discussions of the British.[76] "India was the 'only suitable base' from which the British could sustain military operations on a large scale in the Far East. If India left the Commonwealth, the British position in the North Indian Ocean would be weakened, and oil supplies from the Persian Gulf could not be guaranteed."[77] "In other words, quitting India without securing military bonds with it could lead to the disintegration of British power and the abandonment of many a grand design of imperial strategy."[78]

Withdrawal of British forces

On 5 April 1947 Auchinleck, the Commander-in-Chief, pointed out Mountbatten that neither the British Army nor the British officers of the Indian Army could serve in an India that was neither part of Commonwealth nor a British Dominion.[79] "Accordingly one consequence of secession appeared to be the withdrawal forthwith of all British personnel from the armed forces."[80] The British Government decided to commence the withdrawal of the British Army from India immediately after the transfer of power and planned to complete it the end of 1947.[81] Mountbatten was informed that

"On transfer of power on August 15, British Army Forces will immediately start to be withdrawn from India. This withdrawal will be carried out as rapidly as shipping permits, and is expected to be completed by about the end of this year."[82] It was also decided with concept that British Forces in India, post 15 August 1947, should have no operational function whatever, and that they would therefore not be available to be called upon for such purposes as internal security, use on the North West Frontier or, used in the States.[83] They would be regarded as continuing their training in India until transport arrived to take them back to England.[84] The Viceroy informed all British service personnel in India that "The Indian Armed Forces have now to be reconstituted in accordance with the policy agreed by the Indian leaders. . . . The Commander-in-Chief and Senior Officers of all three Services at Defence Headquarters are staying on for this period. The Commander-in-Chief, who is assuming the title Supreme Commander, will be responsible under the general direction of the Joint Defence Council of the two Dominions for reconstituting the Armed Forces."[85]

The Chiefs of Staff Report of 18 March 1947 said that "The withdrawal of Army and Air Force Stores and equipment could probably be completed within four months. There are no R.N. personnel in India except the C-in-C, Indian Navy. The withdrawal of naval armament stores and the few remaining Admiralty civilians could be completed within the four months mentioned above."[86]

4. Partition of Indian armed forces

At the beginning of 1947, even though the British Government knew that the partition was likely to take place, they did not expect an immediate transfer of power and partition of Armed Forces in India. General Scoon, the Principal Staff Officer, had the opinion that "if the Army is to be handed over to more than one authority it cannot be handed over as an Army but only as communal forces to the respective sides; that once the process starts India will be deprived of any efficient defence and the internal situation will become dangerous."[87] A memorandum by the Secretary of State for India urged the British Government that "A partition of the armed forces will have to be planned in advance and on some definite assumption as regards the political future. . . . a decision on which definite planning and action can be taken would have to be reached by September, 1947, on the assumption that the withdrawal date is June 1948."[88] Further it was stated that:

> It is obvious that if there has to be a division of the Armed Forces, it can only be done on a communal basis. . . . The problem of the Indian Navy will be even more difficult. It is not large enough to stand division into parts which would be effective. The bulk of the personnel come from the Punjab which has no port. The coastline of India is mainly that of Hindustan but, if the Navy were given to Hindustan, Karachi and Calcutta would have no protection.[89]

INDIGENISATION, PARTITION, AND A NEW NAVY

Regarding the division of the armed forces Liaquat Ali Khan wrote to Mountbatten that:

> The division of India implies the division of the Armed Forces to serve Pakistan and Hindustan. Without its own Armed Forces Pakistan would be like a house of cards. But a division of the Armed Forces is a delicate and difficult operation which cannot be carried out in a day.... [T]he Armed Forces should now be reorganised in such a manner that they can be readily split up at the proper time. It is also essential to secure the adequate representation of Muslim officers and men in each branch of the Army, Navy and Air Force by conversion of units and training of personnel. There would then be a self contained and balanced force to serve Pakistan and another to serve Hindustan and these two forces would be held together in a single command till the constitutional issue is decided.
>
> Unless this is done, the Armed Forces which are the ultimate sanction and support for any State will become predominantly Hindu in character and will be completely under the control of the Hindus.[90]

Again on 13 April 1947, Liaquat Ali Khan suggested Mountbatten to secure an adequate representation of the Muslims in each branch of the Army, Navy and Air Force to reorganise the Armed Forces on a communal basis so that they could be split up when a decision on the partition of the country was taken.[91] As a response to Liaquat Ali Khan's request, Field Marshal Auchinleck informed the Viceroy (Mountbatten) that "such re-organization would be a very complicated and difficult process, taking many months if not years."[92] He said that he was not prepared to undertake responsibility for planning such re-organization.[93]

Krishna Menon told the Viceroy that Congress would never agree, if India was given early Dominion status, to the splitting of the Army.[94] Menon expressed had the view that "if Pakistan wanted an Army, it would have to be built up from nothing. Muslims would be released from the Union of India Army for this purpose."[95]

The British Government never wanted the splitting of Indian armed forces, in any event, while the British were responsible for the defence of India.[96] But for Mountbatten the splitting of Army was impossible, and one of his objects was to prove that it was impracticable.[97] Mountbatten, the Governor General of India, had a meeting with General Auchinleck on 14 April 1947 and discussed the balkanisation of India.[98] Mountbatten wanted to have a unified India with a strong centre, and when that was given up, he then wanted to have a united India which would have a weak centre.[99]

Preparation of plan for the partition of the Indian Armed Forces says that "The division of Implies the division of the Armed Forces for no State can exist without its own Armed Forces on whom rests the ultimate responsibility for internal security as well as external defence."[100] "The British forces in India were in no way prepared for the strains and shocks they were to suffer in the final year of their existence. As late as March 1946 there existed not a single contingency plan to prepare the Indian Army for partition."[101]

"Although the British government had accepted the inevitability of partitioning the country, the division of the Armed Forces was considered unthinkable."[102] Lt General Sir Francis Tucker, General Officer Commanding, Eastern Command, came up with a scheme for the division of the Armed Forces on a communal basis.[103] While the British Government was willing to deviate from the Cabinet Mission's plan of unitary India, it did not want to forsake the unity of the Armed Forces.[104] Mountbatten arrived in India on 22 March 1947 as the new Viceroy, and he had been told the objective of the British Government by Atlee, the British Prime Minister:

> It is the definite objective of the His Majesty's Government to obtain a unitary Government for British India and the Indian States, if possible within British Commonwealth, through the medium of a Constituent Assembly, set up and run in accordance with the Cabinet Mission's plan, and you should do the utmost in your power to persuade all Parties to work together to this end, and advise His Majesty's Government, in the light of developments, as to the steps that will have to be taken.[105]

Further Mountbatten was instructed by Atlee:

> If by October 1 you consider that there is no prospect of reaching a settlement on the basis of a unitary government for British India, either with or without the co-operation of the Indian States, you should report to His Majesty's Government on the steps which you consider should be taken for the handing over of power on the due date. . . . You should take every opportunity of stressing the importance of ensuring that the transfer of power is effected with full regard to the defence requirements of India. In the first place you will impress upon the Indian leaders the great importance of avoiding any breach in the continuity of the Indian Army and of maintaining the organisation of defence on an all Indian basis. Secondly you will point out the need for continued collaboration in the security of the Indian Ocean area for which provision might be made in an agreement between the two countries. At a suitable date His Majesty's Government would be ready to send military and other experts to India to assist in discussing the terms of such an agreement.[106]

Mountbatten never wanted the partition of the Indian Armed Forces. He tried all means to persuade the Indian leaders to maintain the unity of the Armed Forces. He maintained that there could be no splitting of the Indian Army before the withdrawal of the British for two reasons. "The mechanics won't permit it, and I won't."[107] The Armed Forces of India was not prepared for a partition in 1947. The Commander-in-Chief, Auchinleck, and most British Officers of the Indian Army were opposed to the division of the Armed Forces. Even when the creation of Pakistan appeared a certainty, Auchinleck argued against the division of the Armed Forces. Field Marshal Auchinleck, the Commander-in-Chief in India had expressed to the Viceroy his view that it would take five to 10 years satisfactorily to divide the Indian Army.[108] The Muslim League's declared policy was that they did not want a unified Army.[109] Mountbatten had the apprehension that "the result of splitting the Army communally would be that the non-Muslim parties would be much stronger. They would be able take over the General Headquarters, the main supply dumps and a large majority of the officers. The Muslims would be left with a greatly inferior share."[110] The Viceroy intended to point out the matter to Jinnah that the Muslims would be left with a greatly inferior share.

A draft broadcast of the Viceroy stated, "the present Armed Forces may have to be divided into two or more separate entities. This is under investigation by the Defence Committee and the difficulties of replacing the 12,000 British Officers by Indian Officers by the end of June 1948 are such that I do not believe that, on top of this, it will be possible to get very far with any partition of the forces before this date. All parties are therefore agreed on the need to keep the present Armed Forces as a single force until plans for their orderly separation can be put into operation."[111]

Regarding the division of the Armed Forces of India, Field Marshal Auchinleck, the Commander-in-Chief, emphasised the continuance of central control of the general administration of the Armed Forces was essential until the process of division was complete and the necessary machinery had been established in the new dominions; and British officers, who held their commissions from the King, could not be required to serve a Dominion Government except with their consent. Such officers as were necessary for effecting the division of the Armed Forces of India and were willing to undertake such service, should therefore be transferred to the British Army or the Royal Navy, and their services thereafter lent to the Indian Governments.[112]

A suitable scale of compensation was sanctioned by the British Government for regular officers of the Royal Indian Navy, the Indian Army and Medical Service, whose appointments were terminated on account of transfer of power.[113] The amount of compensation as provided for in the Viceroy's announcement of 30 April 1947 was on a graduated scale, depending on age. Later, after the Dominions had been constituted, it was decided by the Joint Defence Council on 20 August 1947 that deferred pay should be

INDIGENISATION, PARTITION, AND A NEW NAVY

granted to all Indian ranks of the Armed Forces provided they were fully qualified and were discharged only because they did not elect to serve either of the two dominions.

Each of the existing departments of the Government of India were renamed by adding the word 'India' in brackets at the end of its former designation, to handle cases exclusively or predominantly concerning the future Dominion of India.[114] On 4 July 1947, the Indian Independence Bill was introduced in the House of Commons. The Bill was passed, without any amendment, by the House of Commons on 15 July, and by the House of Lords on the following day, and it received the Royal Assent on 18 July 1947.[115] On 22 July 1947, it was decided that the Partition Council should function temporarily as the Joint Defence Council until 15 August 1947, when the latter would come into full being. All the decisions relating to the Armed Forces were taken by the Partition Council, or the Partition Council functioning as the Provisional Joint Defence Council, or the Joint Defence Council itself after 15 August. The Joint Defence Council was set up by the Joint Defence Council order 1947 (Notification No.G.G.O.2, dated 11 August 1947) which was to be valid up to 01 April 1948.

5. Armed Forces Reconstitution Committee

Immediately after transfer of power and before the consequential administrative readjustments had been completed, India was confronted with problems of formidable magnitude. In August 1947 the Armed Forces Reconstitution Committee was set up. Before the transfer of power, all the higher appointments in command and on the staff had been held by British officers. Indian officers had to be appointed to these posts to replace those who has chosen to retire or had opted to serve in Pakistan. The composition of the Armed Forces Reconstitution Committee and its Sub-Committee for RIN consisted as follows:

H.E Field Marshal Sir Claude Auchinleck, Commander-in-Chief in India as Chairman

1. Vice Admiral Sir Geoffery Miles, Commander-in-Chief, RIN
2. Air Marshal H. S. P Walmsely, Air Officer Commanding-in-Chief in India
3. Lt General Sir Arthur F Smith, Chief of the General Staff
4. Mohammad Ali, Financial Adviser, Defence & Supply, Military Finance Department
5. G. S. Bhalja, Addl Secretary, Defence Department
6. Colonel H. V. S Muller, Secretary, Commanding-in-Chief's Secretariat

Royal Indian Navy Sub-committee

1. Commodore J. W. Jefford.
2. Commander A. B. Goord, Staff Officer (Plans).
3. Commander J. C. Mansell, Commander Administration, NHQ.
4. Commander H. M. S Choudri, Staff Officer (Naval Appointments), NHQ.
5. Commander B. S. Soman.
6. Lt Commander D. Shanker
7. Lt Commander I. K. Mumtaz, Dy Director of Engineering, NHQ
8. Lt Commander A. R. N. Hussain
9. Lt C. J. Munsiff
10. S. Jayasankar, Deputy Financial Adviser, Military Finance
11. Mumtaz Mirza, Deputy Financial Adviser, Military Finance

The Armed Forces Reconstitution Committee decided that the Governments of the Dominions of India and Pakistan should take over responsibility for the government of their respective territories, with effect from 15 August 1947.[116] On 15 August the Army Headquarters of each Dominion would become responsible for the operational control of all Indian formations and units within their respective territories. Indian units overseas would remain under the Supreme Commander and British units would be withdrawn from India and Pakistan over a period commencing in July 1947.[117]

The Partition Council had taken the decision regarding the allotment (reconstitution) of units of the Armed Forces between the future Governments of India and Pakistan in two stages: the first stage, namely, 'a rough and ready division on a communal basis' and the second stage, namely 'the combing out of units on a basis of the voluntary transfer of individuals'.[118] These decisions were based on the unanimous recommendations of the Armed Forces Reconstitution Sub-Committee and the Armed Forces Reconstitution Committee.[119] The Partition Council took up with the reconstitution of the Royal Indian Air Force and Indian Army and much later the reconstitution of the Royal Indian Navy. The Partition Council recommended the following division of the ships of the Royal Indian Navy:[120]

> India: All existing landing craft and 32 ships, of which there will be 4 sloops, 2 frigates, 12 minesweepers, 1 corvette, 1 survey vessel, 4 trawlers, 4 motor minesweepers and 4 harbour defence motor launches.
>
> Pakistan: 16 ships including 2 sloops, 2 frigates, 4 minesweepers, 2 trawlers, 2 motor minesweepers and 4 harbour defence motor launches.

6. Partition and its adverse impact

The Partition of British India in 1947, which created the two independent states of India and Pakistan, was followed by one of the cruellest and bloodiest migrations and ethnic cleansings in history.[121] On 3 June 1947 Lord Mountbatten, the Viceroy of India, had announced the partition of India (what has come to be known as the 3 June Plan or Mountbatten Plan) that was to be achieved within 75 days, and by 26 June a Partition Council was established. The border between India and Pakistan was determined by a British Government–commissioned report usually referred to as the Radcliffe Line after the London lawyer Sir Cyril Radcliffe. Four days later, on 7 June 1947, when this Council announced the guidelines for the division of the armed forces, just about 45 days were left in which to complete the task. This responsibility was entrusted to the Armed Forces Reconstitution Committee (AFRC), chaired by Field Marshal Sir Claude Auchinleck, the then Commanding-in-Chief in India.[122] The Committee recommended the reconstitution of the Armed Forces on the basis of territorial considerations, not on communal ones, and the defence personnel were given a choice of leaving the service or continuing in either the Indian or the Pakistan forces.

Finally the partition was promulgated in the Indian Independence Act of 1947 and resulted in the dissolution of the British Indian Empire. The partition displaced up to 12.5 million people in the former British Indian Empire, with estimates of loss of life varying from several hundred thousand to a million. The partition settlement also included the division of state assets, including the Defence Forces, the Indian Civil Service and other administrative services, the Indian railways, and the central treasury. On 18 July 1947, the British Parliament passed the Indian Independence Act that finalized the partition arrangement. The Government of India Act of 1935 was adapted to provide a legal framework for the two new dominions.

The impact of partition fell on all the state institutions; even the defence forces did not remain untouched. The naval force was divided into Royal Indian Navy and Royal Pakistan Navy. The Royal Indian Navy, which had gained extensive experience in World War II, had to be split in the approximate proportion of two-thirds of the undivided fleet and associated assets to India and one-third to Pakistan. Regarding the placing of the Union Jack in the Naval Ensign of the future Royal Pakistan Navy, Jinnah informed Mountbatten that, he had been unable to find a single supporter for the idea of having the Union Jack in the upper canton of the Muslim League flag. He explained that it would be repugnant to the religious feelings of the Muslims to have a flag with a Christian cross alongside the crescent.[123]

RIN still continued to relay on the Royal Navy for its assistance for quite a few years in the form of loan service of officers to man appointments at various levels including Chiefs of the Naval Staff. The Indian Navy was the last of the tri-service forces to have an Indian Chief of Naval Staff. The way

INDIGENISATION, PARTITION, AND A NEW NAVY

the British handled the so-called transfer of power to India was that they were too exhausted after the Second World War to sustain the empire; they were in a hurry to leave and made no attempt to ensure an orderly transition.

The Indian and Pakistani political leaders do bear some of the responsibility. The Congress and the Muslim League failed to reach a compromise; the reasons for this are argued about to this day. There was much uncertainty in the rush to hand over power. Few people could guess what ideologies the future states would represent, where each state would be created, what the relations would be with the princely states, how the defence forces would be split and so on. It took a few years for conditions to stabilise. Nowadays we are used to a world of nation-states but this was one of the first acts of decolonization.[124]

> Admiral Sreedharan recalls,
> I was then serving onboard HMIS Dhanush, the Boys ship, which was at sea on its way to Aden. The ship was recalled to Bombay and allotted for transfer to Pakistan. Indian officers and sailors were replaced by Pakistanis, except British officers, one of whom was in command – Commander FA Kilburn, R.I.N. The ship was then to continue its training cruise, including the Indian trainees onboard in order not to interrupt sea training, thought to be an unfair decision for the Indian boys. Although there were no incidents, the tension was visible and both nationalities staying on board together during the period of transition was a strain. The ship was renamed Zulfiquer, when it reached Karachi. (See Table 6.2)[125]

Admiral R. D. Katari, the first Indian Chief of the Naval Staff recalls the partition in his book *A Sailor Remembers*:

> On partition the Royal Indian Navy was left with four of the war time built frigates and about seven or eight of the minesweepers also built during the war and little else. The pre war sloops were either scrapped or sunk like the "Pathan" and later "Indus" in Akyab harbour. We lost three well established schools, the Boy's Training Establishment "Bahadur", Gunnery school "Himalya" and Radar school "Chamak" all in Karachi. The rest of the training establishments were left with us, but they were all war rime constructions and needed modernization or replacement.

Training establishments

Proposals for control of training establishments were made jointly for all three services. The AFRC accepted the unanimous recommendations of the Naval Sub-Committee that the technical training establishments fall in three categories.[126]

Table 6.3 Partition of RIN ships

Type of Vessel	India	Pakistan
Frigate	HMIS *Tir*	HMPS *Shamsher*
	HMIS *Kukri*	HMPS *Dhanush*
Sloop	HMIS *Sutlej*	HMPS *Narbada*
	HMIS *Jumna*	HMPS *Godavari*
	HMIS *Kistna*	
	HMIS *Cauvery*	
Corvettes	HMIS *Assam*	–
Minesweeper	HMIS *Orissa*	HMPS *Kathiawar*
	HMIS *Deccan*	HMPS *Baluchistan*
	HMIS *Bihar*	HMPS *Oudh*
	HMIS *Kumaon*	HMPS *Malwa*
	HMIS *Rohilkhand*	
	HMIS *Khyber*	
	HMIS *Carnafic*	
	HMIS *Rajputana*	
	HMIS *Konkan*	
	HMIS *Bombay*	
	HMIS *Bengal*	
	HMIS *Madras*	
Survey vessel	HMIS *Investigator*	–
Trawler	HMIS *Nasik*	HMPS *Rampur*
	HMIS *Calcutta*	HMPS *Baroda*
	HMIS *Cochin*	
	HMIS *Amritsar*	
Motor Minesweeper (MMS)	MMS 130	MMS 129
	MMS 132	MMS 131
	MMS 151	
	MMS 154	
Motor Launch (ML)	ML 420	–
Harbour Defence Motor Launch (HDML)	HDML 1110	HDML 1261
	HDML 1112	HDML 1262
	HDML 1117	HDML 1263
	HDML 1118	HDML 1266
Miscellaneous	All existing landing craft	–

Source: Singh, Rear Admiral Satyindra, *Under Two Ensigns*, Oxford and IBH Publishing Co, New Delhi, 1986.

1   those that can be split almost immediately
2   those that can be split before the end of reconstitution
3   those that will require up to two years to split

Under the first category were supply and secretariat training, cookery training, physical and recreation training, firefighting, and damage control. The second category covered the torpedo and anti-submarine training, electrical and communication training, and the third category consisted of gunnery

INDIGENISATION, PARTITION, AND A NEW NAVY

and radar training, and shipwright training. The Committee recommended that the schools in the second category be split forthwith and that the training in these subjects, after 15 August 1947 would be entirely under the control of the Dominion concerned.[127] It was also recommended that the schools mentioned in the third category would be split by the end of reconstitution.

The Viceroy had expressed his views before the Provisional Joint Defence Council (JDC) on 6 August 1947 that "it was clear that where the two dominions were in a position to set up independent schools at once, this should be done without delay. The problem to be considered was the control of schools which would serve both dominions, both those which could be duplicated before 01 April 1948, and those which would have to continue in joint use after that period."[128] The Indian representatives felt that the training of their armed forces was a vital matter over which they must exercise complete control.[129] This was the view of the Indian Cabinet. The JDC realised that although there were risks involved in transferring the control of training establishments to the respective dominions, however the need of the hour was that they should be prepared to stand on their own, hence the risks were accepted. The other view was that it was preferable to have joint control until such time as the whole layout of training establishments would be reorganised so as to ensure complete equality of treatment to both dominions.

The Commander-in-Chief emphasised that the efficiency and harmony of the training establishments should be maintained. He was sceptical of handling the training establishments of two dominions without resolving the difficulties coming in front. He feared that the both training schools would lose their efficiency if their difficulties were not resolved and he considered that problem of instructors as being one of the most important.[130] Hence, he recommended that the both the training establishments should temporarily controlled by the Joint Defence Council to make them efficient in facing future challenges.[131] The Provisional Joint Defence Council decided that, as soon after 15 August 1947 as possible the Defence Ministers of the two dominions should report to the Joint Defence Council the dates by which they wished to assume control of the various training establishments serving both dominions.[132] The Commander-in-Chief (Supreme Commander) was instructed to prepare a draft charter to govern the conduct of these establishments after they passed to the dominion's control.[133]

7. Effects of transfer of power and partition on RIN

Manpower

With the creation of the Dominion of India on 15 August 1947, British officers of the RIN and its Reserves were compulsorily retired.[134] Regular British officers were granted compensation for loss of career and officers not qualified for full pension were granted proportionate pensions. Consequent on the

INDIGENISATION, PARTITION, AND A NEW NAVY

partition of the Navy, Indian officers were given the option to elect for service with either of the Dominion Navies subject to the following provisions:[135]

1. Muslims residing in India and non-Muslims from Pakistan areas could choose service with either navy
2. Muslims from Pakistan could opt for service only with the RPN and non-Muslims from the Indian Dominion could opt for service only with the RIN.

Officers who did not wish to serve either Navy had the option to retire without any compensatory benefits. British officers (ex-RIN) were invited to volunteer for service in the Armed Forces of India and Pakistan, and those who volunteered were transferred to a special list of the Royal Navy and were placed under the administrative control of the Deputy Supreme Commander (Navy) who detailed them for duty with either the RIN or RPN according to requirements.[136] On the closing down of Supreme Commander's Headquarters on 30 November 1947, the administrative control of British officers passed to the Deputy Commander (Navy), whose appointment lapsed on 31 December 1947. The retirement of British officers caused a serious shortage in the officer cadre, particularly in the senior ranks.[137] The British officers who volunteered were selected for extended service with the RIN on a contract basis for three years from 1 January 1948. Their contracts guaranteed them in the main terms and conditions of service similar to those in force prior to 15 August 1947.[138]

Figure 6.1 Outline of changes in personnel: ratings:[139]

Ratings	Borne on 14-8-47	Opted for Union of India	Borne on 1-7-1948	
CS	3654		1911	NCS
	31		19	
SS	5458	4880	2812	
SS(Ex-Army)	107		3	
HO	152	90	44	
	9402	4970	4789	
Boys	980	441	513	
Apprentices	124	97	121	

The net intake during the period (15 August 1947 to 30 June 1948) was 421 (including Boys and Apprentices) and of these 289 were new recruits (mainly Boys and Apprentices) and 132 other intakes comprising recovered

INDIGENISATION, PARTITION, AND A NEW NAVY

deserters and ratings re-enrolled.[140] The total wastage during the said period was 272 (including Boys and Apprentices); of these 79 were discharged; 187 deserted and 6 died.[141] A total of 940 personnel resigned from the naval service during this period. The number of ratings transferred to Pakistan up to 30 June 1948 are given in Tables 6.4, 6.5 and 6.6.

Table 6.4 Transfer of RIN ratings to Pakistan

Month	Number
August 1947	3,100
September 1947	230
October 1947	24
November 1947	20
December 1947	37
January 1948	8
February 1948	6
March 1948	7
April 1948	17
May 1948	4
June 1948	3
Total	**3,456**

Source: Report on the Royal Indian Navy, 15 August 1947 to 15 August 1948, 1948, Naval Historical Branch, Portsmouth, United Kingdom., p. 24

Table 6.5 Provincial aspect of active service ratings

Province	As on 14–8–1947	As on 01–6–1948
Madras	22.7%	29.0%
Bombay	7.5%	10.5%
CP & Berar	0.9%	1.5%
UP	7.0%	9.2%
Assam	1.2%	1.0%
Bihar	1.7%	1.7%
Orissa	0.8%	1.1%
East Punjab	6.5%	8.6%
West Bengal	2.1%	2.5%
Travancore	8.4%	12.2%
NWFP	2.9%	0.3%
Sind	0.4%	0.1%
West Punjab	21.4%	4.9%
East Bengal	7.7%	5.3%
Others	8.8%	12.1%

Source: Report on the Royal Indian Navy, 15th August 1947 to 15th August 1948, 1948, Naval Historical Branch, Portsmouth, United Kingdom., pp. 24–25

INDIGENISATION, PARTITION, AND A NEW NAVY

Table 6.6 Communal composition of active services ratings

Religion	As on 14–8–1947	As on 01–6–1948
Hindus	38.1%	57.7%
Muslims	40.8%	9.4%
Sikhs	1.7%	4.4%
Others	19.4%	28.5%

Source: Report on the Royal Indian Navy, 15th August 1947 to 15th August 1948, 1948, Naval Historical Branch, Portsmouth, United Kingdom., p. 25

A total of 620 active service ratings (including boys and apprentices) were demobilised during the period 15 August 1947 to 30 June 1948; the total number of active service ratings released up to the end of 30 June 1948 became 11,316.[142] Effective borne strength as on 1 July 1948 was 5,242. See Table 6.7 for the breakdown of officers and Table 6.8 for warrant officers:[143]

Active Service	4,562
Boys and Apprentices	634
Ex HOs	43
Ex-Army	3

Table 6.7 Borne strength of officers in the post-Independence era

	Borne as on 14–08–1947		Opted for Union of India		Borne as on 01–07–1948	
	European	Indian	European	Indian	European	Indian
Executive	130	295	56	225	12	207
Engineer	59	43	30	31	6	29
Electrical	4	19	2	22	2	22
Medical	4	43	2	39	–	33
Supply & Secretariat (S & S)	8	116	3	95	–	85
Special	9	45	5	32	2	25
Instructor	2	12	1	9	2	7
Shipwright	1	–	1	–	2	–
	217	573	100	453	26	408
Total	790		553		434	

Source: Report on the Royal Indian Navy, 15th August 1947 to 15th August 1948, 1948, Naval Historical Branch, Portsmouth, United Kingdom., p. 25

*Commissioned officers (excluding midshipmen and cadets).

*European officers include Royal Navy officers on loan to the RIN and Royal Navy Special List officers.

Table 6.8 Borne strength of warrant officers in the post-Independence era

	Borne as on 14–08–1947		Opted for Union of India		Borne as on 01–07–1948	
	European	*Indian*	*European*	*Indian*	*European*	*Indian*
Cd. Bosun	–	1	–	1	1	1
Bosun	–	7	–	1	–	1
Cd. Gunner	2	–	1	–	2	–
Gunner	1	18	–	–	–	–
Cd. Gunner (T)	1	–	1	–	2	–
Gunner (T)	1	–	1	–	–	–
Cd. Sig Bosun	2	–	1	–	1	2
Sig. Bosun	–	5	1	4	–	3
Cd. Wt. Tel	2	–	–	–	–	1
Wt. Tel	–	8	1	1	2	–
Cd. Wt. Elect.	–	–	–	–	1	–
Wt. Elect.	4	–	4	–	4	–
Wt. Ord. Off	1	1	1	1	–	1
Wt. M.A.A	–	4	–	2	–	3
Cd. Wt. Mech	–	–	–	–	–	1
Wt. Mech	–	7	–	4	–	3
Cd. Wt. Schoolmaster	–	4	–	–	–	–
Wt. Schoolmaster	–	89	–	53	–	54
Cd. Wt. Stores Officer	–	1	–	1	–	1
Wt. Stores Officer	–	9	–	7	–	7
Cd. Wt. Writer Officer	–	2	–	2	–	2
Wt. Writer Officer	–	8	–	8	–	8
Wt. Shipwright	–	–	–	–	1	–
Bosun (P&R.T)	–	2	–	–	–	–
Bosun (A/S)	–	2	–	–	–	–
Wt. Wardmaster	–	2	–	–	–	–
Wt. Engineer	–	23	–	23	3	22
	14	193	11	108	17	110
	207		119		127	

Source: Report on the Royal Indian Navy, 15th August 1947 to 15th August 1948, 1948, Naval Historical Branch, Portsmouth, United Kingdom., p. 26

The communal and provincial representation of Indian officers in the Royal Indian Navy are appended in the following. Table 6.9 gives the provincial composition of Indian commissioned and warrant officers:

Communal composition (Indian commissioned officers)[144]

	As on 14–8–1947	*As on 1–7–1948*
Hindus	38.5%	45.1%
Muslims	14.3%	0.5%

(*Continued*)

(Continued)

	As on 14–8–1947	As on 1–7–1948
Sikhs	5.8%	8.6%
Parsees	8.7%	9.8%
Anglo-Indians	22.3%	16.2%
Indian Christians	7.8%	17.2%
Others	2.6%	2.2%

Communal composition (Indian warrant officers)[145]

	As on 1–7–1948
Hindus	34.5
Muslims	10.9
Sikhs	4.6
Parsees	4.6
Anglo-Indians	2.7
Indian Christians	10.0
Jews	2.7

Table 6.9 Provincial composition of Indian commissioned and warrant officers as on 1 July 1948

Provinces	Commissioned Officers	Warrant Officers
West Bengal	4.9%	1.8%
East Punjab	5.7%	6.4%
Assam	1.0%	–
Madras	11.7%	21.9%
Bombay	34.4%	44.5%
CP & Berar	5.2%	4.6%
UP	6.8%	6.4%
Bihar	1.4%	–
Orissa	0.2%	–
Delhi	4.4%	–
Coorg	0.2%	–
Rajputana & CI	1.7%	–
Jammu & Kashmir	0.2%	–
Patiala	0.2%	–
Hyderabad	0.2%	–
Travancore	2.4%	3.6%
Mysore	1.2%	1.8%
Kathiawar	0.5%	–
Cochin	0.2%	0.9%

INDIGENISATION, PARTITION, AND A NEW NAVY

Provinces	Commissioned Officers	Warrant Officers
Sind	2.4%	0.9%
NWFP	–	0.9%
West Punjab	13.5%	3.6%
East Bengal	1.2%	1.8%
Burma	0.2%	–
South Africa	0.2%	–
Portuguese India	–	9%

Source: Report on the Royal Indian Navy, 15th August 1947 to 15th August 1948, 1948, Naval Historical Branch, Portsmouth, United Kingdom., p. 27

With the partition. the Gunnery, Radar Schools and the New Entry and Boys' Training Establishments went to Pakistan. The Naval Establishments and Boys' Training Establishments which were at Karachi before partition were shifted to Vizagapatam in 1948.

Progress in training all communications ratings was maintained up to 15 August 1947. "As 70 percent of the senior communications ratings were Muslim who opted for Pakistan, India was left almost entirely without instructors and courses in the RIN Signal school had to cease."[146] Accordingly, arrangements were made for higher rate courses in the United Kingdom for RIN communication ratings, and it was planned to restart courses in the RIN Signal School at Cochin by autumn 1948. Four RIN officers were sent to the United Kingdom in November 1947 for the Long Communication course and another six officers were selected to be sent, on completion of the first batch in October 1948.[147] On request of the Government of India, eight vacancies in the Warrant Communication Officers Course, which was commencing on 6 September 1948 in the United Kingdom, were allotted to the RIN.[148]

Captain (E) D. N. Mukerji, RIN, after an initial period in Naval Headquarters (India) where he helped to reorganise the Engineering Branch, assumed command of HMIS *Shivaji* in December 1947. He was the first engineer officer as well as the first Indian to hold this appointment.[149] The RIN Report says that "The engineering branch was the hardest hit by reconstitution."[150] From 108 officers on 14 August 1947 the eventual strength dropped to 35 officers, against a sanctioned cadre of 71. To overcome this shortage, it was decided to grant short service commissions to the personnel possessing suitable qualifications.[151] Thirty vacancies were offered for the year 1948, although about 800 applications were received. In addition, the cadet entry was stopped up to eight per annum, and released engineer officers were re-employed on short service commission. In early 1948 eight special entry engineer officers were recruited and nine more officers were selected in August 1948.[152]

8. Retaining of British personnel

Mountbatten, Nehru and Jinnah realised the serious vacuum and breakdown would affect the defence forces by the removal of trained and experienced British Officers and Service Personnel. Pandit Nehru and Jinnah expressed the desire to have the requisite number of British Officers and other ranks, including technical specialists, to stay back in the service in the post partition period.[153] Accordingly Mountbatten (Viceroy and Chairman of the Joint Defence Council) took up the case for the retaining of British Service Personnel in the new Dominions with the British Government in the United Kingdom and accordingly obtained the approval on the terms and conditions of service under which British officers and other ranks would be asked to volunteer.[154] Nehru requested the British Government that senior Indian officers should be associated immediately with work at the topmost level and their immediate promotion on the basis of the recommendation of the Nationalisation Committee.[155] However, many British officers serving in the two dominions were not keen to continue because of the large-scale disturbances and massacres that took place as a result of partition.[156] In April 1947 Baldev Singh asked Mountbatten about the prospects of retaining of British personnel in the Indian Armed Forces, and he was told that would depend on India's decision to continue in the Commonwealth and her future connection with Britain.[157] Sardar Baldev Singh and Mr. Dundas requested the services of British officers for the Armed Forces of the newly constituted dominions in the post partition period.[158] Mountbatten, the Viceroy, was sceptical that even after three years of independence, the India Armed Forces would not to be fully nationalised and hence would still require British officers.[159]

The Supreme Commander of India was also concerned about the shortage of manpower in the Armed Forces of the two dominions. Therefore he emphasized the retention of the British officers after the period of reconstitution, and he wanted an early decision on the terms and conditions of service of these officers.[160] Approval was accorded in 1948 to the loan of 88 commissioned officers and 61 warrant officers of all branches from the Royal Navy, these numbers including officers already on loan.[161]

Notwithstanding the general policy of nationalisation, RIN had to depend on the Admiralty for the provision of a number of Royal Navy officers for filling certain senior and specialist appointments. Accordingly, a demand was placed on the Admiralty in 1948 for 103 officers, and 75 were provided till August 1949.[162] This was exclusive of 14 RN Special List officers (British officers of the undivided RIN), who were continuing to serve with RIN for specified periods. As on 14 August 1949, the major senior appointments of the RIN which were held by the British Officers on loan were: the Commander-in-Chief RIN, Deputy Commander-in-Chief and Chief of Staff, Commodore Commanding Royal Indian Naval Squadron, Commodore-in-Charge Cochin, Chief of Material, Chief of Naval Aviation, Director of Naval Engineering and Commanding Officer Boys' Training Establishment.[163]

The recommendations of the Armed Forces Reconstitution Committee on the terms of service to be offered to Britishers and men of all three services who were asked to serve on after 15 August 1947 was approved by the Partition Council on 5 July 1947. Initially, all agreements were for one year, but for officers and men of the RIN and Indian Army, the contract was terminable at three months' notice by either party.[164] "For officers and men of the Royal Navy, British Army and Royal Air Force the contract was terminal at three months' notice by the Supreme Commander only, the individual having no choice in the matter."[165] The condition was imposed by the service ministries in the United Kingdom to conform to their general practice elsewhere.[166] The AFRC considered the practicality that many British personnel would be unwilling to be tied down to serve for a year and willing to serve for a shorter period to complete work already in hand which would finish in three or six months. Accordingly the AFRC recommended to the Joint Defence Council that the terms of service for officers and men of the RN, British Army and RAF be altered from one year to engagement for three, six, nine or 12 months, the period to be fixed not liable to notice by either side but to be extendable by periods of not fewer than three months at a time.[167] Those who volunteered would revert to their parent service at the end of the period for which they were engaged. Those volunteering for three or six months would not be eligible for leave, unless they subsequently extended their service to a total of not less than nine months.

Apart from retaining the British officers, to make up the shortage of officers in different branches of the RIN, a scheme for direct recruitment in commissioned ranks on the basis of Short Service Commission of seven years' duration was introduced and 55 Executive, seven Engineering and five Electrical commissions were given between the period August 1948 and August 1949.[168] Fifteen released officers and 14 Reserve Officers were granted five years' Short Service Commission in the RIN under a special scheme.[169] A scheme for the transfer of Short Service Commission (SSC) officers to the Permanent Cadre was introduced in 1948 and subsequently 14 SSC officers and two Reserve Officers were transferred into the permanent cadre.[170] In order to retain the services of many of the officers of the Special Service Branch of the RIN, who were having specialised knowledge in their sphere of work, Government sanction was obtained to the grant of Short Service Commission of three years duration to the selected Special Branch Officers.[171]

9. Post-independence developments

Reorganisation in the post partition era

Rear Admiral J. T. S. Hall, CIE., was selected by the Government of India to command and reorganise the Royal Indian Navy, and assumed his appointment on 15 August 1947. The Government of India decided that the appointment of the Flag Officer Commanding, Royal Indian Navy was to be re-designated Chief of Naval Staff and Commander-in-Chief, Royal Indian Navy.[172] Hall accordingly assumed this new title on 21 June 1948. The appointment of Flag Officer, Bombay, was abolished with effect from 15 August 1947 and Commodore-in-Charge Bombay was created in its place. Commodore H. R. Inigo-Jones, CIE, assumed the duties of Commodore-in-Charge Bombay from that date.[173]

In November 1947, a delegation visited the United Kingdom and made arrangements for 47 officers and 366 ratings to undergo various courses in Royal Navy establishments. Attachments to ships of the home and Mediterranean Fleets for practical sea training were also arranged.[174] Accordingly, 21 cadets in September 1948, 9 in January 1949 and 16 in May 1949 were sent to the United Kingdom for training at the Royal Naval College at Dartmouth.[175] The Indian delegation of November 1947 was sent to the UK with the prime motive to obtain war machines from the British Government. As a guide for the planning of the future of RIN, the Indian delegation asked to be supplied with estimates of the cost of various types of new and secondhand vessels, aircrafts, etc. and their running costs, as set out in the Naval Plan Paper No. 1.[176]

On 1 January 1948, the old Directorate of Training and Education was split into two separate directorates, viz., the Directorate of Weapons and Training (DWT) and the Directorate of Naval Education (DNE).[177] In April 1948, the Education Branch in the RIN was created vide RIN instruction 38/48.[178] The schoolmaster branch merged into the Education Branch and as a result of this change, Headmaster Lieutenant, etc. were re-designated Instructor Lieutenant, etc.

Captain H. G. Hopper, DSO, RN, Director of Weapons and Training on completion of his term of duty with the Royal Indian Navy, relinquished his appointment on 20 May 1948. The Boys' Training Establishment was temporarily transferred from HMIS *Hamla*, Bombay to Vizagapatam in early 1948.[179] On its transfer, there were about 220 boys and since then, however two batches of 130 and 180 were recruited. Different batches were combined and their training was extended by about six months on account of the time that had been lost on transfer of the BTE from Karachi to Bombay and then to Vizagapatam. The first batch of the electrical boys after completing their initial training in the Boys' Training Establishment proceeded to HMIS *Valsura* in June for their technical training. The initial training of Stoker Boys (Marine Engineering ratings) was undertaken in the Boys' Training Establishment and then they proceeded to HMIS *Shivaji* for their technical training.

Between August 1948 and August 1949, 782 boys and 63 Artificer Apprentices were recruited. In order to make up the shortage of manpower in the RIN, the recruitment of Direct Entry ratings was started on 1 October 1948, in the Seaman, Stoker, Communications, Electrical, Cooks, Writers, Stores Assistants, Stewards and Topasses branches and a total of 1,632 were recruited till 14 August 1949.[180] In accordance with the RIN Instruction 26/48, 574 ratings were re-enrolled in various branches up to July 1949.[181] Physical standards in respect of these ratings were relaxed vide RIN Instruction 125/49.[182] In order to overcome the shortage of manpower, created as a result of partition, wide publicity regarding careers in the Navy was given. A pamphlet entitled "India's Navy and How to Join It" and other photographs were published.[183]

On 15 August 1948, a new post designated Flag Officer Commanding Royal Indian Naval Squadron (FOCRINS) was created.[184] The appointment was subsequently re-designated as Commodore Commanding, Royal Indian Naval Squadron (COMRINS) on 4 April 1949.

On 15 January 1949 Naval Headquarters was reorganised into five main departments, each under a Principal Staff Officer, such as Deputy Commander-in-Chief and Chief of Staff, Chief of Personnel, Chief of Administration, Chief of Material and Chief of Naval Aviation.[185] Deputy Commander-in-Chief and Chief of Staff were responsible for planning, operations, communications and intelligence and also for the overall coordination of the staff. Chief of Personnel looked after the recruitment, service conditions, training, welfare and discipline of personnel, and for the appointment of officers and drafting of ratings for the manning of the fleet. Chief of Administration had the task of supply and victualling, stores, pay and allowances, transport and civil engineering. Chief of Material was responsible for engineering, electrical and armament supply and material resources of the Navy. Chief of Naval Aviation was to look after the development of a Naval Air Service.[186]

First Naval plan

The Indian Independence Act of 1947, the partition and the reconstitution of the forces necessitated a number of changes in the law applicable to the Royal Indian Navy. The Naval Discipline Act of the United Kingdom was applied, until 14 August 1947, as a common code of discipline to the Royal Navy and the Royal Indian Navy subject only in the case of the latter to certain modifications made by the Indian Navy (Discipline Act), 1934, as set forth in the Admiralty Fleet order 2810 of 1943 and Royal Navy Instruction 72 of 1943, ceased to apply.[187] British officers of the Royal Indian Navy were transferred to a special list of the Royal Navy. These officers as well as other officers of the Royal Navy attached to the Royal Indian Navy were not subject to the Indian Navy (Discipline) Act.[188]

The Indian Independence Act made provision for the exercise of the power of command by British officers over personnel of the Indian services to which they were attached.[189] The intention was to provide more effectively for the exercise of the disciplinary powers conferred by the Indian Independence Act. This order made provision for the grant of commissions to officers of the Royal Navy attached to the Royal Indian Navy empowering them to convene court-martial under the Indian Navy (Discipline) Act and for the appointment of such officers on court-martial convened under the Act.[190] Due to the shortage of officers in the senior ranks, it was evident that there would be difficulties in convening court-martials as the Indian Navy (Discipline) Act required the appointment of a substantive Captain as President of Court-Martial for the trial of officers below the rank of Captain. It was, therefore, necessary to resort to the wartime expedient and the above mentioned order made provision for the appointment of substantive or acting Commanders as presidents of such Court Martials.[191]

The Admiralty envisaged a force of escort vessels and local flotillas of minesweepers, the extension of base repair facilities at Bombay and possibly Calcutta for the use of large ships of the Commonwealth navies, and the development of considerable assembly and supply arrangements for escort forces at Cochin.[192] However the Indian Government wanted a developed navy, which could prevent a seaborne attack on India in the event of a war. Therefore the Indian Government adopted the policy of securing and maintaining naval superiority over neighbouring nations.[193] "Such a strategic role necessitated a navy possessing the nucleus of a striking force, as well as escort vessels and local flotillas to safeguard the base areas."[194] To modernise the handicapped RIN, a 10-year plan, known as Plan Paper 1, was prepared in late 1947 under the direction of Vice Admiral Parry, the FOCRIN. The naval plan emphasised the immediate indigenisation of RIN and the development of RIN into a carrier navy having two light aircraft carriers, three cruisers, eight destroyers, four submarines and other supportive ships and shore establishments.[195]

Chapter V of the Plans Paper says that, "The eventual role of the Navy of India is to safeguard her shipping on the high seas from interference in war; to ensure that supplies can both reach and leave India by sea in all circumstances; to keep open her ports and coastal shipping routes; to prevent any enemy landing on her shores; and to support the Army in any operations which may be required in the furtherance of the national policy."[196] According to Rear Admiral Satyindra Singh, the first Plan Paper envisaged "the role and the force requirements of the Navy of free India for the next ten years were given a concrete shape for the first time."[197] "Arguments favouring the acquisition of three such cruisers (Leander class) were put up as Plans Paper 2/47 which deliberated on the build-up of the RIN as a balanced naval force, getting out of the sloop stage and for contributing towards India's image in the region."[198] "The force was to be capable of expansion when the necessity arose and, though designed primarily for defensive role, it was to be capable of offense against an enemy in the Indian Ocean."[199]

Increased recruitment The expansion of the RIN after partition called for immediate action to step up recruitment to the officer cadre.

1. Cadet entry: Whilst in the pre partition days the number of cadets who entered every year was 24, the input of cadets during 1948 was increased to 46. It was accepted in principle that the input for the years 1949 and 1950 would be 16 and 17, respectively.[200]
2. Direct recruitment: The planned cadets entry was calculated merely to offset normal wastages through death, discharge, resignation, retirement etc, when the cadre is full. In order to build up the officer cadre of the expanded Navy the only solution was direct recruitment. This was accepted in all the branches of the RIN for an initial period of two years.[201]

Officers of the RIN Reserves who were considered suitable were offered a short service commission of five and three years' duration. The special branch of the RINVR was planned to be abolished by the end of September 1948. However, in view of the experience of some of these officers it was hoped to devise a scheme whereby their services would continue to be available to the RIN.[202] The warrant engineers of RINVR, who were recruited on the T124-X (India) Agreement for the duration of the war were granted extensions from year to year after 31 March 1946, and the last extension expired on 31 March 1948.[203] Such of these officers who were willing and were considered suitable for future retention were offered short service warrants for three years. Officers serving on short service warrants had the opportunity to convert to the permanent cadre.[204]

In August 1947, the highest rank holding by an Indian officer was Commander and rest of all senior officers were British. As a result of the transfer of power, most of the British officers of RIN opted to go back to Britain. To meet the requirements of officers in the senior ranks approval was accorded, in accordance with the RIN Instruction 8/48, to a scheme of promotion of officers to the acting rank of Lieutenant Commander and above in all branches.[205] In view of the acute shortage of ordnance officers in the RIN, the Government agreed to waive the age limit in all deserving cases of promotion from ratings.[206] A preliminary professional examination for promotion of warrant ordnance officer was conducted in October 1948. The over age ratings were also recommended to take the examination.

The Commander-in-Chief explained before the Provisional Joint Defence Council, on 6 August 1947, that his title as Commander-in-Chief (India) was inapplicable after 15 August 1947, as command of the troops of each dominion then passed to the respective Commander-in-Chief. He was therefore given the title of Supreme Commander. Equally, neither the C-in-C RIN nor the AOC-in-C, would exercise command over naval and air forces. It was desirable to have a title by which to refer to them, which would indicate their correct status. He suggested that they should be called Deputy Supreme Commander, Navy and Air Force, and the CGS (Chief of Staff) should be

INDIGENISATION, PARTITION, AND A NEW NAVY

called Deputy Supreme Commander, Army. These proposals were agreed to by the Provisional Joint Defence Council.[207] On 15 August 1947, the Headquarters of the Commander-in-Chief of the undivided Royal Indian Navy was split into three distinct Headquarters as follows:[208]

1. Supreme Commander's Headquarters (Navy) under the Deputy Supreme Commander (Navy) located in Delhi
2. Naval Headquarters (India) under the Flag Officer Commanding Royal Indian Navy (FOCRIN), located in Delhi
3. Naval Headquarters (Pakistan) under the Flag Officer Commanding, Royal Pakistan Navy, located in Karachi

The Flag Officer Commanding Royal Indian Navy, with a nucleus staff of six officers and 18 clerks assumed responsibility for the operational control of the reconstituted Royal Indian Navy from 15 August 1947, and immediately started planning the reorganisation of the Service.[209] The principal function of the Supreme Commander Headquarters (Navy) was then to turn over the remaining subjects to the two new dominion headquarters with minimum disruption and as expeditiously as possible. This task was completed on 30 November 1947 when the Headquarters of the Deputy Supreme Commander (Navy) closed down and Naval Headquarters (India) took over complete responsibility of the RIN.

In 1948 the Naval Headquarters was organised in two main departments, Naval Staff and Naval Administration, under the Chief of Staff and Chief of Administration, respectively.[210] These two departments were further subdivided into directorates, branches and sections. The functions and responsibilities of the two main departments were:

1. Naval Staff: Policy, Planning and Direction of Operations and Training of the Royal Indian Navy, Co-ordination of Operations and Training, Security and Naval Intelligence, Joint Planning with Army and Air Force. Responsible for policy, administration and direction of all personnel questions in the Royal Indian Navy, its Reserves and Ancillary services, excluding civilian personnel. Welfare of commissioned, warrant and subordinate officers, and ratings in the RIN. Inspectional tours and contact with Naval officers-in-charge, and commanding officers of ships and shore establishments.[211]
2. Administrative Staff: Responsible for execution and direction of supply, engineering, electrical engineering, medical, victualing, and financial matters. Liaison with other branches and departments of the Government of India. Provision and supply of equipment and store needs of the RIN, scales, reserves, maintenance and repair of equipment works, quartering, relations with other branches and ministries of Government on material matters.[212]

Partition and the consequent reconstitution of the Armed Forces left the Royal Indian Navy with an unbalanced cadre and denuded the service of many of its finest training establishments which were located in Karachi.[213] During the first year of Independence, Naval Headquarters concentrated on resolving these and the many other problems created by partition. Much attention was also devoted to planning and the foundations for a well-balanced Task Force was laid. The acute shortage of experienced officers was the main burden in reorganising the Service.[214] A few senior officers available had to perform duties and undertake responsibilities far in excess of what would normally be expected from officers of their rank and seniority. Despite the complex problems which had to be overcome, the shortage of experienced staff officers, and the many handicaps under which they had to work, the progress made was very satisfactorily and reflected great credit to those concerned.

Training establishments

As a result of the partition, RIN had lost many training establishments. In the post-independent period RIN started the construction of many training establishments to fulfil the requirement. By mid-1948 many training establishments were created at HMIS *Venduruthy*, Cochin, such as Supply and Secretariat School, Cookery School, Communication School and Anti-Submarine School.[215] "Furthermore partition has necessitated the building in India of a number of training establishments which were originally located in Karachi."[216] The standing Finance Committee recommended the construction of the following projects in 1948 at approximate costs noted against each.[217]

1	Combined torpedo, anti-submarine, communication, electrical and signal schools	95 Lakhs
2	Gunnery school	80 Lakhs
3	Boys' Training Establishment	25 Lakhs
4	Construction of quarters for 400 married and hostel accommodation for 90 single	28 Lakhs

The following major projects, detailed in Tables 6.10, 6.11 and 6.12, were sanctioned and/or progressed in the first year after the partition, between 15 August 1947 to 14 August 1948.

Acquisition of ships

In the meeting of ministers of His Majesty's Government held on 18 March 1947, the First Lord of the Admiralty discussed India's interest in purchasing three cruisers from the Royal Navy at some later date.[218] The pre-Independence Government had already planned to add a cruiser to the

INDIGENISATION, PARTITION, AND A NEW NAVY

Table 6.10 Post-independence major naval plans – Cochin

Name of Project	Estimated cost	Progress
Provision of permanent accommodation for combined torpedo, anti-submarine, communication & electrical schools at naval base, Cochin – Phase I	Rs. 1,972,000	Work suspended in 1948
Piling work for combined schools (Unofficial sanction)	Rs. 1,700,000	Work suspended in 1948
Setting up of temporary gunnery school and training schools shifted from HMIS *Akbar* in HMIS *Venduruthy*.	Rs. 173,000	Work in hand

Source: Report on the Royal Indian Navy, 15th August 1947 to 15th August 1948, Naval Headquarters, New Delhi (1948), Naval Historical Branch of the Royal Navy, Portsmouth, UK, pp. 21–22

Table 6.11 Post-Independence major naval plans – Bombay

Name of Project	Estimated cost	Progress
Modification to the distribution and metering of electricity in HMI Dockyard	139,000	Work not yet started
HMIS *Shivaji* – Repairs and renewals Phase I	187,111	Completed
HMIS *Shivaji* – Water supply (installation of filtration plant)	58,000	Work in hand
HMIS *Shivaji* – Swimming pool	46,000	Completed
HMIS *Shivaji* – Repairs to approach road	67,000	Completed
HMI dockyard capstans	25,500	Work held up due to non-arrival of capstans from UK

Source: Report on the Royal Indian Navy, 15 August 1947 to 15 August 1948, Naval Headquarters, New Delhi (1948), Naval Historical Branch of the Royal Navy, Portsmouth, UK, pp. 21–22

Table 6.12 Post-Independence major naval plans – Vizagapatam

Name of Project	Estimated cost	Progress
Additions and alterations to existing accommodation in HMIS *Circars* to accommodate the temporary Boys' Training Establishment	114,000	Completed

Source: Report on the Royal Indian Navy, 15th August 1947 to 15th August 1948, Naval Headquarters, New Delhi (1948), Naval Historical Branch of the Royal Navy, Portsmouth, UK, pp. 21–22

Royal Indian Navy. This plan was vigorously pursued by the Indian Government.[219] In response to the request for cruiser for RIN, Mountbatten said that "The Interim Government was very anxious to obtain a British cruiser for service with the Indian Navy."[220] According to him, it was essential to the efficiency of the Indian Navy that this request should be met; this would have the further advantage that the Indian Navy would for years be dependent on the British Navy for active help in maintaining in service a naval unit of this size. He thought that it might be possible for a British cruiser to be loaned to the Indian Navy under arrangements similar to those recently made with the Norwegian Government.[221] On account of impending partition, the question of acquiring cruisers was held in abeyance early in 1947 and the acquisition of HMS *Achilles* was cancelled.[222] Naval Headquarters (India), however, raised the proposal anew immediately after partition, and it was decided to acquire one cruiser from the Royal Navy. HMS *Achilles* was accordingly handed over to the Government of India on 5 July 1948 and renamed as HMIS *Delhi*.[223] The ship was taken over on behalf of the Government of India in the United Kingdom. Immediately after the partition it became increasingly evident that unless arrangements could be made to provide facilities for a large number of officers and men to undergo courses and attachments in Royal Navy training establishments and ships, the acquisition of the cruisers and the expansion of the Royal Indian Navy would be considerably retarded.[224] Owing to the assistance accorded by the British Admiralty, the necessary arrangements were completed in December 1947. The next problem which then had to be resolved was the transport of these officers and men to the United Kingdom in sufficient time to complete their courses and to man the cruiser. Five hundred and eight ratings were deputed to the United Kingdom between the months of December 1947 and May 1948, to undergo various courses and attachments in the Royal Navy. The majority of these men were earmarked for the cruiser and after completing their courses were drafted to HMIS *Delhi*.[225]

As a further step in the phased expansion programme, negotiations were completed in 1948 for the acquisition of three 'R' class Destroyers from the Royal Navy, viz., HMS *Rotherham*, *Redoubt* and *Raider*.[226] The modernisation and tropicalisation of these destroyers began in 1948 and they were expected to be commissioned in March 1949. Two oil fuel tankers ex-Empire *Gypsy* and Empire *Bairn* were bought from the British Admiralty on 29 February and 15 March 1948, respectively.[227] Negotiations with the Admiralty for the purchase of Landing Ship Tank (LST) (3) HMS *Avenger* was finalised in 1948.

A case for the acquisition of a second cruiser was initiated in 1949. As the British Government was not able to spare such a ship, it was decided to acquire three Hunt Class Frigates on loan from the British Government to meet India's training and operational requirements, and these ships arrived in India in 1953. In 1954 the Admiralty offered a second cruiser, which was accepted after being modernized. "An overview of the Indian Navy's development after Independence shows peaks and troughs directly related to the 1947–1990 Cold War between 'capitalist America' and the 'communist

INDIGENISATION, PARTITION, AND A NEW NAVY

Soviet Union' for global ideological and commercial dominance."[228] From 1947 to 1957 Britain sold secondhand warships of 1940s vintage (rendered surplus after the end of the 1939–1945 World War) to her erstwhile colonies and dominions as part of its plan for the defence of its 'British Commonwealth' against the Soviet Union.[229] During the World War itself, possible future confrontation with the Soviet Union was foreseeable.

Until 26 January 1950, the RIN was the senior most of the Defence Services in India. In the post-Independence era also RIN continued as the prime service in India as earlier. When India became a sovereign republic state on 26 January 1950, the prefix Royal was discontinued and Service came to be called the Indian Navy.[230] The use of the words, 'His Majesty' was also discontinued and 'His Majesty Indian Ships (HMIS)' got re-designated as 'Indian Naval Ships (INS)'.[231] The White Ensign was replaced by the Indian Naval White Ensign the as Ashoka Sarnath Lion capitol took the place of the Tudor Crown, and the lotus leaf became the surround in naval badges, in which the design of the surmount was altered, depicting the Ashoka Chakra at the centre. The laurel of lotus buds depicts the Indian national flower, symbolizing creation out of water, a great medium on which the Navy operates. See Figure 6.1.

Figure 6.1 Indian Navy receives the President's Color on 26 January 1950
Source: Naval History Division, Indian Navy, New Delhi

Table 6.13 Warships of the Indian Navy in 1950

Class/Type	Name
Cruiser (Flag Ship)	*Delhi*
11th Destroyer Flotilla	*Rajput, Ranjit* and *Rana*
12th Frigate flotilla	*Jumna, Cauvery, Sutlej* and *Kistna*
Boys' training ship	*Tir*
Fleet Minesweepers	*Rajputana, Konkan, Rohilkhand* and *Madras*
Survey ship	*Kukri*
Oceangoing tug	*Hathi*
121st Seaward Defence Motor Launch	1110, 1112, 1113
LSTs	*Avenger*, ML 420

Source: Naval Headquarters (India) records, Naval History Division, New Delhi

As on 31 December 1950, the number of officers in the Indian Navy was 737 and that of ratings was approximately 7,000.[232] The number of Royal Navy (RN) and RN (special list) officers serving with the Indian Navy on 31 December 1950 was 61 and eight, respectively.[233] However, in 1950, the Indian Navy requested the Royal Navy for the loan of 19 more officers. The ships of the Indian Navy in 1950 consisted of those listed in Table 6.13.[234]

10. Conclusion

The RIN was going through a very difficult phase in the postwar period. The post war demobilisation and RIN Revolt of 1946 caused an acute shortage of manpower in the RIN. Due to political pressure, the British Government decided on complete indigenisation of Indian Armed Forces. By the end of the war the RIN ratings cadre was fully indigenised. However, the British did not envisage the complete indigenisation in the near future due to lack of experienced officers. The British Admiralty and the RIN believed that "senior officers are not made in a day, it is experience that counts."[235] The RIN did not favour the immediate indigenisation and quick promotions of Indian officers because they did not have adequate naval service and experience for higher ranks, and the military requirement remained a priority. In 1947 the highest rank of an Indian officer in the RIN was Commander. Had the RIN officer cadre been fully indigenised by August 1947, it would have been a disaster in the post-independence years. The less experienced Indian officers could not have handled a newly borne navy alone.

When the British realised the partition was unavoidable, they tried all their means to abort the division of Indian Armed Forces. They wanted a united defence force in India to continue their colonial hegemony in South Asia. The British considered India as a base in the Far East. Therefore it

INDIGENISATION, PARTITION, AND A NEW NAVY

was in the interest of the British to keep India in the Commonwealth, more than India's interest to be part of it. On arrival in India in the last week of March 1947, Mountbatten's aim was to persuade the Congress to remain in the Commonwealth. "British military interests could not be achieved otherwise, because, Auchinleck pointed out, the British army and indeed the Indian army, with its complement of Indian officers, could not serve in any India that was not under the Crown or was a British Dominion, since the oath of allegiance was to the King."[236] Towards the achievement of this goal, the British officials tried to persuade the Indian leaders to keep India in the Commonwealth by offering military support even after independence. "Anticipating India's requests for military aid to build up her armed forces after independence, the British thought that any discussions on such issues should be linked to a military treaty between the two countries."[237]

When the British Government decided to end colonial rule in India, the Indian Armed Forces were neither prepared for a partition nor for fully nationalised defence forces. Because of late induction of Indians into the officer rank in the RIN, in 1931, the Indian officers could reach only to the rank of Commander by 1947. In 1947, most of the trained, experienced and specialised officers and warrant officers were British. Nationalisation of the RIN at the time of independence was not at all practical due to lack of experienced Indian officers. The partition too played a cardinal role in reducing the experienced personnel of RIN. In the initial stages of the war, recruitment was largely concentrated in the North and NWFP because most of the training establishments were located in Karachi. At the time of partition most of these trained sailors opted for the Pakistan Navy. This caused a large shortage of trained, experienced senior sailors and warrant officers in the RIN. The communal harmony among the RIN ratings, which was the most prominent factor during the RIN Revolt, was lost as a result of the partition.[238] The handicapped RIN had to depend upon the British Admiralty for assistance in manpower and material. Even after independence RIN had to be dependent on British officers till Vice Admiral R. D. Katari became the first Indian Chief of the Naval Staff in 1956.

"Though India had gained political independence, Britain still envisaged exerting a controlling influence over its Navy."[239] The RIN's development in the post-Independence period was directly related to the British fear of the Russian threat. From 1947 to 1957 Britain sold secondhand warships of 1940s vintage (rendered surplus after the end of the 1939–1945 World War) to her erstwhile colonies and dominions as part of her plan for the defence of its 'British Commonwealth' against the Soviet Union.[240] "Though nationalists called for the immediate 'Indianisation' of the service and replacement of its British officers, these plans were scuppered by Partition and the resultant division of naval resources into two navies. This perpetuated the need for British personnel and equipment and continued a culture of dependence in spite of political independence."[241] Under Admiral William Parry, the

RIN envisaged its future development, including aircraft carriers and submarines, in Plan Paper 01/48.[242] The perspective planning was linked with India's membership in the Commonwealth. The Naval Plan Paper 10/48 entitled 'Proposed Strength of Indian Navy' described that "At the time of writing (as earlier paper), it was assumed that India would remain inside the Commonwealth of Nations and that substantial naval help could be excepted from other Commonwealth countries in the event of hostilities."[243]

In 1948, the Government of India had requested Professor P. M. S. Blackett to conduct a study and submit a report on the future of the Indian Armed Forces, and he had submitted his report to the Defence Minister in September 1948. However, this report did not envisage a larger Navy in India. The report concluded that "if India's navy were planned as complementary to some great power to fight in a major war rather than as an independent unit to fight in a small war, a not very different programme of expansion would be advisable. For it would clearly be most efficient militarily for India to look after the coast and local defences."[244] The post-independent Indian Government's defence policy was mainly focused on the land frontier and most of the naval proposals were turned down, as the Government failed to understand the importance of a balanced naval force in the Indian Ocean.

Notes

1 A. G. Noorani, 'The Partition of India', *Frontline*, Vol. 18, No. 26, 22 December, 2001–04 January, 2002.
2 Nehru's Letter to Auchinleck dated 12 September 1946 (John Ryland University Library, Manchester), File LXXI, MUL 1193, quoted in Sharmila Singh's, unpublished Ph.D Thesis titled, *Partition of the Indian Armed Forces between India and Pakistan*, JNU, New Delhi, p. 75.
3 Quoted in Connell, n.57, pp. 854–855, quoted in Sharmila Singh's, unpublished Ph.D Thesis titled, *Partition of the Indian Armed Forces between India and Pakistan*, JNU, New Delhi, 1994, p. 75.
4 File Minutes, Royal Indian Navy-Demobilisation Planning: Recommendations for Regular and Reserve Forces and Requirements in Immediate Post-War Period Admiralty Observation, Requirement of R.N Officers for Secondment to R.I.N, 1945, The National Archives, Kew Gardens, UK, ADM 1/18488.
5 File on Committee for the Nationalisation of the Indian Army, dated 15 October 1946, File SEC/11/192/H, History Division, Ministry of Defence, New Delhi.
6 File on 'Armed Forces Nationalisation Committee', Naval Headquarters, New Delhi.
7 Ibid., Circular No. NC/32, Signed by the Lt Col B. M. Kaul, Secretary, A.F.N.C dated 09 January 1946.
8 Lt Col Gautam Sharma, Nationalisation of the Indian Army (1885–1947), Allied Publishers Limited, New Delhi, 1996, p. 187.
9 Ibid.
10 Naval Headquarters Letter Signed by Chief of Staff dated 21 January 1947, File on 'Armed Forces Nationalisation Committee', Naval Headquarters, New Delhi.

11 File on 'Armed Forces Nationalisation Committee', 1947, Naval Headquarters, New Delhi.
12 Ibid.
13 Commodore J Lawrence, Chief of Staff's Correspondence to the Armed Forces Nationalisation Committee, dated 23 January 1947, Naval Headquarters, New Delhi.
14 File on 'Armed Forces Nationalisation Committee', 1947, Naval Headquarters, New Delhi.
15 Sharmila Singh, unpublished Ph.D Thesis titled, *Partition of the Indian Armed Forces between India and Pakistan*, JNU, New Delhi, p. 77.
16 Ibid.
17 Record Interview between Rear Admiral Viscount Mountbatten of Burma and Mr. Rajagopalachari, held on 11 April 1947, Mountbatten Papers, Viceroy's Interview No.48, Constitutional Relations between Britain and India: Transfer of Power 1942–47, Nicholas Mansergh (Ed.), (here in after *TOP*), Vol. 10, p. 195.
18 Ibid.
19 Ibid.
20 Record of Interview between Rear Admiral Viscount Mountbatten of Burma and Group Captain S. Mukherjee, dated 01 May 1947, Mountbatten Papers, Viceroy's Interview No. 10, *TOP*, Vol. 10, p. 521.
21 Ibid., pp. 521–522.
22 Record Interview between Rear Admiral Viscount Mountbatten of Burma and Mr. Rajagopalachari, held on 11 April 1947, Mountbatten Papers, Viceroy's Interview No. 48, *TOP*, Vol. 10, p. 195.
23 Record Interview between Rear Admiral Viscount Mountbatten of Burma and Mr. C. H. Bhabha, held on 23 April 1947, Mountbatten Papers, Viceroy's Interview No. 89, *TOP*, Vol. 10, p. 375.
24 Liaquat Ali Khan to Mountbatten, Letter dated 07 April 1947, *TOP*, Vol. 10, p. 151.
25 Ibid., pp. 151–152.
26 Liaquat Ali Khan to Mountbatten, 07 April 1947, Mountbatten to Liaquat Ali Khan, 09 April 1947, Interview between Liaquat Ali Khan and Mountbatten, 11 April 1947, Liaquat Ali Khan to Mountbatten, 13 April 1947, ibid., pp. 153, 165, 200–201, 220–221. Quoted by Anita Inder Singh in her article 'Imperial Defence and the Transfer of Power in India, 1946–1947', *The International History Review*, Vol. 4, No. 4, November 1982, p. 585.
27 Armed Forces Nationalisation Committee (No. NC/23 of 29th January 1947): General Views on Nationalisation of the Armed Forces by the Flag Officer Commanding the Royal Indian Navy, Naval Headquarters, New Delhi.
28 Ibid.
29 Ibid.
30 Ibid.
31 Ibid.
32 Pradeep P. Barua, *Gentlemen of the Raj: The Indian Army Officer Corps 1817–1949*, Pentagon Press, London, 2008, p. 46.
33 Armed Forces Nationalisation Committee (No. NC/23 of 29th January 1947): General views on nationalisation of the armed forces by the Flag Officer Commanding the Royal Indian Navy.
34 Ibid.
35 Ibid.
36 Report Submitted by the FOCRIN on Armed Forces Nationalisation Committee's Questionnaire No. NC/32 of 09 January 1947, Appendix-C, dated 08 February 1947, Naval Headquarters, New Delhi.

INDIGENISATION, PARTITION, AND A NEW NAVY

37 Ibid.
38 Ibid.
39 File on 'Armed Forces Nationalisation Committee', 1947, Naval Headquarters, New Delhi.
40 Preparation of Plan for the Partition of the Indian Armed Forces, dated 25 April 1947, Note by Indian Cabinet Secretariat, Mountbatten Papers, Official Correspondence Files: Armed Forces, Indian, Vol. 1, Part 1, *TOP*, Vol. 10, p. 419.
41 Viceroy's Staff Meeting held on19 April 1947, Uncirculated Record of Discussion No. 10, Mountbatten Papers, *TOP*, Vol. 10, p. 329.
42 Minutes of Viceroy's Twenty Second Staff Meeting held on 25 April 1947, Mountbatten Papers, *TOP*, Vol. 10, p. 414.
43 Ibid.
44 Ibid.
45 Minutes of Viceroy's Twenty-Fourth Staff Meeting held on 01 May 1947, Mountbatten Papers, *TOP*, Vol. 10, p. 523.
46 Viceroy's Staff Meeting, held on 10 April 1947, Uncirculated Record of Discussion No. 5, Mountbatten Papers, *TOP*, Vol. 10, p. 179.
47 Record Interview between Rear Admiral Viscount Mountbatten of Burma and Mr. Rajagopalachari, held on 11 April 1947, Mountbatten Papers, Viceroy's Interview No. 48, *TOP*, Vol. 10, p. 195.
   Ibid.
48 Minutes of Viceroy's Twenty Third Staff Meeting, held on 26 April 1947, Mountbatten Papers, *TOP*, Vol. 10, p. 442.
49 Minutes of Viceroy's Twenty Fourth Staff Meeting, held on 1 May 1947, Mountbatten Papers, *TOP*, Vol. 10, p. 523.
50 Record Interview between Rear Admiral Viscount Mountbatten of Burma and Mr. C. H. Bhabha, held on 23 April 1947, Mountbatten Papers, Viceroy's Interview No. 89, *TOP*, Vol. 10, p. 376.
51 Viceroy's Personal Report No. 5, dated 1 May 1947, *TOP*, Vol. 10, p. 542.
52 Minutes of Viceroy's Twenty Third Staff Meeting, held on 26 April 1947, Mountbatten Papers, *TOP*, Vol. 10, p. 442.
53 Lieutenant-General A. Nye to Rear-Admiral Viscount Mountbatten of Burma, dated 02 May 1947, *TOP*, Vol. 10, p. 560.
54 Record Interview between Rear Admiral Viscount Mountbatten of Burma and Mr. O. P. Ramaswami Reddiar, held on 2 May 1947, Mountbatten Papers, Viceroy's Interview No. 108, *TOP*, Vol. 10, p. 376.
55 Atlee to General Hollis, dated 10 May 1947, Prime Minister's Personal Minute: Serial No. D. 1/47, *TOP*, Vol. 10, p. 741.
56 Heaton Nicholls to Atlee, dated 26 May 1947, *TOP*, Vol. 10, p. 988.
57 Peter Low, Book Review on 'The Limits of British Influence: South Asia and the Anglo-American Relationship, 1947–56' by Anita Inder Singh, *A Quarterly Journal Concerned with British Studies*, Vol. 26, No. 3, Autumn, 1994, p. 578.
58 Ibid.
59 Eric Mieville Expressed His Views to Mountbatten, Minutes of Viceroy's Twenty Ninth Staff Meeting held on 09 May 1947, Mountbatten Papers, *TOP*, Vol. 10, p. 703.
60 Ibid.
61 Minutes of Viceroy's Twenty Ninth Staff Meeting held on 09 May 1947, Mountbatten Papers, *TOP*, Vol. 10, p. 703.
62 Ibid.
63 Ibid.
64 Ibid.

65 Anita Inder Singh, 'Imperial Defence and the Transfer of Power in India, 1946–1947: Notes, Bibliographies, and Documents', *The International History Review*, Vol. 4, No. 4, November 1982, p. 568.
66 Ibid.
67 Ibid.
68 Ibid., p. 569.
69 Ibid.
70 Ibid., p. 571.
71 Ibid., Amery to Eden, 09 May 1943, ibid., pp. 956–957. Quoted by Anita Inder Singh.
72 First Draft of a Paper for the War Cabinet, Secret, dated 21 June 1943, quoted in Amit Kumar Gupta (Ed.), *Myth and Reality: The Struggle for Freedom in India, 1945–47*, Manohar Publications, New Delhi, 1987. The Chapter on *Imperial Strategy and the Transfer of Power, 1939–51*, by Partha Sarathi Gupta, p. 5.
73 Ibid., p. 5.
74 A. Martin Wainwright, Book Review on The 'Limits of British Influence: South Asia and the Anglo-American Relationship, 1947–56' by Anita Inder Singh, *The American Historical Review*, Vol. 100, No. 3, June 1995, pp. 932–933.
75 Anita Inder Singh, 'Imperial Defence and the Transfer of Power in India, 1946–1947 Notes, Bibliographies, and Documents', *The International History Review*, Vol. 4, No. 4, November 1982, p. 572.
76 Ibid.
77 Ibid., p. 580.
78 Ibid.
79 Mountbatten Papers, Record of Interview between Rear Admiral Viscount Mountbatten of Burma and Field Marshal Auchinleck, dated 05 April 1947, *TOP*, Vol. 10, p. 134.
80 Ibid., p. xvii.
81 Mountbatten Papers, Partition Papers, Transfer of Power, Vol. 12, p. 195 and The Earl of Listowel to Mountbatten, Telegram dated 09 July 1947, *TOP*, Vol. 12, p. 62.
82 The Earl of Listowel to Mountbatten, Telegram dated 09 July 1947, *TOP*, Vol. 12, p. 62.
83 Note by Rear Admiral Viscount Mountbatten of Burma, Mountbatten Papers, Partition Council Papers, undated, *TOP*, Vol. 12, p. 195.
84 Ibid.
85 Mountbatten's (Viceroy) Open Letter to All British Service Personnel in India, dated 12 July 1947, *TOP*, Vol. 12, p. 116.
86 Report by the Chiefs of Staff, Chief of Staff Committee Paper C.O.S (47)59(0), dated 18 March 1947, *TOP*, Vol. 9, pp. 979–980.
87 India and Burma Committee, Paper I.B (47) 27, India: Transfer of Power to More Than One Authority, Memorandum by the Secretary of State for India, dated 04 March 1947, Note by India Office, Secret Enclosure, *TOP*, Vol. 9, p. 843.
88 Ibid.
89 Ibid.
90 Liaquat Ali Khan to Mountbatten, Letter dated 07 April 1947, *TOP*, Vol. 10, p. 152.
91 Liaquat Ali Khan to Mountbatten, Letter dated 13 April 1947, *TOP*, Vol. 10, p. 220.
92 Record of Interview between Rear Admiral Viscount Mountbatten of Burma and Field Marshal Auchinleck, Mountbatten Papers, Viceroy's Interview No. 64 dated 14 April 1947, *TOP*, Vol. 10, p. 224.

INDIGENISATION, PARTITION, AND A NEW NAVY

93 Ibid.
94 Minutes of Viceroy's Twenty Ninth Staff Meeting, held on 09 May 1947, Mountbatten Papers, *TOP*, Vol. 10, p. 703.
95 Ibid.
96 Report by the Chiefs of Staff, Chief of Staff Committee Paper C.O.S (47)59(0), dated 18 March 1947, *TOP*, Vol. 9, p. 978.
97 Record of Interview between Rear Admiral Viscount Mountbatten of Burma and Field Marshal Auchinleck, Mountbatten Papers, Viceroy's Interview No. 64 dated 14 April 1947, *TOP*, Vol. 10, p. 224.
98 Ibid., p. 225.
99 Viceroy's Staff Meeting held on 11 April 1947, Uncirculated Record of Discussion No. 6, Mountbatten Papers, *TOP*, Vol. 10, p. 190.
100 Note by Indian Cabinet Secretariat, Mountbatten Papers, Official Correspondence Files: Armed Forces, Indian, Vol. 1, Part 1, dated 25 April 1947, *TOP*, Vol. 10, p. 419.
101 Byron Farwell's work *Armies of the Raj, from the Great Indian Mutiny to Independence: 1858–1947*, Viking, New York, 1989, p. 348.
102 Sharmila Singh, unpublished Ph.D Thesis titled, *Partition of the Indian Armed Forces between India and Pakistan*, JNU, New Delhi, p. 81.
103 Ibid., p. 85.
104 Ibid., p. 82.
105 Atlee to Lord Pethick Lawrence, dated 18 March 1947, Enclosure to No. 543, Atlee to Rear Admiral Viscount Mountbatten of Burma, *TOP*, Vol. 9, p. 972.
106 Ibid., pp. 973–974.
107 Alan Campbell Johnson, *Mission with Mountbatten*, Robert Hale Limited, London, 1953, p. 58.
108 Auchinleck Expressed His Views to Mountbatten, Minutes of Viceroy's Fourth Staff Meetings, held on 28 March 1947, *TOP*, Vol. 10, p. 35.
109 Ibid.
110 Ibid.
111 Draft of Broadcast Statement by the Viceroy, Annexure II, Viceroy's Personal Report No. 5, dated 1 May 1947, *TOP*, Vol. 10, p. 547.
112 The Division of the Armed Forces of India, Minute 8, India and Burma Committee. I.B. (47) 28th Meeting, held on 28 May 1947, *TOP*, Vol. 10, p. 1020.
113 A. L. Venkateswaran, *Defence Organisation in India*, Publication Division, Ministry of Information and Broadcasting, Government of India, New Delhi, 1967, p. 38.
114 Executive Council (Transitional Provisions) Order, Notification No. G.G.O.1, dated 19 July 1947, National Archives of India, New Delhi.
115 R. C. Majumdar (Ed.), *The History and Culture of the Indian People: Struggle for Freedom*, Bharatiya Vidya Bhavan, Bombay, 1969, p. 786.
116 Chief of the General Staff Letter No. 6385/150/SDI dated 10 July 1947, *TOP*, Vol. 12, p. 75.
117 Ibid.
118 Government of India, Press Information Bureau to India Office, Telegram, L/P&J/10/81:f15 dated 12 July 1947, *TOP*, Vol. 12, p. 113.
119 Ibid.
120 Ibid., p. 114.
121 Ishtiaq Ahmed, 'The 1947 Partition of India: A Paradigm for Pathological Politics in India and Pakistan', *Published in Asian Ethnicity*, Vol. 3, No. 1, March 2002, pp. 9–28.
122 Jaswant Singh, *Defending India*, Macmillan India Ltd, Bangalore, 1999, p. 96.

123 Record of Interview between Rear Admiral Viscount Mountbatten of Burma and Jinnah, Mountbatten Papers, Viceroy's Interview No. 162, 12 July 1947, *TOP*, Vol. 12, p. 122.
124 Yasmin Khan, *The Great Partition: The Making of India and Pakistan*, Yale University Press, New Haven and London, 2007.
125 Rear Admiral Sridharan, *A Maritime History of India*, Ministry of Information & Broadcasting, Government of India, New Delhi, p. 317.
126 Partition Proceedings, Vol. 5, Part 1, Decision on Military items of the Partition Council, and Proceedings of the Provisional Joint Defence Council and the Joint Defence Council, 1947, History Division, Ministry of Defence, New Delhi, 601/14476/H, p. 166.
127 Ibid.
128 Ibid., p. 174.
129 Ibid.
130 Ibid.
131 Ibid.
132 Ibid., p. 175.
133 Ibid.
134 Report on the Royal Indian Navy, 15th August 1947 to 15th August 1948, 1948, Naval Historical Branch, Portsmouth, UK, p. 9.
135 Ibid.
136 Ibid., p. 10.
137 Ibid.
138 Ibid.
139 Ibid., p. 24.
140 Ibid.
141 Ibid.
142 Ibid., p. 25.
143 Ibid.
144 Ibid., p. 26.
145 Ibid.
146 Ibid., p. 14.
147 Ibid.
148 Ibid.
149 Ibid., p. 18.
150 Ibid.
151 Ibid.
152 Ibid.
153 Nehru to Mountbatten, dated 11 July 1947, *TOP*, Vol. 12, p. 105 and Mountbatten's (Viceroy) Open Letter to All British Service Personnel in India, dated 12 July 1947, *TOP*, Vol. 12, p. 117.
154 Ibid.
155 Ibid., p. 106.
156 Partition Proceedings, Vol. 5, Part 1, Decision on Military Items of the Partition Council, and Proceedings of the Provisional Joint Defence Council and the Joint Defence Council, 1947, History Division, Ministry of Defence, New Delhi, 601/14476/H, p. 364.
157 Record of Interview between Rear Admiral Viscount Mountbatten of Burma and Sardar Baldev Singh, Mountbatten Papers, dated 16 April 1947, Viceroy's Interview No. 70, *TOP*, Vol. 10, p. 284.
158 Partition Proceedings, Vol. 5, Part 1, Decision on Military Items of the Partition Council, and Proceedings of the Provisional Joint Defence Council and

INDIGENISATION, PARTITION, AND A NEW NAVY

the Joint Defence Council, 1947, History Division, Ministry of Defence, New Delhi, 601/14476/H, p. 364.
159 Minutes of Viceroy's Twenty Ninth Staff Meeting held on 09 May 1947, Mountbatten Papers, *TOP*, Vol. 10, p. 704.
160 Partition Proceedings, Vol. 5, Part 1, Decision on Military Items of the Partition Council, and Proceedings of the Provisional Joint Defence Council and the Joint Defence Council, 1947, History Division, Ministry of Defence, New Delhi, 601/14476/H, p. 364.
161 Report on the Royal Indian Navy, 15th August 1947 to 15th August 1948, Naval Headquarters, New Delhi, 1948, Historical Branch of the Royal Navy, Portsmouth, UK, p. 10.
162 Report on the Royal Indian Navy, 15th August 1948 to 14th August 1949, Naval Headquarters, New Delhi, 1949, Naval Historical Branch of the Royal Navy, Portsmouth, UK, p. 3.
163 Ibid.
164 Partition Proceedings, Vol. 5, Part 1, Decision on Military Items of the Partition Council, and Proceedings of the Provisional Joint Defence Council and the Joint Defence Council, 1947, History Division, Ministry of Defence, New Delhi, 601/14476/H, p. 164.
165 Ibid.
166 Ibid.
167 Ibid.
168 Report on the Royal Indian Navy, 15th August 1948 to 14th August 1949, Naval Headquarters, New Delhi, 1949, Naval Historical Branch of the Royal Navy, Portsmouth, UK, p. 4.
169 Ibid.
170 Ibid.
171 Ibid.
172 Report on the Royal Indian Navy, 15th August 1947 to 15th August 1948, Naval Headquarters, New Delhi, 1948, Historical Branch of the Royal Navy, Portsmouth, UK, p. 5.
173 Ibid.
174 Ibid., p. 9.
175 Report on the Royal Indian Navy, 15th August 1947 to 14th August 1949, Naval Headquarters, New Delhi, 1949, Historical Branch of the Royal Navy, Portsmouth, UK, p. 4.
176 Military Branch File Minutes, dated 02 September 1948, ADM 116/5852/114293, The National Archives, Kew, UK.
177 Report on the Royal Indian Navy, 15th August 1947 to 15th August 1948, Naval Headquarters, New Delhi, 1948, Naval Historical Branch of the Royal Navy, Portsmouth, UK, p. 7.
178 Ibid.
179 Ibid., p. 8.
180 Report on the Royal Indian Navy, 15th August 1948 to 14th August 1949, Naval Headquarters, New Delhi, 1949, Naval Historical Branch of the Royal Navy, Portsmouth, UK, p. 5.
181 Ibid.
182 Ibid.
183 Ibid.
184 Ibid., p. 1.
185 Ibid.
186 Ibid.

187 Ibid., p. 13.
188 Report on the Royal Indian Navy, 15th August 1947 to 15th August 1948, 1948, Naval Historical Branch, Portsmouth, UK, p. 13.
189 Ibid.
190 Ibid.
191 Ibid.
192 Tughlak, 'The Birth of the Indian Navy', *Naval Review*, 44:2, April 1956, pp. 173–174.
193 Lorne J. Kavic, *India's Quest for Security: Defence Policies, 1947–1965*, University of California Press, Berkeley, 1967, p. 117.
194 Ibid.
195 Naval Plan Paper No. 1, 1947, ADM 116/ 5852, The National Archives, Kew, UK.
196 Ibid.
197 Rear Admiral Satyindra Singh, *Under Two Ensigns: The Indian Navy 1945–1950*, Oxford & IBH Publishing Co., New Delhi, 1986, p. 36.
198 Ibid.
199 Vice Admiral W. E. Parry, 'India and the Sea Power', *USI Journal*, 79:334-335, January–April 1949, p. 27.
200 Report on the Royal Indian Navy, 15th August 1947 to 15th August 1948, 1948, Naval Historical Branch, Portsmouth, UK, p. 10.
201 Ibid.
202 Ibid.
203 Ibid.
204 Ibid.
205 Ibid.
206 Ibid., p. 11.
207 Partition Proceedings, Vol. 5, Part 1, Decision on Military Items of the Partition Council, and Proceedings of the Provisional Joint Defence Council and the Joint Defence Council, 1947, History Division, Ministry of Defence, New Delhi, 601/14476/H, p. 173.
208 Report on the Royal Indian Navy, 15th August 1947 to 15th August 1948, Naval Headquarters, New Delhi, 1948, p. 6, Caird Library, National Maritime Museum, Greenwich, UK.
209 Ibid.
210 Ibid.
211 Ibid.
212 Ibid.
213 Ibid.
214 Ibid., p. 7.
215 Ibid., Naval Historical Branch of the Royal Navy, Portsmouth, UK, p. 9.
216 Ibid., p. 21.
217 Ibid.
218 Meeting of Ministers, MISC/M (47)8, dated 18 March 1947, *TOP*, Vol. 9, p. 982.
219 Royal Indian Navy Club Report, London, p. 319. USI, New Delhi.
220 India and Burma Committee. I.B. (47) 28th Meeting, held on 28 May 1947, Minute 10, *TOP*, Vol. 10, p. 1022.
221 Ibid.
222 Report on the Royal Indian Navy, 15th August 1947 to 15th August 1948, Naval Headquarters, New Delhi, 1948, Caird Library, National Maritime Museum, Greenwich, UK, p. 2.

INDIGENISATION, PARTITION, AND A NEW NAVY

223 Ibid.
224 Ibid., p. 3.
225 Ibid., p. 10.
226 Ibid., p. 2.
227 Ibid.
228 Vice Admiral G. M. Hiranandani, *Transition to Triumph: Indian Navy:1965–1990*, Lancer Publishers, New Delhi, 1996.
229 Ibid.
230 Report on the Royal Indian Navy, 15th August 1949 to 31st December 1950, Naval Headquarters, New Delhi, 1948, p. 1, Caird Library, National Maritime Museum, Greenwich, UK.
231 Ibid.
232 Ibid., p. 3.
233 Ibid., p. 5.
234 Ibid., pp. 2–3.
235 Ibid.
236 Mountbatten Papers, Record of Interview between Rear Admiral Viscount Mountbatten of Burma and Field Marshal Auchinleck, dated 05 April 1947, *TOP*, Vol. 10, p. 134.
237 Anita Inder Singh, 'Keeping India in the Commonwealth: British Political and Military Aims, 1947–49', *Journal of Contemporary History*, Vol. 20, No. 3, July 1985, p. 474.
238 Miles to Admiralty, dated 14 Jan 1948, ADM 1/21104, National Archives, UK, p. 5.
239 Daniel Owen Spence, 'Imperial Transition, Indianisation and Race: Developing National Navies in the Subcontinent, 1947–64', *Journal of South Asian Studies*, Vol. 37, No. 2, 2014, p. 329.
240 Vice Admiral G. M. Hiranandani, *Transition to Triumph: Indian Navy: 1965–1990*, Lancer Publishers, New Delhi, 1996.
241 Daniel Owen Spence, 'Imperial Transition, Indianisation and Race: Developing National Navies in the Subcontinent, 1947–64', *Journal of South Asian Studies*, Vol. 37, No. 2, 2014, p. 323.
242 Indian Navy's First 10 Years Plan, Known as Naval Plan of 01/48.
243 'A Report to the Hon'ble the Defence Minister on Scientific Problem of Defence in Relation to the Needs of the Indian Armed Forces' by Prof P.M.S Blackett, 10 September 1948, New Delhi (Known as Blackett Report), p. 3, MoD History Division, New Delhi.
244 Ibid., p. 11.

BIBLIOGRAPHY

Primary sources

In India

(a) History division, ministry of defence, New Delhi

Committee of Imperial Defence Report, 1938, Paper No. 198-D.
Expansion of the Armed Forces, Naval Headquarters, Secret Document, 1944.
General Robert Cassels's Correspondence & Telegram between the Viceroy and Secretary of State for India dated 24 August 1938 Dealing with Defence Expenditure Matters, File No. 601/7478/H.
General State of RIN on Outbreak of War in 1939 & RIN Expansion, OSD/C10/ii.
Monograph Approved by FOCRIN on the RIN Man-Power Situation 1939–1945 (Secret) dated 10 October 1945, MoD History Division, New Delhi.
Proceedings of a Conference held at General Headquarters on the 19th, 20th and 21st March 1942 to Consider Methods of Enhancing India's Recruiting Effort.
Report on Progress in Training in Royal Indian Navy, 26th July 1943 to 30th September 1944, Report by the Flag Officer Commanding Royal Indian Navy, Secret Document, 1944.

(b) Naval Headquarters, New Delhi

Changes in the International Situation Affecting India's Defence Policy and Commitments, Submitted by the GOI to the Secretary of State, dated 04 November 1937.
Committee of Imperial Defence Memorandum, by the Secretary of State for India (W. Wedgwood Benn), 'Control of Royal Indian Marine in War', December 1931.
Composition and State of Training of the Royal Indian Navy, 30th September 1943.
Defence Policy of India 1936–37, General Staff Paper Entitled 'Memorandum on the Defence Forces', 1936.
General Staff Memorandum Entitled 'India's Defence Commitments and Her Ability to Implement Them' dated 24 March 1937, Submitted by the Defence Department, GOI.
Historical Background of the Royal Indian Navy.
Memorandum by the Marine Department of the Government of India, Simla, 08 September 1932.

BIBLIOGRAPHY

Minutes of Viceroy's Staff Meetings, 4th Meeting held on 28 March 1947.
The Navy and Its Job, Royal Indian Navy Recruitment Brochure, Undated, Naval Headquarters, New Delhi.
Press Release, Information Officer, India Office, 'The Indian Navy (Discipline) Bill', 05 September 1934 and Minutes of Brown to the Under Secretary of State for India, 07 October 1934.
RIN Job Advertisement Booklet, 1940.
RIN Memorandum, OSD/F6.
RIN Revolt, Inquiry Commission Report, Part III, GF62/86 PR II, Naval Headquarters, New Delhi.
RIN Training, Naval Headquarters, New Delhi.
Royal Defence Forces Officers' Recruitment Brochure, Undated.
The Royal Indian Navy: A Review, 1945.
Royal Indian Navy Club Report, 1950.
Royal Indian Navy Lists of 1936, 1937 and 1938.
Second Report of the Cabinet Committee, dated 29 July 1938, CID Paper No. 198-D.
War Department History (RIN Section), Head 3: Defence of India.

(c) National Archives of India, New Delhi

Defence of India Act 1939 & Other Rules, 351.7502 IN 2D, 6052.
Executive Council (Transitional Provisions) Order, Notification No. G.G.O.1, dated 19 July 1947.
Indian Naval Reserve Force (Discipline Act) 1939, Cd-112, 1939, 153954, National Archives of India, New Delhi.
RIN Revolt, Inquiry Commission Report, Part III, GF62/86 PR II, Naval Headquarters, New Delhi, 1946.
Summary of the Report of the Commission of Enquiry in to the RIN Mutiny, February 1946, War Department, GOI, New Delhi, National Archives of India, New Delhi.

Primary sources from the UK

(a) The National Archives, Kew, UK

ADM 1/12791, Post War Problems.
ADM 1/13978, Demobilisation.
ADM 1/13996, Recruitment of Officers for RINR & RINVR.
ADM 1/16359, Report on the Royal Indian Navy for the Year Ending, 1st May 1944.
ADM 1/18488, Royal Indian Navy Demobilisation Planning.
ADM 1/18488, Royal Indian Navy: Demobilisation Planning, Recommendations for Regular and Reserve Forces and Requirements in Immediate Post War Period Admiralty Observations, Requirement of RN Officers for Secondment to RIN, 1945.
ADM 1/18527, The Royal Indian Navy: Review of History, Operations and Future of RIN, dated 2 April 1945 by FOCRIN Vice Admiral J.H. Godfrey.

BIBLIOGRAPHY

ADM 1/19411, Royal Indian Navy Dairy February 1946.
ADM 1/19411, Royal Navy Personnel Loaned to Royal Indian Navy for Instructional Duties.
ADM 1/19413, Report on the Royal Indian Navy, July–December 1945.
ADM 1/20815, Royal Navy Personnel Loaned to Royal Indian Navy for Instructional Duties.
ADM 1/21163, Royal Indian and Pakistan Navies in Transition Period 1946–1948.
ADM 1/8419/112, Indian Troops Mutiny at Singapore.
ADM 1/8737/96, Report to the Government of India on the Royal Indian Marine.
ADM 1/8797, Conversion of Royal Indian Marine into Royal Indian Navy.
ADM 1/9829, Royal Indian Navy War Organisation.
ADM 116/1815, Naval Defence of the British Empire.
ADM 116/2596, Royal Indian Navy and Royal Indian Marine: Recruitment, Training, Pay etc. of Executive and Engineer Officers.
ADM/1/13996, Recruitment of Officers for Royal Indian Navy Reserve and Royal Indian Naval Volunteer Reserve and Transfer of RNR and RNVR Officers Requested by Indian Authorities.
ADM/1/18527, RIN Review by FOCRIN.
ADM/1/9829, Royal Indian Navy War Organisation.
CAB 11/159, Report of Viscount Jellicoe's Naval Mission to India, (Generally Known as Lord Jellicoe Report), 1919.
CAB 129/7/38, Post War Pay, Allowances.
CAB 6/4, 6/5, 6/6, Report of the Committee of Imperial Defence on Defence of India.
CAB 6/5, CAB 6/6, Committee of Imperial Defence, Defence of India, 'D' Series.
CAB 79/45, Chiefs of Staff Committee, Minutes of the Meeting held on 22 February 1946.
CAB/129/1/37, Future Provision of Officers.
CAB/16/78, Committee of Imperial Defence: Sub-Committee on the Indianisation of the Indian Army Report, Report, Proceedings, Memoranda and Appendix.
CAB/21/3428, Commonwealth War Planning Concerning India, Pakistan and Ceylon.
CAB/23/3/51, Kings Commission to Indians.
CAB/23/39, Rawlinson Committee Report, 1922.
CAB/23/55, Naval Construction Plan.
CAB/24/112, Esher Committee Report.
CAB/24/133, Report of the Indian Retrenchment Committee 1922–23: The Inchcape Report.
CAB/24/185/9, Indian Navy Bill.
CAB/24/190, Committee of Imperial Defence: Sub-Committee on the Indianisation of the Indian Army Report.
CAB/24/190, Indianisation of the Indian Army: The Report of the Sub-Committee of the Committee of Imperial Defence.
CAB/24/259, Committee of Imperial Defence: Programmes of the Defence Services (The Sub-Committee on Defence Policy and Requirements), 1935.
CAB/24/259/26, Programmes of the Defence Services.
CAB/44/239, Administrative Narrative 1945–1946; Events in India Command up to 1 April 1946 When India Ceased to be the Base for SEAC.
CAB/65/34/26, War Cabinet Propaganda Policy.

BIBLIOGRAPHY

CAB/66/21/34, India's War Effort.
CAB/68/1/5, War Cabinet Report on 'India at the Outbreak of War'.
CAB/79/45/5, RIN Mutiny.
CAB/80/95/47, Future Officering of the RIN.
CSC/6/40, Army and Navy Recruitment in India: Civil Service Commission, Open and Limited Competitions, Regulations, Rules and Memoranda.
DO 35/2232, India: Constitution, Policy of India Remaining in Commonwealth.
DO 35/2249, India's Relation with the Commonwealth, Commonwealth Relations Official Committee, 1949.
DO/121/69, 1947-India and Pakistan: Report on Departure of Sir Claude Auchinleck, Commander-in-Chief in India.
DO/142/279, King's Colour of RIN: Disposal Off.
DO/142/343, India and Pakistan: Advantages of Membership of the British Commonwealth (Objectives).
DO/142/364, Lord Mountbatten's Report on His Viceroyalty.
DO/35/1251, Position of India in Relation to British Commonwealth.
MT 40/126, Sea Transport Organisation in India Possible Change in View of Indianisation of RIN.
MT/40/126, Sea Transport & Indianisation.
T 162/993, Expert Committee Report (Chatfield Committee Report), 1939.
WO 208/3816, RIN Mutiny Situation Report.
WO 32/10664, Formation of Womans Auxiliary Corps (India).
WO 32/3864, Garran Tribunal Report of 1933.
WO/208/3816, Composition of Naval Forces.
WO/208/3816, RIN Mutiny Situation Report.

(b) British Library, London

IOR/V/24/3042, Administrative Report of the Royal Indian Marine Including That of the Marine Survey of India for the Year 1928–1929.
IOR/V/25/211/1, Pamphlet for the Competition for the Indian Civil Service and Defence Services, 1931 to 1937.
L/I/1/540, Recruitment of Commissioned Rank of the RIN, Press Release dated 15 May 1939.
L/I/1/540/1, Press Release.
L/1/1/838, India's War Effort.
L/MIL/17/9/373 and Microfilm IOR NEG 50555, Report of the Subcommittee of the Indian Defence Committee on Local Naval Defence.
L/WS/1/8, Naval Mobilisation: Telegram to the Govt of India, Army Dept; From Secretary of State to Governor of Burma, Defence Dept, 1939.
L/WS/1/116, Russian threat to India-Counter Measures.
L/WS/1/290, Japanese Activities in the Far East Waters.
L/WS/1/292, Memorandum on India's Defence Commitments, 1937.
L/WS/1/293, Japanese Aggression against India.
L/WS/1/519, Expansion of Defence Services in India.
L/WS/1/957, India Terms: Finding Volunteers for Royal Indian Navy.
L/WS/1/1115, 1117, 1118 and 1119, Continued Service of British Personnel in the Armed Forces of India and Pakistan.

BIBLIOGRAPHY

L/WS/1/1335, Demobilisation Scheme.
L/WS/1/1580, Colonial Defence (Post Hostilities) Committee.
L/WS/1/1587, Indian Defence Expenditure: 1940–47.
MLS/10/1, Admiral Sir Geoffrey John Audley Miles.
Monograph on WRINS.

(c) Caird Library, National Maritime Museum, Greenwich

GOD/34, 35, 42, 43, 45, 47, Papers of Admiral John Henry Godfrey.
GOD/42, Vol II, J.H. Godfrey Report, India, 1943–46.
GOD/54, 55 and 56, RIN LOG Magazine.
IOR/V/25/211/1, Pamphlet for the Competition for the Indian Civil Service and Defence Services, 1931 to 1937.
MLS/10/1, Admiral Sir Geoffrey John Audley Miles.
RIN/1/13, HMIS Rajputana.
RIN/1/14/1 Papers of Lt Walter George Cotham.
RIN/2/2, Five Navies Fight for Burma.
RIN/2/3, 4, Papers of Lt Cdr Mac Donald.
RIN/3/12, RIN Inquiry Commission Press Cuttings.
RIN/3/2, 4, 6, 8, Papers of Cdr EC Streatfield James.
RIN/8/1 and RIN/8/2, Cooper Papers.
RIN/8/1, 2, Cooper Papers.
RIN/8/3, Regulations for the WRINS.
RIN/9/1, RIN Photographs.
RIN/15/2, Memoir of Commander A.G. Goord.
RIN/16/2, Papers of Commander G.E. Walker.
RIN/41/1 to RIN/41/13, Memoirs of RN and RIN Officers.
RIN/61, Report of the Indian Retrenchment Committee.
RIN/62, Nine Years Plan for the Royal Indian Navy.
RIN/74, Creeds and Customs in the Royal Indian Navy.
RIN/76, Leadership and Discipline: Royal Indian Navy.
RIN/77, RN and RIN: A Historical Link.
RIN/111, Paper of Rear Admiral Mawbey, Director RIM.

(d) Naval Historical Branch, Royal Navy, Portsmouth

Indian Marine, 1868–1896.
Indian Navy Act, 1927.
Placing Indian Minesweeping Vessels under Admiralty. Discussions as to Commissioning, 1917.
Rawlinson Committee Report, 'Re-Organisation of the Royal Indian Marine, Report of the Departmental Committee', March 1925.
Report and Appendices of the Royal Indian Marine Committee, 1912.
Report of the Departmental Committee Appointed to Prepare a Scheme for the Reorganisation of the Royal Indian Marine, 1926.
Report of the Mesopotamian Commission, 1917.
Report on the Royal Indian Navy, 15th August 1947 to 15th August 1948.

BIBLIOGRAPHY

Report on the Royal Indian Navy, 15 August 1948 to 14 August 1949.
Royal Indian Marine: Conclusions of the Inchape Committee, 1922–23.
Royal Indian Marine: Summary of Past and Present, 1919.
Secret Appendix to the Report of Naval Mission to India (Generally Known as Lord Jellicoe Report), 1919.

Interviews

Mrs. ML Cooper, Who Was the Chief Officer, Womens Royal Indian Navy Service (WRINS) during the Second World War, at New Delhi, Interviewed on 15 September 2013 at New Delhi.
Mrs. Ray, Daughter of (Late) Lt Commander Ram Mohan Ray (Who Joined the Royal Indian Navy Volunteer Reserve in 1941 after His Ph.D and Serve the Navy Till 1946), Interviewed on 08 October 2014 at New Delhi.

Secondary sources
Books

Allen, Robert L., *The Port Chicago Mutiny*, Penguin, New York, USA, 1993.
Aloysius, G., *Nationalism without a Nation in India*, Oxford University Press, New Delhi, 1997.
Anthony, Irvin, *Revolt at Sea: A Narration of Many Mutinies*, G.P. Putnam's Sons, New York, 1937.
Azad, Maulana Abul Kalam, *India Wins Freedom*, Orient Longman, New Delhi, 1988.
Aziz, K. K., *History of Partition of India*, Vol. 1, Atlantic Publishers and Distributors, New Delhi, 1995.
Banerjee, Subrata, *The R.I.N. Strike*, People's Pub. House, New Delhi, 1981.
Barrow, John and Gavin Kennedy, *The Mutiny of the Bounty*, 1st U.S. ed., D. R. Godine, Boston, 1980.
Barua, Pradeep P., *Gentlemen of the Raj: The Indian Army Officer Corps 1817–1949*, Pentagon Press, London, 2008.
Belcher, Diana Jolliffe, *Mutineers of the Bounty*, AMS Press, New York, 1980.
Blackburn, Terence R., *A Miscellany of Mutinies and Massacres in India*, APH Publishing Corporation, New Delhi, 2007.
Bligh, William and Edward Christian, *The Bounty Mutiny*, Penguin Classics and Penguin Books, New York, 2001.
Bose, Biswanath, *RIN Mutiny: 1946*, Northern Book Centre, New Delhi, 1988.
Bullocke, John Greville, *Sailors Rebellion: A Century of Naval Mutinies*, Eyre & Spottiswoode, London, 1938.
Butalia, Urvashi, *The Other Side of Silence: Voices from the Partition of India*, Duke University Press, Durham, NC, 1998.
Cardew, Alexander Gordon, *The White Mutiny, a Forgotten Episode in the History of the Indian Army*, Constable, London, 1929.
Chandra, Bipan, *Nationalism and, Colonialism in Modern India*, Orient Longman, Hyderabad, 1979.

BIBLIOGRAPHY

——, *India's Struggle for Independence*, Penguin Books, New Delhi, 1987.

Chinnian, P., *The Vellore Mutiny, 1806, the First Uprising against the British*, Chinnian, Madras, 1982.

Collins, Larry and Dominique Lapierre, *Mountbatten and the Partition of India, Vol. 1: March 22–August 15, 1947*, Vikas Publishing House, New Delhi, 1982.

Das, Dipak Kumar, *Revisiting Talwar: A Study in the Royal Indian Navy Uprising of February 1946*, Ajanta Publications, New Delhi, 1993.

Dutt, R. P., *India To-Day*, People's Publishing House, New Delhi, 1947.

Edwards, Dudley Keith, *The Soldiers' Revolt*, Spokesman Books, Nottingham, 1978.

Goldrick, James, *No Easy Answers: The Development of the Navies of India, Pakistan, Bangladesh and Sri Lanka, 1945–1996*, Lancer, New Delhi, 1997.

Gupta, Amit Kumar (ed.), *Myth and Reality: The Struggle for Freedom in India, 1945–47*, Manohar Publications, New Delhi, 1987.

Gupta, Maya, *Lord William Bentinck in Madras and the Vellore Mutiny: 1803–7*, Capital Publishers & Distributors, New Delhi, 1986.

Gupta, Partha Sarathi and Anirudh Deshpande (eds.), *The British Raj and Its Indian Armed Forces, 1857–1939*, Oxford University Press, New Delhi, 2002.

Guttridge, Leonard F., *Mutiny: A History of Naval Insurrection*, Berkley Books, New York, 2002.

Habibulla, Major General E., *The Sinews of Indian Defence*, Lancer Publishers, New Delhi, 1981.

Hadfield, Robert L., *Mutiny at Sea, Seafaring Men, Their Ships and Times Series*, Stanfordville, E. M. Coleman, New York, 1979.

Haine, Edgar A., *Mutiny on the High Seas*, Cornwall Books, New York, 1992.

Haq, Noor-ul, *Making of Pakistan: The Military Perspective*, Reliance Publishing House, New Delhi, 1997.

Harper, R. W. E. and Harry Miller, *Singapore Mutiny*, Oxford University Press, New York, 1984.

Hasan, Mushirul, *Legacy of a Divided Nation*, Hurst & Company, London, 1997.

——, *India's Partition: Process, Strategy and Mobilization*, Oxford University Press, New Delhi, 2001.

Hastings, Commander D. J., *The Royal Indian Navy, 1612–1950*, McFarland & Company, Inc., Publishers, London, 1988.

Hathaway, Jane, *Rebellion, Repression, Reinvention: Mutiny in Comparative Perspective*, Praeger, Westport, 2001.

Hiranandani, Vice Admiral G. M., *Transition to Triumph: Indian Navy 1965–75*, Lancer Publishers, New Delhi, 1999.

——, *Transition to Eminence: The Indian Navy 1976–90*, Lancer Publishers, New Delhi, 2004.

Hooker, James R., *Anatomy of a Mutiny*, American Universities Field Staff, Hanover, 1972.

Horn, Daniel, *The German Naval Mutinies of World War I*, Rutgers University Press, New Brunswick, 1969.

Hoyt, Edwin Palmer, *Mutiny on the Globe*, Barker, London, 1976.

Hyam, Ronald, *Britain's Declining Empire: The Road to Decolonisation, 1918–1968*, Cambridge University Press, Cambridge, 2007.

James, Lawrence, *Mutiny in the British and Commonwealth Forces, 1797–1956*, Buchan & Enright Publishers, London, 1987.

BIBLIOGRAPHY

Katari, R. D., *A Sailor Remembers*, Naval Headquarters, New Delhi, 1981.

Kavic, Lorne J., *India's Quest for Security: Defence Policies, 1947–1965*, University of California Press, Berkeley, 1967.

Khan, Yasmin, *The Great Partition: The Making of India and Pakistan*, Yale University Press, New Haven and London, 2007.

Khosla, G. D., *Stern Reckoning: A Survey of the Events Leading Up to and Following the Partition of India*, Oxford University Press, New Delhi, 1990.

Mahajan, Sucheta, *Independence and Partition: The Erosion of Colonial Power in India*, Sage Publications, New Delhi, 2000.

Marty, André, *The Epic of the Black Sea Revolt*, Workers Library Publishers, New York, 1941.

Metcalf, Barbara and Thomas R. Metcalf, *A Concise History of Modern India*, Cambridge University Press, Cambridge and New York, 2006.

Mohanan, Kalesh, *Maritime Heritage of India*, Alchemy Publication, Indian Navy, Coimbatore, 2016.

Nayyar, Vice Admiral K. K. (ed.), *Maritime India*, Rupa & Co, New Delhi, 2005.

Page, David, Anita Inder Singh, Penderel Moon, G. D. Khosla, and Mushirul Hasan, *The Partition Omnibus: Prelude to Partition/the Origins of the Partition of India 1936–1947*, Oxford University Press, Oxford, 2001.

Pakistan Navy History Section. *Story of the Pakistan Navy: 1947–72*, Compiled by Pakistan Navy History Section, History Section, Naval Headquarters, Islamabad, 1991.

Pandey, Gyanendra, *Remembering Partition: Violence, Nationalism and History in India*, Cambridge University Press, Cambridge, 2002.

Prasad, Bisheshwar, *Defence of India: Policy and Plans*, MoD History Division, New Delhi, 1963.

Ray, Nisith Ranjan (ed.), *Challenge: A Saga of India's Struggle for Freedom*, People's Publishing House, New Delhi, 1984.

Raza, Hashim S., *Mountbatten and the Partition of India*, Atlantic, New Delhi, 1989.

Rubin, Gerry R., *Durban 1942: A British Troopship Revolt*, Hambledon Press, London, 1992.

Sahai, Dr. Baldeo, *Indian Navy – A Perspective*, Publication Division, New Delhi, 2006.

Sareen, Tilak Raj, *Secret Documents on Singapore Mutiny, 1915*, Mounto Publishing House, New Delhi, 1995.

Sarma, Vice Admiral S. H., *My Years at Sea*, Lancer Publications, New Delhi, 2001.

Seervai, H. M., *Partition of India: Legend and Reality*, Emmanem Publications, Bombay, 1989.

Sho, Kuwajima, *Indian Mutiny in Singapore: 1915*, Ratna Prakashan, Calcutta, 1991.

Singh, Rear Admiral Satyindra, *Under Two Ensigns, the Indian Navy 1945–50*, Oxford & IBH Publishing Co., New Delhi, 1986.

———, *Blue Print to Blue Water, the Indian Navy 1951–65*, Lancer International, New Delhi, 1991.

Smith, A. D., *Theories of Nationalism*, Duckworth, London, 1971.

Smith, Leonard V., *Between Mutiny and Obedience: The Case of the French Fifth Infantry Division during World War I*, Princeton University Press, Princeton, 1994.

Sridharan, Rear Admiral K., *A Maritime History of India*, Publication Division, Government of India, New Delhi, 1982.

Tracy, Nicholas, *The Collective Naval Defence of the Empire, 1900–1940*, The Navy Records Society, London, 1997.

Venkateswaran, A. L., *Defence Organisation in India*, Publication Division, Ministry of Information and Broadcasting, GoI, New Delhi, 1967.

Verma, Capt Bharat and Vice Admiral G. M. Hiranandani, *Indian Armed Forces*, Lancer Publishers, New Delhi, 2008.

Vijayasree, C., and others, *Nation in Imagination: Essays on Nationalism, Sub-Nationalism and Narration*, Orient Longman, Hyderabad, 2007.

Wolpert, Stanley, *Shameful Flight: The Last Years of the British Empire in India*, Oxford University Press, Oxford, 2006.

Woodward, David, *The Collapse of Power: Mutiny in the High Seas Fleet*, A Barker, London, 1973.

Articles

Ashton, S. R., 'Mountbatten, the Royal Family, and British Influence in Post-Independence India and Burma', *The Journal of Imperial and Commonwealth History*, Vol. 33, No. 1, January, 2005.

Chatterji, Admiral A. K., 'The Indian Navy-How Army Dominance Inhibited Its Development', *Indo-British Review*, Vol. 16, No. 1, March, 1989.

Davies, Andrew, 'From "Landsman" to "Seaman"? Colonial Discipline, Organisation and Resistance in the Royal Indian Navy, 1946', *Social & Cultural Geography*, Vol. 14, No. 8, 2013.

Deshpande, Anirudh, 'Remembering RIN Revolt: Popular Celebration of Nationalism Fifty Year Ago', *Mainstream*, 24 February, 1996.

Farooqui, Amar, 'Divide and Rule? Race, Military Recruitment and Society in Late Nineteenth Century Colonial India', *Social Scientist*, Vol. 43, Nos. 3/4, March–April, 2015.

Greenhut, Jeffrey, 'Sahib and Sepoy: An Inquiry into the Relationship between the British Officers and Native Soldiers of the British Indian Army', *Military Affairs*, Vol. 48, No. 1, 1984.

Jones, Morris, 'Thirty-Six Years Later: The Mixed Legacies of Mountbatten's Transfer of Power', *International Affairs (Royal Institute of International Affairs)*, Vol. 59, No. 4, 1983.

Krishnan, Commodore N., 'Strategic Concepts of Indian Naval Expansion', *USI Journal*, Vol. LXXXVIII, No.372, July–September, 1958.

Kumarasingham, Harshan, 'The "New Commonwealth" 1947–49: A New Zealand Perspective on India Joining the Commonwealth', *The Round Table*, Vol. 95, No. 385, July, 2006.

Lammers, C. J., 'Strikes and Mutinies: A Comparative Study of Organizational Conflicts between Rulers and Ruled', *Administrative Science Quarterly*, Vol. 14, No. 4, 1966, pp. 558–572.

BIBLIOGRAPHY

Meyer, John M., 'The Royal Indian Navy Mutiny of 1946: Nationalist Competition and Civil-Military Relations in Postwar India', *The Journal of Imperial and Commonwealth History*, Vol. 45, No. 1, 2017.

Mohanan, Kalesh, 'War, Revolt and End of the Raj', *Journal of Indian Ocean Studies*, New Delhi, Vol. 21, No. 1, April, 2013.

———, 'Mutiny or Revolt? A Study of RIN Mutiny of 1946', *Maritime History Society 35th Annual Seminar Proceedings*, Mumbai, October 2014, pp. 103–114.

Parry, Vice Admiral W. E., 'India and the Sea Power', *USI Journal*, January–April, 1949.

Rand, Gavin and Kim A. Wagner, 'Recruiting the "Martial Races": Identities and Military Service in Colonial India', *Patterns of Prejudice*, Vol. 46, Nos. 3–4, 2012.

Singh, Anita Inder, 'Imperial Defence and the Transfer of Power in India, 1946–1947 Notes, Bibliographies, and Documents', *The International History Review*, Vol. 4, No. 4, November, 1982.

———, 'Keeping India in the Commonwealth: British Political and Military Aims, 1947–49', *Journal of Contemporary History*, Vol. 20, No. 3, July, 1985.

Spear, Percival, 'Britain's Transfer of Power in India', *Pacific Affairs*, Vol. 31, No. 2, 1958.

Spence, Daniel Owen, 'Imperial Transition, Indianisation and Race: Developing National Navies in the Subcontinent, 1947–64', *South Asia: Journal of South Asian Studies*, Vol. 37, No. 2, 2014.

Tughlak, 'The Birth of the Indian Navy', *Naval Review*, Vol. 44, No. 2, April, 1956.

INDEX

Note: Page numbers in *italic* indicate a figure and page numbers in **bold** indicate a table on the corresponding page

active service ratings 68; borne strengths of **69**; pay and allowances 79–80
Admiralty Fleet order 2810 of 1943 209
American Heritage Dictionary 164
anti-British slogans 150
armed forces 46, 136; commonwealth and 185–190; reconstitution of 213
Armed Forces Nationalisation Committee (AFNC) 178, 181, 185
Armed Forces Reconstitution Committee (AFRC) 207
Ashoka Sarnath Lion capitol 216
Asif Ali, Aruna 7, 163, 164
Auchinleck, Sir Claude 71, 165, 178, 179, 191
Australia 110, 156
Australian Cadets Training College, Jervis Bay 182
Axis and Allied Powers 3
Ayyangar, Gopalaswamy 178
Azad, Maulana Abdul Kalam 156
Azad Maidan 152

Banerjee, Subrata 8, 153
Barlow, J. A. 28
Barua, Padeep P. 182
Bedford, A. E. F. 23, 27
Best, Thomas 1
Bevin, Ernest 189
Bhagwatkar, V. M. 7, 165, 168
birth, Royal Indian Navy 22–24

Blackett, P. M. S. 219
Bombay 1, 44, 45, 87, 101, 111, 153
Bose, Biswanath 8, 155
Boxer Rebellion 15
British commonwealth 26, 180; *see also* commonwealth
British commonwealth defence policy 146
British Indian Armed Forces 5
British Military Policy in India, 1900–1945: Colonial Constraints and Declining Power 6
British Raj 9, 150

Cabinet Mission Plan 178
Calcutta 30, 45, 153, 210
Cariappa, Brigadier 180
Central Strike Committee 8
Chamberlain, Neville 26
Chatfield Committee, 1938 31–33, 39, 40, 47; local naval defence, priority 35; recommendations of 33–34; Royal Indian Navy, reorganization 39–42; scale of attack, measuring 35–36; strong naval force, major dangers 36–37
Chatfield Expert Committee 18
Chatterji, Admiral 21
Chetty, Shanmukham 23
Chiefs of Staff (COS) Committee 87, 136, 138, 140; recommendations of 136, 140–141; report 137, 138
Choudhury, Commander 180

INDEX

Choudri, H. M. S. 178
coastal trade, India 137
Collins, D. J. E. 4
Combined Inter-Services Historical Section (India and Pakistan) 4
COMCRIN 113
Committee of Imperial Defence 22, 35, 139
Commodore Commanding, Royal Indian Naval Squadron (COMRINS) 209
commonwealth 9, 218; armed forces and 185–190; British forces, withdrawal of 189–190
Congress leadership 7
Cooper, Duff 29
Cooper, M. L. 92
Corbett, T. N. 4
Cunningham, P. 92

Das, Dipak Kumar 8
Defence Authority in India 30–31
Defence Book provisions: auxiliary craft, fitting out 43; closure of ports 43; disposition, RIN Vessels 43; examination service 43; mobilisation, RIN 43; naval intelligence 44; port war signal stations 43
defence budget of India 21
defence policy of India 18
demobilisation 141–146; lower limit (stage III) 143; officers **145**; planning 144; upper limit (stage I) 142–143
Demobilization Committee 154
desertion 96–99
Deshpande, Anirudh 6, 7, 66
development plans, RIN: Chatfield Committee, 1938 31–34; committees and recommendations 24–45; Garran Award 24–25; Government of India proposal of 1934 25–29; Nine Year Plan of 1937 29–31
direct entry recruits 78
Directive for Reorganization Committee (India) of 1944 136
Directorate of Naval Education (DNE) 208
Directorate of Weapons and Training (DWT) 208

Dunedin, Viscount 24
Dutt, B. C. 7, 8, 150, 151, 155–157, 161, 162, 164

East India Company (EIC) 1
economic factors 20–22
education 130–131
Esher Committee of 1920 16, 17; recommendations 6
establishments 112
ethnic types 66–67
Europeanisation, army 9
expansion, RIN 110–135; anti-submarine training 124–125; boys (sailors) 117–119; composition and strength 111–112; electrical mechanics 125–126; equipment shortage 132; gunnery training 121–124; instructors 132; mechanical training establishment 120–121; officers training 114–115; ratings training 115–116; reserve officers' training 119–120; seamen training 116–119; sea training 131–132; specialised training 126–131; special service ratings 116–117; torpedo and electrical training 125; training of wartime 113–114; training wastage 133–134
Expansion of the Armed Forces and Defence Organisation, 1939-1945 4
Expert Committee 32, 47

Farwell, Byron 9
First World War 1, 15, 16
Fitzherbert, Vice Admiral 29
Flag Officer Commanding Royal Indian Naval Squadron (FOCRINS) 209
Flag Officer Commanding Royal Indian Navy (FOCRIN) 23, 27, 55, 58, 64, 84, 112, 140, 158, 159, 181–184

Gandhi, Mahatma 7, 163, 164, 178
Garden Reach Workshop, Calcutta 110
Garran, Sir Robert Randolph 24
Garran Award 24–25, 42
Garran Tribunal Report 18
geo-political situation 18–20

INDEX

Goldrick, James 5
Gourgey, P. S. 8, 165
Government's Rehabilitation Scheme 147
Gupta, S. C. 4

Hall, T. S. 207
Herbert, Fitz 162
'His Majesty Indian Ships (HMIS)' 216
History Division 4
History of the Pakistan Navy 5
HMIS *Akbar* 71, 88, 117
HMIS *Bahadur* 126
HMIS *Cheetah* 158
HMIS *Dalhousie* 115, 116
HMIS *Feroze* 88
HMIS *Investigator* 119
HMIS *Kakauri* 161
HMIS *Kakauri* 142
HMIS *Salsette* 129
HMIS *Talwar* 150–152, 167
Hopper, H. G. 208

IMMTS *Dufferin* 64
IMMTS (Indian Mercantile Marine Training Ship) *Dufferin* 58
Imperial Defence Budget 16
Imperial War Office 25
Inchcape, Lord 21
Inchcape Committee 21
Indian Air Force 138
Indian Air Force Volunteer Reserve (IAFVR) 4
Indian Armed Forces 4, 9, 190
Indian Coastal Reservation Act 23
Indian Defence Forces 19, 162
Indian Independence Act of 1947 209
Indianisation 9, 58, 170, 178–180, 182
Indian Marine 1
Indian Marine Act of 1884, Section 6 16
Indian Marine Act of 1887 14
Indian Marine Service Act of 1884 14
Indian Mercantile Marine 183
Indian National Army (INA) trials 6
Indian Naval Reserve Officers 185
'Indian Naval Ships (INS)' 216
Indian Navy (Discipline Act), 1934 209
"Indian Navy" 154, 157
Indian Navy (Discipline) Act 210

Indian Navy Discipline Bill 23
Indian Retrenchment Committee 6–7
India's Defence Commitments and Her Ability to Implement Them 29
indigenisation 9; of armed forces of India 178–181; RIN and 181–185
Inigo-Jones, H. R. 208
intermediate demobilisation 144
international political situation 19
Inter Service Recruiting Organisation 72
Inter-Services Demobilisation Planning Staff (ISDPS) 141, 142

James, Streatfield 5, 81, 82
Japan 19, 20, 136, 142
Jellicoe, Lord 6, 16, 21
Jinnah, Mohammed Ali 7, 153, 163, 178, 187
Joint Defence Council 207
joint responsibility principle 34

Karachi 45, 87, 88
Katari, R. D. 162
Kaul, B. M. 178
Khan, Liaquat Ali 181, 191
Khan, M. S. 8, 151, 153, 163, 165
Khan, Muhammad Ismail 178
Kunzru, Hriday Nath 178

labour exchanges 147
Lal, Sir Shadi 24
Lammers, D. J. 148
Landing Craft Wing 73, 74, 97, 112
locality-wise representation 95

Madras 15, 28, 30, 36, 113, 124
Mahajan, Sucheta 5, 6
Major Danger 19
Making of Pakistan: The Military Perspective 5
manpower 55–109; development **102**; situation, progress 99–101; state at outbreak of war 56–58; status **73**; status of hostilities only ratings **98**; supply 75–77
Manpower Recruitment Directorate 71
Marquis of Zetland 29
martial theory 103

INDEX

Mason, Philip 66
Mawbey, H. L. 21, 22
Memorandum on the Defence Forces (1936) 19, 29
Menezes, S. L. 8
Menon, Krishna 191
Mesopotamian Commission of 1917 16
modern warfare 18
Mountbatten, Lord 180, 181, 185–189, 191, 218
Mukherjee, Subrato 180
Mukherji, D. N. 9
Murray 28
Muslim League 7, 11, 153, 163, 167, 193, 197
mutinies 148–150, 152, 164–166, 182; categories 148

nationalisation 184, 185, 218
Nationalisation Committee 185
Nationalisation of the Indian Army 9
National Service (European British Subjects) Act 59
Naval Administration 212
Naval Central Strike Committee (NCSC) 151–153
naval defence of India 20
Naval Discipline Act of 1884 14
Naval Discipline (Dominion Naval Forces) Act of 1911 14
Naval Discipline Act of the United Kingdom 209
Naval History Cell 4
Naval Plan Paper 10/48 219
Naval Revolt of 1946 150
Naval Staff 212
"The Navy and Its Job" 154, 157
Nehru, Jawaharlal 150, 178
Nehru, Motilal 9
net capital cost 40
net total capital cost 41
Nicholls, Heaton 187
North Western Frontier Provinces (NWFP) 66
Nye, A. 187

Oxford Encyclopaedia of Maritime History 148

Pakistan 152, 163, 186–188
Parry, William 218
partition 213; of India 185; of Indian armed forces 190–194
Patel, Sardar 153, 163, 164
pay and allowances 79–80; active service ratings 79–80; HO ratings 79
permanent cadre 67; continuous service ratings 67; non-continuous service ratings 67
Pilani 159
Plan Paper 1 210
Plan Paper 01/48 219
post-first world war era (1920-1939) 14
post-independence developments: First Naval plan 209–213; post partition era, reorganisation 207–209; ships acquisition 213–217; training establishments 213
post-independence major naval plans **214**
post-war development plan 136–141
post-war economic situation 2
Pownall Sub-Committee recommendation 4
Pownall Sub-Committee's Report 33
Prasad, Bisheshwar 4
Prasad, Sri Nandan 4
'Proposed Strength of Indian Navy' 219
Provisional Joint Defence Council 211, 212
Public Accounts Committee 26, 27
Punjab 101

Quit India Movement 162, 168, 170

racial discrimination 7, 154
Rajagopalachari, Mr. 180, 186
Rawlinson, Lord 22
Rawlinson Committee 22, 23
Ray, Mrs. 147
Ray, Ram Mohan 147
recruitment 55–109, 210; active service ratings 68; cadet entry 211; desertion 96–99; direct recruitment 211; of Indian officers 60, 61–62; inter-provincial and communal development 93–96; from mercantile

INDEX

marine 68–70; naval recruiting organisation 59–60; Naval Selection Board 61; permanent cadre 67; publicity 80–90; of ratings 65–77; Recruiting Directorate of Adjutant General's Branch 60–65; reserve cadre formation 90; RINR & RINVR 63–64; Royal Indian Navy Fleet Reserve (RINFR) 64–65; Royal Indian Navy selection board 60–65; selection of officers 58–65; status in 1942 62; temporary cadre 67–68; warrant officers 62–63; women, induction of 90–92

Reddiar, O. P. Ramaswami 187
Regimental Medical Officer (RMO) 77
Registration (Emergency Powers) Act (I of 1940) 59
relaxation, medical examination 77–78
research methodology 11
Reserve Scheme (Act No. I of 1933) 26
resettlement 146–148
retrenchment programme 22
RIN Enquiry Commission 155, 160–162, 164, 166
RIN Enquiry Commission Report 7, 149, 152
RIN Enquiry Committee 163
RIN Enquiry Report 148, 156, 160, 161
RIN Mutiny Enquiry Report 156
RIN Report of 1945 146, 147
RIN revolt 3, 6, 148–168, 217; causes of 153–162; countries and navies, exposure 156–157; demobilisation 160–161; divisional system and discipline, failure 161–162; events prior to 150; impact of 169; nationalism, question of 162–163; political influence, question of 163–164; racial discrimination 156; recruitment advertisements 157–160
RIN Strike Committee 155
RIN Uprising Memorial 169
Royal Army Ordnance Corps (RAOC) 63
Royal Indian Air Force (RIAF) 76, 82, 180

Royal Indian Fleet Reserve (RIFR) 67, 68, 90
Royal Indian Marine (RIM) 1, 2, 6, 9, 15, 21, 28
The Royal Indian Navy 4
Royal Indian Navy Fleet Reserve (RINFR) 64–65
Royal Indian Navy Reserve (RINR) 60, 63–64, 90, 114
Royal Indian Navy Volunteer Reserve (RINVR) 25, 26, 60, 63–64, 90, 114
Royal Indian Navy War Organisation 44
Royal Naval Volunteer Reserve (RNVR) 62
Royal Navy Instruction 72 of 1943 209
Royal Navy Reserve (RNR) 58, 62

sea borne raids 19
Second World War 2–4, 6, 110–135, 137, 150, 188
Sen, K. 92
Sepoy mutiny 148
Sharma, Gautam 9
ships acquisition 213–217
short service commission (SSC) 207, 211
Simon, Sir John 29
Simpson, J. A. 29
Singapore 19, 26, 27, 110
Singh, Anita Inder 188
Singh, Madan 151
Singh, Mehr 178
Singh, R. K. 150
Singh, Sardar Sampuran 178
Singh, Satyindra 5, 9, 210
Singh, S. Baldev 179
Singh, Sharmila 180
Somaliland Expeditions 15
Soviet Russian-German Treaty of August 1939 19
specialised training 126–131; coastal forces 129; domestic training 128; education 130–131; firefighting and damage control 129; landing craft wing 128–129; radar training 126–127; radio mechanics 127–128; sick berth attendants 128; signals training 126

INDEX

standing Finance Committee 213
"The Story of Kishore and Khalil" 160
Sulaiman, Sir Shah Muhammad 24
Surat 1
Swarajists 23

T124-X (India) Agreement 211
temporary cadre 67–68; hostilities only ratings 68; special service ratings 67–68
Thimayya, K. S. 178
Tomlin, Lord 24
training, growth 110–135

*Under Two Ensigns: Indian Navy, 1945-1950*5
Union Jack 152
United Kingdom 42, 62, 82, 141, 156, 215

Wade, A. L. 178
Walker, Sir Charles 21
Walwyn, Sir Humphery 23, 26
War Book (India) 1939 42–45
War Department Historical Section 4
war mortality 8
warrant officers 62–63
warships: Indian Navy **217**; planned strength **146**
wartime advertisements **84–86**
Wavell, Lord 188
women, induction of 90–92
Women Auxiliary Corps (India) 91
Women's Royal Indian Naval Service (WRINS) 91, 92

zone-wise manpower representation 93

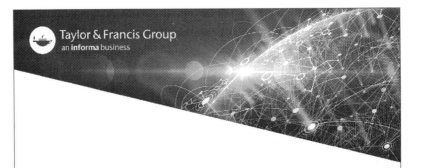

Printed in the United States
by Baker & Taylor Publisher Services